Preface

A concept which stretches across the paranormal and extraterrestrial fields, is the one that there are portals through which strange beings visit us. Sometimes these are called star gates or vortexes, but the basic idea is the same: There are portals through which they enter and exit, as they go back to their mind-boggling home realities.

However, few of us stop to really examine and investigate this idea; we mention the word "vortex" and then wander onward in our confusion. In **"UFOs, Portals and Gateways,"** Nigel Mortimer explores this fascinating possibility in depth and gives his many years of experience, proof, and conclusions. Are these visitors actually inter-dimensional rather than from far distant star systems? After all, long distance space travel imposes intense radiation which might be impossible to overcome, and the distances are so vast as to be incomprehensible.

Nigel Mortimer suggests that other dimensions are layered right on top of ours; all that is needed is a door through to the other layer. Yes, this involves advanced quantum knowledge, no doubt, but if those other-dimensional beings are more advanced scientifically or can travel through the powers within their minds, they can simply use the portals which exist in the fabric of space/time or which can be created through quantum engineering.

In childhood, I was visited by a being who said he was a human from Earth's future. This possibility has become my favorite theory, not through emotional bias but because of my detailed scientific research throughout the years. If humans from the future are among our visitors, they too would use dimensional gateways because they too are right on top of us in a different layer of time - and time is the 4th dimension.

They are dimensional visitors. In our future, will we discover and use dimensional portals? Can someone even today, find a gateway to elsewhere or else-when?

Nigel Mortimer and I first communicated in the 1990s. Nigel was receiving messages and information from "elsewhere or else-when." I was happy to give him a bit of guidance and reassurance along his path. He has learned and accomplished much since then. I have worked with thousands of people but I always remember Nigel and am pleased we have reconnected in these times of great change and challenge for Earth.

"UFOs Gateways and Portals" is an intriguing book which may well hold the key to where they come from and who they are! How many other-dimensions are out there? There are exotic beings we cannot even imagine - that is, until they visit us. Come along with Nigel Mortimer as he tells us of their incredible gateways!

<u>Diane Tessman</u>

Also by Nigel Mortimer

ISAAC NEWTON & THE SECRET SUN DIAL
Portal to Another World.
THE CIRCLE & THE SWORD

Published by Ancient Mail Verlag

UFOs, Portals & Gateways

Exploring the evidence for

Inter-Dimensional Beings

& bringing about a new UFO awareness.

Nigel Mortimer

Wisdom Books

A Wisdom Books Publication

UFOs, Portals & Gateways

First published in Great Britain in 2013 by Wisdom Books
This edition published in 2013 by Wisdom Books

ISBN-13: 978-1500588854
ISBN-10: 1500588857

Typeset in Garamond by M Rules
Wisdom Books
A division of House of Books Yorkshire
Sutcliffe Buildings
Settle
North Yorkshire
England BD24 9EZ

FOR MY WIFE HELEN,
*Who not only gave me the love and support
to write this book, but became herself witness to the
extraordinary events at the Settle portal.*

"Time waits for no one,
It just dances on.
Wait for a dream,
When you wake up,
It's gone."

Contents

Foreword
BY MALCOLM ROBINSON

There are a number of British Ufologists who in their own ways are researching the UFO enigma here in the U.K. However there is one man who takes his research to another level and that man is Nigel Mortimer. Nigel has been involved in UFO research since 1980 when he was fortunate enough to have his own encounter with a strange aerial object. Ever since then he has been a man on a mission dedicated to seeking out the answers to the UFO Mystery.

As the years have progressed and his investigations have continued, Nigel has managed to channel what he describes as 'Other Worldly Intelligences' One of the main intelligences that Nigel has channeled is a Celestial Being known as Sharlek who has imparted to Nigel many interesting and thought provoking things which have a major bearing on mankind. This in itself is of course staggering but is in keeping with similar channeled messages from similar beings across the world, so Nigel does not stand along in this regard. However, things took a major turn for Nigel when in the summer of 2011 near his home town of Settle in North Yorkshire he and his wife Helen discovered a 'Star Gate' to another dimension. This was to prove not only enlightening to Nigel but took his Investigations onto a whole new level. Finding this 'portal' or 'gateway' to another world was of colossal importance not just to Nigel and his wife but to mankind as a whole and he just knew that this information just simply had to come out. And come out it did in Nigel's previous book, *'Isaac Newton and the Secret Sundial. Portal to another world'*
However Nigel brings the reader up to speed in this new book with some astounding revelations about this 'portal' Not only does Nigel deal with the finding of the 'portal' and the messages received therein, but it looks at UFO cases in relation to 'portals' all over the landscape of which Nigel draws cleverly together in regards to his own findings at the Settle 'portal.' The book also takes a look at the science behind how dimensions might work and how the ancients would have approached

their own 'portals' and how they interacted with them. Another major facet of the UFO enigma is of course the 'Shape Shifting' phenomenon that of humans turning into 'something else', either a small grey 'being' or lizard like entity which of course sounds crazy but when you weigh up all the many worldwide reports, then you soon come to realise that here is something which has a lot to back it up and Nigel gives you his own thoughts and research on this here in this fine book. There are a number of researchers who believe that those 'alien visitors' which are being seen throughout the skies of the world may not necessarily be coming to us from deepest space, rather, they may be coming through some inter dimensional doorway, a doorway similar to what Nigel and his wife uncovered near Settle back in 2011. I personally believe that the dimensional theory is probably the one to which we all should be looking towards for answers regarding the UFO mystery. We know so little about ourselves and our place in the cosmos and the dimensional theory, those inter-dimensional doorways and portals that Nigel so cleverly writes about here, will certainly open your eyes and make you question how little we really know about our standing and place in the grand scheme of things. Needless to say this book takes a look at Inter-dimensional doorways and entities and how dimensions might work all of which makes for interesting and thought provoking reading. Of course one of the main portal doorways here in the United Kingdom is said to be located in the very heart of Rosslyn Chapel near Edinburgh Central Scotland and Nigel takes a look at the history and relevance of this particular 'doorway'. I found the book all neatly tied together providing the reader with the science and physics of dimensions and 'portals' and if to show how massive a subject 'portals' can be then the chapter on the Skinwalker Ranch southeast of Ballard, Utah in the United States of America which has seen an incredible amount of strange phenomena occurring around it such as UFO sightings, Bigfoot, Crop Circles, poltergeist activity and glowing balls of light will simply astound you. But its Nigel's own study and information regarding 'portals' which I found most fascinating and of which I'm sure you will too. Nigel also takes a look at some of the Freemason secrets which has a bearing on the very nature and subject of this book. As stated, Nigel has been involved with these subjects for a big part of his life and has spoken and written about these subjects up and down the U.K. He was a regional UFO investigator and researcher for the Northern UFO Network, (NUFON) and was the Director of Regional Investigations for BUFORA during the early 1990's.

I have known Nigel for many years now and have respected his work and I am pleased to call him a friend. His dedication and passion for his research is second to none and his time spent on this subject is not only a labour of love for him but a desire to invite people to look at this subject in a different light. UFO research is not just about researching lights in the sky, things have moved on, we are now looking at a subject which appears more complex than we can ever imagine. Some may see the UFO subject as nothing more than wishful imagination, but what this book clearly does, is to show the reader the complexity of the subject and how things are not so black and white. Nigel and his wife Helen have spent many hours researching this subject their passion to get some answers has seen them take time out of their own valuable life to pursue those answers. UFO researchers tend to spend their own time and money on this subject (I know, I am one of them) and this has been the case with Nigel. The findings that you will come across in this book just had to be presented here. Research is not all about placing your research in filing cabinets. Research is to be shown to people like you, the reader of this book. Some may disagree with the findings in this book, and Nigel would be the first to accept this. But we have to remember that science is all about looking for answers. Many new and amazing discoveries have been made by looking and thinking 'out of the box' and this is most certainly the case here. What may sound and look absurd in one century might not be the case in the next.

With the publication of this book, Nigel brings forward a new way for the public to share in his most fascinating findings. You will soon see that the UFO phenomenon is not quite what it appears to be. Mankind may have been looking at this subject in completely the wrong way and this fine book leads you onto a different path of Ufology, a path of adventure, a path of thought and mystery, of channeling, of 'portals' and dimensions and Celestial Beings. It's a book you'll find hard to put down. It is my hope, that the findings in this book, will lead you to view the UFO phenomenon in a new light. So sit back pour yourself a drink as you will soon be entering a world of 'portals', dimensions and mystery.

Malcolm Robinson
Founder of Strange Phenomena Investigations

Acknowledgments

I am indebted to the following UFO & Portal Researchers for their help and opinions concerning the ongoing search for the truth about inter-dimensional realities. Special thanks goes to Patricia Hession, Cathy Bilsky, Samantha Mansi, Tony Topping, Leah Watterson, Valerie Walters, Melanie Cameron, Jackie Taylor, Luara & Mike Sayers, Sam Wright, Ian Popple, James Garry Dick, Jonny Camilleri, Bobby Sullivan, Kevin Goodman, Michael Rutherford, Danni Mattes, Ronnie Betts, Peter Robbins, Nigel Watson, Steve Mera, Neil Munnerley, Steve Wills, Cindy Bennett, Susanne Klimt, Christopher Woods, Steve Burnand, David Boyle, UFO Portugal, Juanita & Jez Cox, Ruth Ablett Tina Laurent RIP, & Kevin Darkstorm RIP.

"There is much more going on at these portals than we are currently aware of. It's not just UFO's that people see, but many different types of phenomena."
Thank You Derek Savory

"I feel that portals are a mirror of our own consciousness and process of existence. Creation is a frequency that we seek to experience in many life times. Many doorways of a universal effect have created these portals that you may not be aware of, but are happening in the now. "
Thank You Aaron Turner

"I was a solid nuts and bolts UFO researcher for many years. Opening Portals and Nigel Mortimer have given me a new avenue to continue my journey through this multi faceted subject."
Thank You Garry Moore.

"UFO's have always been an interest of mine and I have joined a lot of Facebook groups to further my knowledge in the subject, but none of them compared to Opening Portals. Nigel Mortimer has really opened up the field of study and taken us in a whole new direction."
Thank You Christyn Lingham

And thank you to everyone else who has been so kind to support both Helen & I in our portal adventures.

Introduction

POR-TAL : A doorway, entrance, or gate, especially one that is large and imposing, sometimes found in large buildings, at other times found between dimensions.

Since writing my last book about an ancient site which was regarded by some, including myself and my wife, as being an inter-dimensional portal I have investigated a number of other possibilities as to whether portals really exist, what they may be, and in fact, how long they have been situated on this planet? This book is very different to my previous ones, in that I have tried to present here all of the evidence that has come to light in recent times to indicate the possible reality for portals. This runs alongside research that shows a possible link between these portal locations and the UFO phenomenon; from the point of view that some Extraterrestrial life-forms may indeed be travelling through such portals, moving from other dimensional states to our own reality, which of course is yet just another dimensional state.

The idea that portals could exist is a very long held one and goes back to the earliest of times. It was a pagan religious notion that gateways between this world of the living and that of the dead, although unseen by most, was a possibility that the human mind could not say with any certainty did not exist. Some scholars state that this was born out of fear and superstition, a need within early man to know better his mortality and reason for existence on this planet. However, other gateways into places where mankind played no conscious part, like the dream-worlds of sleep-time and the world-wide lore of the Faery Realms, underline the human conception that some time and space in which other denizens exist, is not all of pure fantasy and the imagination.

Having myself been an investigator and researcher of the UFO phenomenon for over 30 years, I have been in the fortuitous position to have been able to monitor how the enigma has transcended from people reporting strange lights in the skies above this planet Earth, to one which includes the possibility that dimensional travel could be (and would be) a more direct approach to moving between vast distances whether that be in space or time. It has been proven beyond reasonable doubt within scientific institutions that the movement of matter between physical locations without the need for transport as we recognise it, is reality, albeit at the microscopic level of neutrinos. Recent announcements from the scientific community suggest that these minute particles are capable of moving faster than the speed of light, yet Einstein's theory of Relativity states that this is impossible as all things cannot move faster than light in our three known dimensional states. So, what is happening here? The only possible answer to this 'impossibility' is that either Einstein's theory is wrong, or that other dimensions exist apart from the three known ones, in order for this to take place, by neutrino particles taking short cuts in and out of our dimension. Mind blowing stuff!

At this point in the illusion we call time, as I write this book, we begin to venture into a world where acceptable scientific research draws closer to the mysteries of the unexplained. I am in no doubt that some Newtonian scientist will kick and scream their way in any other direction than the one in which their own results are taking them closer to what was once termed magic superstition. This has more to do with a problem attached to the human ego than anything else related to any kind of scientific approach. I do not think it will be too long before science in the traditional sense and the unexplained phenomenon that has up until now entrenched itself in the fringes of social acceptability, will be one and the same thing.

That is the real aim of this book. To be able to present enough viable information and evidence for the reality of portals and then to suggest, until another time, how best we can better and more fully understand what use there was, and is, for these gateways into the unknown? On a local level we have been working since 2010 at the ancient site of the Settle Sun Dial Portal to bring this about. We have documented all of our finds on video and camera stills (some of which are presented in this book for the first time) in written reports and on site evaluations.

Investigating portals take in much more experimentation that the old school ufologists sometimes comprehend. Yes, the same kinds of phenomena can and do take place at these portals (which used to be called Window Areas) that we find in UFO reports, but it is also essential that we look at other factors including the physical make up of the landscape, environmental aspects, the known and unknown history of the location and the attitudes of those who actually live close to these portals, for example.

When we accept that everything in this known reality (the dimensional state) is energy of one form or another, we can be reasonably certain that other dimensions may take form from similar energies. This would of course include worlds, planets, plants, life-forms and anything else as yet unimagined by us, that has potential to fill such a void by the manipulation of this energy. We do not know the rules of reality in these other places, it may be that there are no other recognised living entities in them, or it may be that these locations are full of beings which regard our own dimension as we regard the simplicity of those who once dwelt in caves in this world.

Mankind has long been able to form things, objects and tools from other forms of energy on this planet since those early times. As we have progressed on the physical plane of humanity, simpler forms of energy like trees and plants, rock and oils, and even animal life forms, have all been used & changed by us to make other more suitable things to fit our human needs. The plastics found in abundance in the world today, some would say essential to our modern way of life, are all in themselves forms of energy (matter) which has been changed by human hands or the technology science has allowed him.

The keyboard that my fingers are writing this book upon was once a collection of oils and chemicals arranged into a different form and then by design given a purpose which stemmed from the human consciousness. When I look down at it now with its rows of dust covered buttons, themselves imprinted with the symbols of our language, it can be difficult to imagine this apparatus in any other form than the one in front of me. Yet, science and not the imaginations of magic allowed that amazing transference of energy to take place in such a common place object like this keyboard, that we often forget that this method of shape-shifting (albeit at the hands of human technology) is not only real to us in this dimension, but also demonstrates how energy forms can be manipulated once the science and reasoning behind it becomes known.

A common thread as to what portals are, is that they are being recognised the world over in very similar places and situations. I gave an account in my previous book about the Settle Sun Dial Portal, that Portals can be both very small or very large areas within the physical landscape. They can even be found in spaces where buildings exist today, but were probably not constructed when the portal pre-existed it. There is a very ancient element to the origins of such portals and some indication exists that at least Neolithic Man was aware of the positioning of these inter-dimensional gateways which he would mark out with standing stones and megalithic structures. Some researchers go as far as to say that there is a world energy grid of portals and that these line up in linear and geometric formation around the globe. This network of portals not only allows life-forms, some like us and some not, to travel vast distances in the blink of an eye, but are also being used by secretive human military forces to travel to and fro, between portal entrances positioned in this dimensional world. Does a top secret establishment know already the secret of the portals and if so, what intentions do they have for using them? In other words, is Stargate a reality?

I have lost count of the amount of people who have jokingly said to me, 'If these portals exist, why don't you go through one and prove it!'. To be honest, that is a fair point and although many of these people will have had their tongue firmly stuck in cheek when they say that to me, maybe they do not realise the actual significance of this. Of course there has never been a time yet where I have been able to physically enter a portal vortex (*simplified: the place where energies cross in portals*) and travel through it into another dimensional state, but there may have been numerous times in which I have certainly found my mind being able to access these other realities when standing in a portal vortex.

There is a very good scientific reason why, at this present time, most of us would be unable to move physically through portals (although, I do think as mentioned, there might be secret groups of humans existing now who have overcome this problem) and that is to do with how we work with energy and perceptions of mind to physical body limitations which I will explain about in the book. I quoted at the beginning of this introduction the definition of what the dictionary states a portal to be; *a doorway*, implying that this is either an entrance to somewhere else or a door to this dimension from somewhere else..., or *a gate*, implying a barrier that maybe separates realities....., especially one that *is large and imposing*, implying that portals are something of significance and impose something upon us all. In my own opinion, I would suggest that portals impose upon us a truth. This truth relates to who we are and our own position in this known dimensional state we call 'our world'. Upon investigating Portals together in this book, we will see with some degree of certainty that the only thing holding most of humanity back from the acknowledgement of portal reality is that which has been imposed upon us, a lack of freewill and the ability to think for ourselves out of the box.

If you read this book and take from it nothing more than a sense of awareness that you might not be alone in this energy called the dimensional multi-verse, the recognition that humanity may be sharing this and other dimensions with life-forms that understood this problem millions of years ago (and some only seconds ago in another reality!) and overcame it, then I will be happy to have pointed you in a direction encompassing all dimensions.

CHAPTER ONE

The Ancients & The Portal

A basic theme of science fiction is the portal, a door or gateway through which human beings can travel from this reality of three dimensions to others which may be here on Earth, back in time, in the future or maybe on another world somewhere else. However, we must ask ourselves where did the idea of the portal originate even in the fantastic writings of science fiction? Who first comprehended the idea that there may be unseen entrances which connect our known reality to another that has been, up until modern day at least, a 'figment of the human imagination'?

The concept that we may be able to travel further than the five known senses allow, is as ancient as the origin of Mankind. It aligns itself with the awe and wonder that early humans appreciated in their attempt to understand and organise a reality in which they found themselves and the very real and instinctive notion of fear that accompanied those early thoughts, that he may be the only intelligent being in the vast space of the universe and beyond.

Out of this, grew the first mystery schools and basis for later man-manipulated religions which we find all over this planet today. At the core of these concepts, we find descriptive allowances for 'another place', a heaven maybe, or even a wonderland where things are very different to those found in this three dimensional reality. Within most of the known religions of the world, this other place just out of the reach of human appreciation, exists as somewhere only achievable after death or a transference of the human spirit. But why should we even allow ourselves to be fooled for millennia into thinking that such a place unseen to most if not all of us, should even exist within the boundaries of religion, if there is indeed no basis for anywhere else other than the physical world that we live in? For, in doing so, this would either indicate that most of mankind for thousands of years has been deluding himself about the thoughts in his own mindset, or that the fear of being alone in the universe is so entrenched within, that we have been happy to be-fool ourselves with a fantasy for that length of time! There is of course another option. Other realities really do exist and somehow, we have been aware of them but on a level of consciousness that very few actually appreciate in a factual way.

The true and basic notion for other dimensional states, other worlds and other realities that we may be able to comprehend, is best evidenced by the realisation that all of us have (and anyone who has ever lived on this planet)has the conscious knowledge that we have been here, living as a part of this reality and this dimension. We know without exception that dimensions exist because we are a part of this one, and so is everything else that we can understand at this time. The fact remains that we are dimensional beings, due to the realisation that we exist in a dimensional state of being.

The greatest of all mysteries must be that of aliens and UFOs. For thousands of years, people have looked to the heavens and wondered if there is other intelligent life like ours out there. If so, we ponder on where 'they' might come from?

Today, it seems without doubt that the universe should be teeming with life and planets like our own and some of those, may be home to beings which are more intelligent than ourselves, having mastered the problems of space travel in their distant past. There never seems to be a day in which someone , somewhere in the world, sees or reports a UFO, people from all walks of life, from all countries and cultures, all ages and genders, and through the instant access to information via the internet, the scales are tipping towards the UFO phenomenon becoming a reality and truly scientific consideration.

I have held the opinion for some time, that some UFOs and other worldly beings are not of the same physical energy or dimensional state that our reality is a part of here on planet Earth. They seem to operate in a different kind of state of being, from another reality which may be much closer to home than many of us realise. Physical science finds the concept of UFOs visiting this planet a difficult one to evaluate as the phenomenon is mostly a transient one and sightings do not normally last for long periods of time. The main argument that science puts forward for it being very unlikely that UFOs and aliens visiting this planet is due to the vast distances involved. What if these UFOs were operating to different laws of science to ours? What if these UFOs do not travel through space, but get here through dimensional gateways in time and space?

We must look towards the knowledge of the ancients and the metaphysical if we are to find answers that may confirm that E.T.'s are not just E.T.'s, but dimensional beings like you and me. I say, like you and me, because we too, are dimensional beings living in the dimensional reality we perceive and understand. Many of the beings that we have encountered all seem to have a similar message, that they come from and operate in a different place, a higher dimension, and that the true nature of realities in all of these dimensions is consciousness. Dimensions are different and unobserved by us because they are of a higher vibration frequency and may even consist of less dense matter like we have here on Earth, making them a more thought like state of reality in which the concept of solid matter is alien.

The idea of another world that is unseen by man, but just out of reach, is ancient. The concept is something which fires the imagination of young children and adults alike, that there really could be another civilisation out there that is living alongside us all in secret and separate from our understanding of life and our place in the physical universe. In the most ancient of texts we find the repeated mention of portals and gateways into other realms in cultures from all over the world. In Meso-American folklore we find this interesting account about the ancient Mayan peoples,

'The Maya believed that there were portals or doors, Tzeltal, that, at certain times, would open to allow visitors from the stars into their world.'

One of these portal visitors was Quetzalcóatl, the feathered serpent, who brought with him the knowledge of how and where to build pyramids, which consisted of very well thought out patterns in the landscape to imitate the placement of different stars and planets. This was also found to be the case in ancient Egypt too. It is written in ancient texts that these Mayan pyramids and temples were perfectly designed and constructed, with a plan in mind: high vibration, special energy and a message that we still can't understand fully today. It is said that there are twelve major inter-dimensional portals of ancient origin still located around the world. I suspect that there were many more than this and most of their actual locations have been lost to time. It seems that these major portals have been remembered due to the ancients building stone monuments, temples and arches at the sites.

In September 1996, a huge carved structure that resembled a doorway was discovered at Hayu Marca mountains of southern Peru, close to Puno and Lake Titicaca. It has been revered by the locals for many generations as the Gate of the Gods to the City of the Gods within the massive rock, yet to date, no physical city exists in the locality. The doorway measuring some seven meters in height and as wide, has been carved out some time in the distant past from the natural rock face. There is a smaller entrance-like alcove in the base of the door, itself just over two meters high.

The discovery of 'Puerta de Hayu Marca', the Gate of the Gods or Spirits, was made by Jose Luis Delgado Mamani while he was trekking through the surrounding foothills. When he saw the enigmatic structure for the first time he remarked that it was so mind blowing that he almost passed out. What is interesting is something else he said shortly after making the discovery,

"I have dreamed of such a construction over the year, but in the dream the path to the door was paved with pink marbles statues lining either side of the path. In the dream, I also saw that the smaller door was open and there was a brilliant blue light coming from what looked like a shimmering tunnel. I have commented to my family many times about these dreams, and so when I finally gazed upon the doorway, it was like a revelation from God. How do you make order of such a strange occurrence?"

Legend says that in times long past, great heroes had gone to join their gods by passing through the gate to spend immortality there and on special occasions, those men were allowed to travel back with the gods for a short time to inspect all the lands of the kingdom in the physical world. Who were these gods that occupied a hidden realm that was seemingly none physical, maybe another dimension, and how could they offer those heroes of the Incas temporary immortality?

In another account of old from that same region we learn that around the time that the Spanish Conquistadors landed in Peru the gateway to the gods once more became active. An Inca priest from the temple of the seven rays named Aramu Mara fled from the temple taking with him a sacred golden disk known as the 'key of the gods' and hid in the mountains of Hayu Marca. Eventually he reached the doorway carved into the rock face which was being guarded by shaman priests. When they saw that he had the 'key' (golden disk) they took it from him and a ritual was performed and a wonderful blue light emerged from the opening portal. Inside they found a tunnel and when the key was handed to one of the shaman, he passed through it never to be seen again. It has been noted that when archaeologists visited the site in 1996, they found a small round depression hollowed out of the door rock surface which was about the size of a hand. A small saucer shaped disk would snugly fit into this.

Researcher Ellen Lloyd states, *'Amaru Muru and his wife arrived in light ships in a Peruvian valley. Several temples and cities such as for example Machu Picchu, Cuzco, and Tiahuanako were deliberately built over powerful vortexes. In time Amaru Muru's empire included not only Peru, but stretched all over South America. He also established the so-called Brotherhood of the Seven Rays. Hidden in a monastery deep in the Andes, this mystery school continued to follow the sacred Lemurian teachings. In addition, the monastery also preserved the valuable objects brought by Amaru from the motherland. Among one of these objects was a certain sacred solar disc. The disc was rarely seen and most of the time it was stored in a hidden chamber.'*

As you will see, the two aspects mentioned in the account of portal activation at Hayu Marca, the bright blue light and the mention of a 'key' to open the portal (in this case it seems to have been a golden disk), have been observed in modern times too at other portal sites including the one currently under investigation by my wife and I here in Settle. Also note that it is said on certain days in the afternoons, the door of Hayu Marca becomes semi-transparent and that sightings of tall men with light hair and fair skin have been observed close by, accompanied by blue and orange balls of light. Is it by coincidence and nothing more, that an increasing number of UFO sightings have been made around the shores of Lake Titicaca, resembling glowing disk-shaped spheres, mainly blue and golden in colour. Further, the legend states a prophecy. In the future (now?) the door of the gods will one day open ' many times bigger than it actually is, and allow the gods to return in their sun ships'.

Rumours have been circulating for some time now that a star gate exists in Libya . World renowned researcher, Dr Michael E. Salla, who held academic appointments at a number of universities including the School of International Service, Washington DC (1996-2001), Dept. of Political Science, Australian National University, Canberra (1994-96) and who taught Peace as a Researcher in Residence at the Centre for Global Peace (2001-2003), holds a PhD in Government from the University of Queensland, Australia and an MA in Philosophy from the University of Melbourne, Australia, had this to say in his somewhat controversial thesis in 2003 called "An Exopolitical Perspective on the Pre-emptive War against Iraq",

"An independent archaeologist that discusses a direct link between the ancient ET presence in Sumer (southern Iraq) and current US focus on the regime of Saddam Hussein, is William Henry. Henry's main thesis is that there existed in Sumerian times a technological device which he describes as a 'Stargate', that the Anunnaki / Nephilim used to travel back and forth from their home world and the Earth, and also how they travel around the galaxy.

If there is a Stargate existing in Southern Iraq that will play a role in such a 'prophesied return of the gods', then it is most likely that clandestine government organizations that greatly influence or control the Bush administration, are aware of the existence and the role of this Stargate. Iraq's President Hussein is most likely also aware of such a Stargate's existence as might be inferred by his architectural projects intent on reviving the grandeur of early Mesopotamian civilizations, and cementing his place as the restorer of Iraq's past glory.

More significantly, his permission for a German team of archaeologists to resume excavations in the Sumerian city of Uruk after detailed underground mapping, suggests that this may be the location of the Sumerian Stargate. This knowledge of a buried Stargate, may also be part of the reason why the German government has been publicly opposed to a US pre-emptive war against Iraq. If in fact both the Hussein regime and the Bush administration believe that a Stargate lies buried in the sands of Southern Iraq, then there most likely exists a race to gain access to it and to control it. William Henry's thesis is that this is indeed the political underpinning of the continuing military conflict in Iraq."

Should a Stargate or portal have ever existed in Iraq then it would surely be something that any government of the world would want to secure for its own gain. The comments made by Salla suggest that this portal was a physical device of some kind, maybe similar to the one described in the cult TV series and film Stargate. There certainly is no reason why such a device could not have been constructed at some point in history and if so, probably encompasses the same ideas about EM fields and electro-magnetism that seems to be at the heart of the theory for inter-dimensional natural portals. If this is the case, then it would suggest that in ancient times someone on or off this planet had the means to construct such a Stargate, which in itself suggests an even bigger mystery. Some suggest it was the Annunaki (those who fell from the heavens) who helped the ancient Sumerians in that region to use advanced technology including the Stargate. Over 6000 years ago, the Sumerians claimed that their own civilisation was born out of the teachings given to them from beings that came to Earth from their home planet Nibiru. Sumerian texts tell us that more than 400,000 years ago these beings landed in the Tigress-Eurphrates region and set up a colony called E-Den. There seems to be some evidence for this monumental happening found in the Apocryphal Book of Baruch: ' Then the Lord created the great flood destroying all life, including the 409,000 giants! 'Again in the Book of Enoch: "Two huge men appeared to me, the like of which I had never seen on Earth. Their faces were shining like the Sun, their eyes too, were like a burning light. And they took me up and carried me to the 'first heaven', and they fly with their wings and do the rounds of all the planets. They led before my face the elders, the rulers of the stellar orders."

In the 1980's, Saddam Hussein ordered a massive restoration project at the Ziggurat Temple where it had been rumoured for generations that the Stargate was housed. After the invasion of Iraq and the downfall of Hussein, it is known that the crack US forces were directed to plunder and secure many museums in Iraq. Those same US forces took control of the Great Ziggurat Temple and stayed there for the next ten years after Hussein had been overthrown.

Perhaps the most enigmatic of all portals is the supposed Stargate of Babylon, which in biblical times connects with the Temple of Solomon. We will examine the temple further in this book, but for now let us consider that after sacking the temple and conquering Jerusalem around 600BC, King Nebuchadnezzar returned to Babylon with treasures including the Ark of the Covenant and three wise men as hostages. Included were a young man and 'master magician' named Daniel, and another prominent prophet, Ezekiel, who had visions of 'the kingdom of Heaven on Earth while imprisoned in Babylon. After acquiring a sense of the hidden secret knowledge from the Temple of Solomon, Nebuchadnezzar built the hanging gardens of Babylon and restored the fantastic Ziggart of Marduk known as the Tower of Babel. The word Babel originates from *Bab-li,* which in the Babylonian language meant 'Gate of God '. This is our first tip-off that Nebuchadnezzar attempted to construct by means a Stargate or a portal to heaven. According to the Bible, Nebuchadnezzar was a wise man, a sage , an alchemist and a seer. He surrounded himself with such as Daniel who he considered to be able to gain insight from prophetic dreams and asked him to interpret a dream in which Nebuchadnezzar saw:

'a tree in the midst of the Earth, and the height thereof was great. The tree grew, and was strong, and the height thereof reached into heaven, and the sight thereof to the end of the Earth. There was great fruit in this tree and the birds of Heaven lived in its branches. From this tree the king saw a "watcher" and a "holy one" from Heaven emerge. They told him to destroy the tree, and leave its 'stump' in the Earth.'

Although this dream was confusing for the King, with hindsight today we are able to look at other aspects found in accounts concerning portals from around the biblical landscape of that time. The word 'watcher' suggests someone who is 'from this other place (heaven)' and is accompanied by a 'holy one'. They both 'emerge' from this other place. Watcher is a name given to the Nephilim, giant mysterious beings who first appeared in the early cultures of the Middle East and derives from the Egyptian name for "divine being" or "god", neter, which means 'one who watches.' Neter-neter land is the name of the place in the stars where these beings dwell. Sumeria, another earthly land of the An-un-naki, was known as the land of 'ones who watch'. To find out more as to why Nebuchadnezzar wanted this dream to be deciphered in haste, we need to look at another account involving the King:

'Nebuchadnezzar sets up an image of gold to worship in Babylon. The image is a massive three score (60) cubits high and six cubits wide. A cubit is 18 inches, making the image 540 inches high (three score or thirty times 18 inches high). 540 inches is 45 feet high, about the size of a four and a half story building. This project was big Whatever it was, the massive structure could be seen from miles around.

This image depicts one who spoke like a dragon, *the first beast, who's deadly wound was healed. And he does great wonders. He makes fire come down from heaven. And he tells the people to construct an image to the beast, which had been wounded by the sword, but did live.'* The person who 'speaks like a dragon' has the power to give life to this image, in other words to make it speak. Anyone who would not worship the image of the beast should be killed', says Revelation. The problem that Nebuchadnezzar had, was that he could not make the gleaming head of gold speak. He tried using musical vibrations to get it to work, but this was to no avail. Eventually the King summoned three wise Jews from Babylon who were friends of Daniel and Abednegor - who worked at the Temple of Solomon - but when they saw the bulking image, they refused to help him. It has been suggested that these three wise men possessed something that Nebuchadnezzar needed to make the image speak, for while in the temple they were able to accomplish this. So what was this golden image that could, if you knew what to do, speak? While conquering Jerusalem, Nebuchadnezzar was known to have pillaged the Temple of Solomon and removed the holy objects to take back to Babylon. It is possible that these would have included the Ark of the

Covenant and the ultimate Secret of the Temple, the Golden Head of God. The clue in understanding what the dream meant comes from the ancient Egyptian accounts of Osiris and the journeys into the Otherworld.

Osiris' ladder (later to become Jacobs Ladder) into the heavens is a pillar atop a platform (or 'stump') that resembles the Ark of the Covenant (which the ancients said was made of gold). If this is the tree atop the stump of Nebuchadnezzar's dream, and if this is his golden image of the beast, then what these stories relate, is Nebuchadnezzar's attempt to open a Stargate. The story goes on that the king is so annoyed at the lack of cooperation from the three wise men, that he has them thrown into the burning furnace at the foot of the golden image, but only after they all don highly unusual helmets and protective clothing! Nebuchadnezzar is astonished that when he goes to inspect the burned up bodies, he sees the men walking out of the furnace quite unharmed, accompanied by a fourth man who looks like an angel.

It has been suggested that the Temple Of Solomon housed more than material treasures, including the sacred Ark of the Covenant and that is why powerful leaders and wise men like Nebuchadnezzar considered the temple an important spoil of war. Although the temple was destroyed by his forces, it is claimed in biblical texts that the Ark was secreted away to Babylon. This was no simple ornate wooden chest, but something altogether more valuable to those who knew how to work it. There seems to be a sense when describing the Ark, that it was of a higher technology, a device that could as easily allow men to communicate with God as it could destroy them with its fiery blast. Was the Ark of the Covenant some kind of portal generator, and if so, where did it originate from?

The answer may be forthcoming if we apply the same logic that we currently do to locating portals today, for upon examination of sacred texts and biblical references to the Ark and where it was housed, we find it is the actual site of Solomon's Temple that may reveal this truth. There have in fact been at least three buildings that we refer to as the Temple of Jerusalem, that were built at or close to Jerusalem's Temple Mount. Scholars have, for centuries searched in vain for any remnant of the sacred sanctuary of Solomon as described in 1.Kings:6 of the Bible. However, a number of Iron Age temple remains have been discovered throughout the Levant which bare a striking resemblance to the description given for Solomon's Temple, the closest of which are the black basalt ruins at 'Ain Dara' in northern Syria.

In my previous book about the Settle portal, I proposed and discovered that ancient landscape markers in the form of standing stones and stone circles were placed at the positions known to some Neolithic descendants of a long lost race of humans called the 'first peoples'. In an era before our current history, these evolved humans had full knowledge of the natural workings of the dimensional portals found all over the world and interacted with the beings that travelled through them, gaining more and more knowledge that is hidden today. Due to Earth changes on a massively destructive scale, the first peoples were all but wiped out, but those few who survived, passed on through the generations the technological workings of the portals and star-gates to the Stone and Bronze Aged peoples. In time, the real reason for these important energy sites and vortexes became lost to the ancients, but instinct took over, which enabled them to feel that these were sacred places of power. So they built megalithic structures and stone circles to help remember that which they once knew, yet in doing so, religion and worship was born out of the science of how to travel to other worlds and realities using human & natural energy fields, enforcing further secrets and hidden knowledge for the few who had held onto the truth.

In the legends of Mu & Atlantis, we find clues to the superior knowledge and sciences held by the first peoples. They understood a level of science that we have yet to know and worked closely with the natural elements, free energy and the creational forces. Amongst them were adepts of what we would call magic, really a level of science that relied on the manifestation of matter and form. They understood that we were no different to all energies found in all the universe and indeed, in all other dimensions. The wisdom that the Ancient Egyptians attained seems to have arrived from some place else which has yet to be determined by historical scholars. This is evident in the mathematical genius of the dimensions and geographical layout of temples and the Great Pyramid in particular. Historical tradition states that Thoth, the architect of the Universe embraced by the masonic fraternities even today, was the carrier of a secret knowledge and wisdom; a level of scientific understanding that seems lost to the modern era. Down the centuries this hidden knowledge had been passed down through the hands of those supposedly worthy of it, guarded by an enclosed mind-set which believed that it contained information that the masses in general would not, or could not, understand. Certain historic individuals are said to have tapped in to this level of awareness which helped mankind to progress back towards that knowledge they once were already fully aware of. It is said that Copernicus replaced the earth-centred complacency of the Middle Ages with his heliocentric universe model, after openly stating that he had arrived at his revolutionary insight only after studying the secret writings of the ancient Egyptians. In my book 'Isaac Newton & The Secret Sun Dial', I allude to Newton being aware of a hidden level of awareness which helped him to understand the scientific principles of the Universe, gravity and light in a revolutionary way. Of course evidence points towards Newton being fascinated by Time and Portals and there is a degree of evidence to support that he visited the Settle portal in his life. With this in mind, it is interesting to learn that Newton once stated that,

"the Egyptians concealed mysteries that were above the capacity of the common herd under the veil of religious rites and hieroglyphic symbols"

Much less well known about Newton than his major advancements in the laying down of the foundations for modern physics, was that he was obsessed with the hermetic traditions of the east and alchemical discoveries, in particular the quest for the Philosopher's Stone. He also believed and wrote about a tenth of all his works on the subject, that secrets to life and Man's place in the known universe, could be found in the secret wisdom concealed within the pages of Daniel in the Old Testament. From intense study, Newton's biblical findings led him towards the realisation for him personally, that a hidden code of science could be found within the floor plan and building structure of the Temple Of Solomon. The code brought the sudden revelation to him that within the Temple were all of the elements of the universe and he believed that by gaining knowledge of this, it would be possible to know the mind of God. There is no doubt that Newton was of great mind, but at the angst of many modern day scientists, even the great man himself had to concede in his own words that, *'he had drawn not only upon his own genius, but also upon some very old and secret repository of wisdom, that the law of gravitation expounded in his greatest writing, the Principia was not new but rather had been known and fully understood in ancient times.'*

One such sacred site which I believe was a major portal, existed close to what we know today and in biblical times as the Dome of the Rock in Jerusalem. This was close to the site of the original Solomon's Temple, which when it existed in its original form, became a vortex for the portal due to something that it housed; the Ark of the Covenant. The Bible says that it was the sons of D'Anu, the people of Daniel, who had originally brought this device to Earth. The angel who appeared to king Nebuchadnezzar was related to the people of Daniel, but the king was of a different kind of people (who remained outside of the hidden knowledge of the portals) and they would not want Nebuchadnezzar to enter their realm uninvited. The only evidence we have about this 'device' called the Ark is taken from sources within the Old Testament of the Bible and other religious texts. There is no accurate historic evidence for the Ark of the Covenant, but we do have similar Ancient Egyptian and Babylonian 'chests' which look like the object being described in the holy scriptures. We need to determine what this Ark really was and where it came from? Who were the mysterious D'Anu who brought the device to Earth, implying that it came from somewhere other than this planet and if so, what was it really used for?

The Ark of the Covenant is first mentioned in the Bible in Exodus 25. Following Israel's deliverance from slavery in Egypt, God instructs Moses to build a Tabernacle (or tent) in which the Israelites will worship God. Placed in a special area known as "the Holy of Holies," the Ark of the Covenant was the most sacred object in the Tabernacle. Detailed instructions were given by God to construct the Ark. It was to be made with acacia wood and overlaid with gold. Dimensionally, the Ark was to be 2.5 cubits (1 cubit is approximately 18 in.) long and 1.5 cubits wide and high. Atop the Ark were two gold cherubim that stood with their wings covering an area of the Ark known as the "Mercy Seat." There remains a confusion between the actual Ark and the chest or box in which it was carried from place to place. The construction that we read about (above) for the wooden acacia and gold lined chest was not the Ark device. This was something else that 'was brought to this planet' by the D'Anu. Just what the Ark device itself looked like is not described, but it seems that the appendages like the two cherubim and the Mercy seat (that were a constructed part of the carrying chest) may have been needed to make the Ark device work. The chest-like box seems to have been some kind of transmitter of high frequencies and maybe the Mercy seat was a place on the chest where certain living beings, human or not, could have been transported to and from this dimensional state when sat on that part of the chest. This seems like utter speculation, but may not be that too far fetched.

Researcher Steve Burnand speculates that,

*'If this is a wave based device it might be both a power generator and a portal device. Most religions inherit ideas from elsewhere and take over previous sacred sites as in the UK with many churches on the sites of previous stone circles and even using the circle stones in there construction and plunder the sacred relic's of others, as in the crusades.. I would imagine there was much abandoned technology around the great pyramids that was first discovered by the ancient Egyptians. As this technology came from thousands of years earlier, it went into decline in ancient Egypt and as in the Indiana Jones type scenario, what's left of it today, is stashed away in places like the Vatican vaults. Could this device - the Ark - have come from the kings chamber in the great pyramid?' *

Certainly we know that the Ark had connections in its early earth life with Ancient Egypt, through its mention in the biblical texts of the Old Testament concerning Moses, who was said to have been brought up as a child in the house of Pharaohs daughter. Even the very fact that the building of the Great Pyramid which supposedly pre-dates the reign of the nearest Pharaoh of the 18th Dynasty (which seems to fit with what we know about the character Moses in the bible) who is Akhenaten, would suggest that some kind of long lost knowledge and ability in design and geometrics was employed in such a fantastic feat. We read that Moses, after receiving the ten commandments from God on Mount Sinai, instructed 'Bezaleel, a man filled with the spirit of God in wisdom and in understanding, and in the knowledge, and in all manner of workmanship to devise cunning works' to build the carrying chest for the Ark device. In his book 'The Sign and the Seal', Graham Hancock gives his account as to what the Ark may be and suggests that three options seem most apparent.

1. That the account of the Ark in the Old Testament is correct and it was a repository of divine energies from God, which were capable for all of the miracles that it performed.

2. The Ark was just an ordinary ornate wooden & gold casket that its originators used to dupe generations of the children of Israel, possibly through mass-hallucination and hysteria.

3. The Old Testament description of the Ark was both right and wrong at the same time. The Ark delivered genuine powers, but these were more man-made than supernatural or the will of God.

We need to look at these 'miracles' that the Ark was said to perform and try to decide whether they were genuine, tricks or indeed supernatural in nature? One of the most mentioned of the miracles was that the Ark was able to levitate itself off the ground. It could also lift its bearers off the ground and other objects around it. Yet, it is said that it required bearers to lift and carry it from place to place in the wilderness and it was constructed with wooden poles for them to do so. It was said to emit a strange light and a cloud which materialised out of thin air between the two cherubim on the Mercy Seat. It was able to afflict ailments on people that was similar to leprosy and tumours. If touched by the wrong people or by accident, it killed them. Hancock is correct in noting that the Ark behaved more like a machine than like a 'miracle maker'; it carried out certain tasks which only seemed to work effectively within certain parameters and to certain conditions. This suggested to Hancock that it was likely that the Ark was some kind of device that had been designed and constructed by Man, with all the defects that machinery brings from time to time, and was the result of human skill and ingenuity. I beg to differ due to the fact that this does not answer where the knowledge for constructing such an amazing 'machine' first came from and why only the followers of Moses and the ancestors of the D'Anu were capable of developing and using such a device in those early times?

As mentioned, I feel that the confusion as to whether the Ark of the Covenant was supernatural in origin or man-made, comes down to another confusion of details which show that the Ark described in the story of Moses, was a wooden and gold box much like the one found in Tutankhamen's tomb. The actual Ark of the Covenant was 'housed' in this chest and it was a device that came to earth from somewhere else. To discover where this place was 'off this earth' we really need to discover who the D'Anu were and how they came by the Ark?

"The Anunnaki (also transcribed as: Anunna, Anunnaku, Ananaki and other variations) are a group of deities in ancient Mesopotamian cultures (i.e. Sumerian, Akkadian, Assyrian, and Babylonian). The name is variously written "da-nuna", "da-nuna-ke-ne", or "da-nun-na", meaning something to the effect of "those of royal blood" or "princely offspring". According to The Oxford Companion to World Mythology, the Anunnaki "are the Sumerian deities of the old primordial line; they are chthonic deities of fertility, associated eventually with the underworld, where they became judges. They take their name from the old sky god An (Anu). "

The Anunnaki appear in the Babylonian creation myth. After the creation of mankind, Marduk divides the Anunnaki and assigns them to their proper stations, three hundred in heaven, three hundred on the earth. The Anunnaki are mentioned in the story of Gilgamesh around the time of the great flood and were watchers over the seven flames of hell. In Assyrian and Babylonian mythology, the Anunnaki were the children of the Gods, Anu & Ki.

The Anunnaki seem to have been the same beings as the fallen angels that we find in the biblical texts. They are often described as a giant race, almost a kind of super human and are able to mate with the daughters of Man to produce 'different' offspring with psychic powers. It is from this race of angel-human hybrids that some believe the 'children of Israel' descended and why they continued to have a close relationship with God through the angels. We can turn to both the scriptures and the historical records to find examples of Giant beings at the dawn of time stemming from the pre-flood era. Archaeologist, Dr Carl Baugh states: " Optimal genetic expression means the best that the organism has within its DNA is expressed because of favourable atmospheric conditions." Under such conditions in the early period of the planet, plants and animals would live longer and grow much bigger. This is exactly what we find in the geological column records, all living systems were much larger. A greater O-Zone layer around the planet prior to the flood, which has now diminished to one seventh of what it once was, is evidence that gigantism may have been the norm as this would have filtered out more solar radiation which could have slowed down cell growth in less favourable circumstances.

It is almost as if the Annunaki were looking after their experiment down the ages, given hidden information and protection to the 'humans' that they had first created, different to other human beings in certain areas of the world. The secrets of this high tech belonging to the Anunnaki was given over to their 'creations' and their descendants in lineage, whenever there was a threat to the continuity of it by famine, war or natural disaster. They certainly were, in respect to this, the chosen ones.

By the time that Moses walked the earth, the connection with the angels had been well established. From time to time they would give signs to members of their hybrid offspring, to keep the connection alive that they were different from other humans in one particular region of the planet or another. Religious texts from all over the world, indicate that amongst these 'differences' were the ability to use psychic means to make prophecy, to understand matter and make miracles, to visit other dimensional states and visit the heavens of their 'father'. The amazingly detailed stories of Enoch, Ezekiel, & Daniel are testament to this. Sometimes the angels would put signs in the sky for those with the psychic connection to recognise, and one of those was the hybrid Akhenaten, a contemporary of Moses in the 18th Dynasty Egypt.

The Orange Balls of Lights phenomena is well entrenched within the subject of modern day UFO sightings. I have experienced this kind of phenomenon myself, in fact it was through such an experience with an OBOL in 1980 that I first became aware of UFO reality. Thousands of years before, Akehnaten was having his own encounter with a similar, if not the same, phenomena.

Akhenaten became Pharaoh after his father Amenhotep III's sudden death in Thebes. He was crowned Amenhotep IV (a Pharaoh of Amun). For some unknown reason Akhenaten removed all traces of his father's name from the Stele and monuments of Upper Egypt, which may have come about due to something which happened in the deserts, something so unusual, that it changed forever the concepts of religion in Ancient

Egypt. Even before this 'happening', Akhenaten's family had started to embrace a new awareness towards the pantheon of Gods that their ancestors had worshipped for generations. It was as if, the rulers of that land were beginning to wake up to the fact that something which connected them to the gods, operated as a go-between, unseen, but ever present when called upon. Little is known about Akhenaten's young life and some historians suggest that he may not have been living with his Royal family or with his mother Queen Tiye at that time, but may have been visiting what is now Syria where his mother had connections with the rulers of that land.

If we are to take the physical descriptions of Akhenaten (and his children) at face value, then it seems we are dealing with someone who certainly would have stood out amongst the crowd. Most paintings and carvings have him portrayed with an elongated head at the age of twenty five, when he came to power, his abdomen being elongated and pendulous, his thighs long and swollen, very female-like in shape and form. It has been suggested that this is a deformation caused by inter-breeding (which certainly did happen within the royal line), and also maybe the results of progressive lipodstrophy, 'where there is a progressive & eventual complete disappearance of the subcutaneous fat of the upper part of the body, and, or the other, by a marked increase of the adipose tissue below the loins.' However, this condition remained extremely rare in adult men and mostly none existent today. We know that the royal family surrounding Akhenaten were exhibitionists and used to appear in public in the nude, some say quite normal for that period in time. Or was it? Could this not have been an intended statement in celebration of the fact that they looked physically different from other humans, something which served as a reminder to the masses under that particular rule, that this Royal family were of the Gods and Men. Not only was Akhenaten different to other people in the physical sense, his outlook and appreciation of life and the wonders of the world around him, made statements in his time that were very modern. He has been called 'the world's first idealist, the first individual, and the first prophet of history. Even comparisons with Christ have not been lacking, known in his time as a 'carer for life' and 'the King living in Truth'.

Before we look at the OBOL experience that the young Akhenaten 'reported' in his Stele, much in the way that modern day UFO witnesses report their accounts with the unexplained, I think it is right to look at comparisons made between his person (as known to history) and that of the biblical character, Moses. There are many parallels between both and it would not be too far fetched to suggest that they are either one and the same, or that the latter was based upon the former. Both seem to be intrinsically woven into elements we find within our studies of the portals and devices that may exist to allow inter-dimensional travel and an earlier than normal knowledge about them. Akhenaten was born about 1394BC, the time that biblical scholars place Moses being born at the frontier city of Zarw. In his book 'Moses and Monotheism' Sigmund Freud argued that Moses had been an Atenist priest forced to leave Egypt with his followers after Akhenaten's death. Freud argued that Akhenaten was striving to promote monotheism, something that the biblical Moses was able to achieve. The argument for Moses and Akhenaten being connected at some level was furthered by Ahmed Osman, who claimed that Yuya, the maternal grandfather of the king was the same person as the biblical Joseph, which would cement if true, the line of David within the royal Egyptian household. Another fact of history that is given in support of the duality of the two personages, is found within the content of the

'Great Hymn to the Aten' , said to have been written by Akhenaten and the biblical Psalm 104 in which lines of verse seem almost identical. However, the most significant correlation must be in the way that Akhenaten changed thousands of years of worshipping various god forms to the first ever monotheistic religion, the worship of the sun god deity, the Aten.

What we call Amarna, or el-Amarna today was the city of Akhetaten which means "The Horizon of the Aten". This was the ancient capital of Akhetaten. It lies some 365 miles south of Cairo in a natural amphitheatre between inhospitable cliffs. This narrow opening exists for some twelve kilometres along the Nile River and has a half rounded depth of about five kilometres. This is the place where, in about the fifth year of the king's reign, we are told that by divine inspiration, Akhenaten had to build his capital and move all of his people to live in the middle of the desert. We have a good description handed down in the stele of Amarna as to why this happened and what was behind the divine inspiration, which ultimately enforced the notion that Akhenaten was in communion with the OBOL phenomenon at one particular place. Could that place have been a portal?

On the boundary stele of Akhet-aten, there features the 'Earlier Proclamation', Akhenaten emphasis's, *"Now, it is the Orb, my father, who advised me concerning it, namely the Horizon of the Orb"* (Akhet-Aten, the name of the place where he was to build his new city in the desert) and states further that there is no need for earthly advice on this matter. If, as historians suggest, that Akhenaten was advised by 'the Orb' (his father), how might the sun have advised him? It has been suggested that a gap in the cliffs to the east of the site (the 'Royal Wadi') resembles the hieroglyph for 'horizon' over which the sun rises . Another is that Akhenaten wished to locate his capital in the true geodetic center of the country. However, in his own words we find that Akhenaten refers to a time in his earlier years when he was at that very spot and sighted the Aten between a cleft in the cliffs, as the living 'sun disk' which spoke to his thoughts. We know that the ancient Egyptian term for the disk of the sun was the Aten, which had been first mentioned and evidenced in the Middle Kingdom, though of course simpler solar worship began much earlier in the country's history. It should be noted that the term 'Aten' could be applied to any kind of disk, including even the surface of a mirror or the Moon. In the story of Sinuhe (from the Middle Kingdom), Amenemhat is described as 'soaring into the sky and uniting with Aten (a disk), his creator.'

This has often been described as a vision, but when we read what took place in his choosing the site of Akhenaten's new city, there seems more to it. After observing the 'sun disk' (Orange Ball of Light?) between the two mountains, he felt as if God was speaking directly to him and guiding him to make change in the land. Akhenaten further emphasises his special relationship with the Aten by stating in the Hymn that the Aten has taught the king its "ways" and its "mind." In these teachings, the importance of equality between humans and all creatures alike is also further espoused in the Short (version of the)Hymn. There seems to have been some kind of special relationship between the king and the Aten, for example, the Aten was indeed 'hidden' to the common people as only the king could make offerings before the Aten within its temple. Did this imply that Akhenaten had been given knowledge that allowed only him to understand how to communicate with the Aten. A knowledge that was hidden from the masses (the common people)?

Throughout the whole of the Amarna period, there is not one single reference to the Aten speaking out as a God and in that, it was very odd compared to the previous gods of the ancient Egyptians. If anything, it is a rather hollow and inactive god. Yet, as we know, through Akhenaten, the Aten affected the historic progression of Egypt in a monumental way, the change in concept from the worship of many deities to the monotheistic religion of the one sole creator God. Further the Aten does not physically undertake any form of action and does not show any true compassion for the subjects of the earth it maintains. The Aten seems only to be a name and symbol for the light of the solar orb. It is not a living, thinking entity but only the solar energy that allows life to exist on earth. Therefore Aten cannot be described as a god in the truest sense as it is nothing more than an abstraction. We are only told by the king what the Aten supposedly believes or has done in the past. It is almost as if the King is the intermediary between the Aten (whatever that is) and the people. Akhenaten, Pharaoh or not, is a chosen channel for the ball of light!

Now, let us look at the story of Moses once again to see how the religious reforms in Egypt under Akhenaten that had brought about Monotheism, correlate with the vision of the Aten. In the King James version of the Bible we read in Exodus 3:

"Now Moses kept the flock of Jethro his father in law, the priest of Midian: and he led the flock to the backside of the desert, and came to the mountain of God, even to Horeb.

2 And the angel of the Lord appeared unto him in a flame of fire out of the midst of a bush: and he looked, and, behold, the bush burned with fire, and the bush was not consumed.

3 And Moses said, I will now turn aside, and see this great sight, why the bush is not burnt.

4 And when the Lord saw that he turned aside to see, God called unto him out of the midst of the bush, and said, Moses, Moses. And he said, Here am I.

5 And he said, Draw not nigh hither: put off thy shoes from off thy feet, for the place whereon thou standest is holy ground.

6 Moreover he said, I am the God of thy father, the God of Abraham, the God of Isaac, and the God of Jacob. And Moses hid his face; for he was afraid to look upon God."

If we were to write out the above passages in shorthand script, we would highlight the most important points being made here, mostly from the converse between the burning bush phenomenon and Moses. These are:

a) The situation - (the location) on the mountain of God (Horeb) found at the backside of the desert.

b) The 'angel of the lord' appears to Moses in a flame of fire out of the midst of a bush. The bush looks as if it is on fire, but it is not burnt or consumed by that fire.

c) Moses decides to investigate, to find out why the bush has not burnt away.

d) When the Lord (the angel)saw that he was coming to investigate, a voice supposed to be that of God called out to Moses, telling him where he was (in the bush). This God knew Moses' name.

e) 'God' warns Moses not to come any closer and to take off his shoes, as the place he is standing on, is holy (sacred) ground.

f) 'God' introduces himself to Moses as the God of his father and of Abraham, Isaac & Jacob.

Most importantly in this account there are a number of factors that jump out at me that describe well the types of supernatural phenomena that we find on investigations at the portal sites today. We have suggested that the Anunnaki (Angels) were a race of beings separate from mankind, but after interbreeding with humans at the dawn of time, they left certain individuals with the ability to communicate with them in a psychic way. These hybrids became the bloodline of David in the bible (and many other races of people throughout the world at that time) and so, they were the 'angels of the lord' or the messengers of Anu; the D'anu.

This supernatural being, the angel of the lord, appears to Moses from a position in the landscape which he is told is holy ground. Yet, he is not told why it is such. Another name for 'holy ground' would be sacred ground or 'sacred site' and we know again from research, that the positions of portals were once marked out in the distant past by Neolithic's with standing stones and megalithic structures, stone circles, etc., upon unseen energy lines that criss-cross the globe. Whatever Moses came across on the mountainsides of Horeb, it was probably something that allowed anyone 'with the knowledge and ability' to recognise the place for what it really was. The key word is 'appears' and that is what the phenomenon at portals do. They manifest into this reality seemingly from out of thin air and are often witnessed and described as having a luminous or fiery glow surrounding them; a kind of energy that is not fire and does not burn the immediate landscape. It is interesting too, that 'God' requests of Moses to not come any closer and to take off his shoes. We will examine the possible reasons for this in a later chapter, as this important aspect may support the theory that we are dealing with the grounding of energies at portal sites, in order for them to 'operate' correctly.

Evidence that there was something special about the site of the burning bush on the mountain is given again, by the account that Moses is instructed to re-visit the same location in order to 'communicate and gain instruction' from God. In Exodus 17:

6 Behold, I will stand before thee there upon the rock in Horeb; and thou shalt smite the rock, and there shall come water out of it, that the people may drink. And Moses did so in the sight of the elders of Israel.

7 And he called the name of the place Massah, and Meribah, because of the chiding of the children of Israel, and because they tempted the Lord, saying, Is the Lord among us, or not?

As mentioned, in Neolithic times, before even the lifetimes of even Akhenaten or Moses, the angels of the lord were busy instructing the holders of the sacred and hidden knowledge of the portals to mark out in natural stones (i.e. standing stones) such placements where dimensions meet. Further scriptural information suggests that this was continuing when Moses met with God on Mount Sinai. In Exodus 20:25

'And if thou wilt make me an altar of stone, thou shalt not build it of hewn stone: for if thou lift up thy tool upon it, thou hast polluted it.'

While in the wilderness, Moses sent out scouts to look for a favourable place for his peoples to settle after being exiled from Egypt. Some went to the north, to Hebron and on their return they reported that, "All the people we saw there are men of gigantic size. We felt no bigger than grasshoppers and that is how we looked to them." (Numbers 13:33). Then, again as the people of Moses came to the mountains of what is now Petra in Jordan they found that the place had been settled by giants, the Nephilim, the offspring of the Annunaki. In the later story of David and Goliath, we are told that the giant runs off with the Ark on his shoulders and takes it back to his gigantic brothers in the camp of the Philistines! It almost seems as if the Ark device might belong to the race of the 'giants', or that the Nephilim want to acquire it for there own use? The name Goliath probably comes from the Philistine giant of Gath (I Sam. xvii. 4) and "Goliath" is probably connected with the Assyro-Babylonian "Guzali" which means "running, ravaging spirits & the throne carriers" What were these mysterious 'thrones' that these giants were known to be carriers of? We can read in the bible that the Giant Gath and the Philistines lost the Ark once more, but only after having use it in their own battles before the Ark seemingly turns on them with death and destruction, mutilating the bodies of the priests looking after it. Eventually, the Ark makes its way back to Jerusalem and nothing is then said about it in the Old Testament after the return from Babylon, but the Apocrypha states that the Ark could not be found when the Jewish people rebuilt the Temple at the time of Ezra and Zechariah. The explanation in the Apocrypha was that Jeremiah hid the Ark in a cave in Mt. Nebo before the Babylonian invasion, and that its location would not be revealed until God was ready for it to be found.

The next time that the Ark device is mentioned is in the New Testament which seems to indicate that it was not being housed in the second Temple in Jerusalem under Roman occupation in 63BC. The Ark was so important in Israel from the time of Moses to the First Temple era, that it seems highly unusual that nothing is said of it in the Bible after the Babylonian Captivity, until the Letter to the Hebrews and the Book of Revelation in the New Testament. In Hebrews it is described as it was in the original Tabernacle made by Moses in the desert and in the book of Revelation, the Ark is seen by John in heaven. In neither case is the Ark mentioned as something that remains on the earth now. It seems that whatever the Ark device was, it had now returned back to 'heaven', another place not of this world. The Second Temple stood for over 500 years without containing an Ark, so this would suggest that the Temple site is not dependent on the Ark device being installed within the Holy of Holies, for it to be sacred. But, as we have seen, the device works equally well, wherever it is transported to and does not rely on any particular loyalty to one religion or another, to make it work. This gives the Ark as a device, an almost mechanical feel, a technological apparatus that although used by at least three separate races of people who were aware of the 'fallen angels' in biblical times, it was something that had been brought into the world by a supernatural force.

So where did the Ark go? There persists a legend that the Ark does exist on earth, but is hidden in a cave beneath the Temple Mount or at some secret location close to the site of the Dome. Some of the traditions place the Ark outside of Israel, such as at Mt. Nebo, at Akhetaten in

Egypt and even far-off Ethiopia. But all of these traditions have problems and seem unlikely, since there is a lack of any firm historical or scriptural evidence for them. Having just said that, however, it may seem like a contradiction when I now state that the Ark device may have been in those mentioned places at some time or another and even at all of those places at the same time! A clue to this comes from the fact that Ethiopian priests have stated that when they look at the Ark, it appears and disappears in front of their eyes...'like a mirror'.

I think that from the circumstantial biblical records and partly from the actual historical records, it is safe to say that the Ark device was real in the sense that it could be seen as a real physical thing which had to be transported in a box like chest whenever it was moved from place to place in ancient times. It remains a puzzle as to why it has to be carried by people, when it is said that one of its abilities was to levitate off the ground. The Ark device could not be touched by human hands and had to be viewed when activated at a distance, otherwise it could cause death and destruction. Whatever the device was, it was small enough to fit into the box made by Moses under the instruction of God and it does not seem to have been particularly heavy. When it was placed at certain sites, and it has been noted that two of these sites at least included natural bedrock on which it had to be placed; within the Dome on the Rock and in Ethiopia) the device gave off a mist like glow and a cloud above it and between the two cherubim positioned on the Mercy seat of gold. God was said to be present within this cloud and communicated (channelling?) with Moses and the priests who attended it. When in active mode, the device was said to look and act like a mirror, that would appear and then suddenly vanish into thin air. Of course, until it is either found or fully established as a real object/device the Ark remains an elusive mystery, but the above descriptions should be kept in mind, when we examine further how portals can be activated at certain sacred sites, where seemingly some kind of device is needed to better interact with the phenomena recorded there. With this concept in mind for now, I do not think it would harm us to reason that there is the possibility that world leaders and governments would like to get their hands on such a device, should it really exist, and it seems that at least in ancient and biblical times, this may have already happened. For in doing so, whoever owns and activates the Ark device, may have at their disposal, not only the secrets to the portals and inter-dimensional travel, but also a fuller awareness of who we are and where we might have originated from.

Above: *White Wells on Ilklet Moor as it was in 1993. The tumulus situated directly behind the old healing bath house, seems to be another example of the portal vortex.*

CHAPTER TWO

Positioning Portals

Back in the 1980's the term used for a location where many UFO and other strange unexplained phenomenon occur was a 'Window Area', implying that these locations allowed such manifestations into our reality from somewhere else, through a kind of unseen window or opening. There were many famous window areas around the world at that time, recognised for their high numbers of UFO related events which seemed to have a long history and overlapped previous encounters with the unknown. It soon became apparent that UFOs and the like, appeared to be reported in clusters at certain places more than at others and many of these window areas held similar and sometimes identical attributes in the physical make-up of the landscape and geology where they were to be found.

One such window, was Ilkley Moor in West Yorkshire, England. I was fortunate to have been very much involved with on site UFO investigations during a time when the Ilkley Moor window was actively open for business and I spent hundreds of hours investigating and researching that particular UFO hot-spot for sightings.

The Victorians referred to Ilkley Moor as the 'Place Of Horrors'. a reputation which seems to have built upon local accounts of strange unexplained happenings including multi-coloured lights in the skies, druid-like looking beings, and the moorlands' famous Black Dog encounters. Accounts of these supernatural manifestations exist in written records from Ilkley's past; including the White Wells 'Fairies' encounter of 1815. Interestingly, William Butterfield who recorded what happened at the Wells on midsummer morning of that year, underwent a kind of Oz-Factor experience prior to witnessing several diminutive green-clad men (DGM's). The 'Oz-Factor' was a term coined by Jenny Randles in the 1980s and refers to the onset of an altered state of consciousness often experienced before a UFO or other paranormal experience.

It was in 1981 that I lived in Otley, about 6 miles from Ilkley Moor and had now been several months since I observed an Orange Ball of Light type UFO which many other people had witnessed around the Ilkley Moor region at that time. The sighting inspired in me the compulsion to take up an interest in the UFO phenomenon and from this time, my inquisitiveness grew. I would often sit reading UFO books on the front doorstep of my home in Otley, from time to time, my gaze would wander off the text and over towards the western horizon, in the direction of the moors' Cow & Calf Rocks. The book would be quickly forgotten about at times when l would, by chance, observe very bright luminous objects resembling toothpaste' that squeezed out of thin air to descend from about 1000ft onto the summit of the moorlands. These toothpaste UFOs really did look like they emerged through some kind of invisible open window.

In his book called 'The Haunted Moor', written in 1934, Ilkley's respected business man, Nicholas Size re-counted his somewhat strange experiences whilst out walking the moorland slopes above the town. Even before he reached a location on the moor he would later call the 'Place of Horrors', he felt that he had been there before, that part of the moors being strangely familiar. He points out certain areas like White Wells and 'the clumps of trees which cover the Northern slopes'. Here, he was attracted in a way that left him feeling that he should not continue on his journey but did not know why.

Nicholas Size was forty years old and had travelled the world before coming home to Ilkley with the intention to retire and rest, but at different times, quite unexpectedly, he kept coming across particular parts of the moors which 'seemed to be trying to remind him of things long ago forgotten'. He spent a great deal of time examining the cup and ring carved stones of the moor and speculated for what use they really were made? Whilst in the Cow and Calf rocks region, he came across a place called the 'fairies church'. Size thought that these 'fairies' may have been a small race of humans of the Neolithic period who proceeded the ancient Britons living on the higher ground of the moors back then. He speculates that these may have been the roots of all the traditions of gnomes, pixies, and the 'good people' or the 'little people'.

On one occasion in his book Size relates how he 'felt compelled' to visit the 'Place of Horrors' for reasons he does not know. On top of the Cow Rock, he could see several figures and bright flames in the night air, This was most unusual, and he felt that he was made to noticed that the figures were wearing cloaks like monks. As he gazed at the scene, he describes a kind of phosphorescence, and even more unusual, that the rock was whole, not in two parts, one being the Calf rock as it is found today and the other the Cow rock, as was still the case in 1934.

It was very late into the night and Size was getting tired, but worried that the light on the moors was too bright considering that normally it 'did not appear to be so vivid'. Battling with his sudden tiredness, Size made a hasty retreat off the moor to the safety of the township below. At a later date, Size records the same type of phenomena again. This time, he came quite close to what was going on. To his utter horror he describes the same cloaked figures moving around a blazing fire, which bellowed a sinister 'swirling mist instead of smoke, and as he watched, it became obvious to him (he writes) that this was a scene from the distant past; an actual ritual of small druid-like beings, who were ignorantly busy in their act of sacrificial killing!

"You are not of this realm," Size shouted out in horror at what he was witnessing only meters away.

As he began to turn to run, he found his mind 'in a whirl', and his actions began to lack any purpose. "My hands and feet seemed to be fastened in some way, and I was hauled and 'lifted hither and thither by hands which 'were irresistible'

Size goes on to explain that he thought that something had been put over his face, as 'he could not see anything at all, nothing but blackness'. Battling with his wits, he was eventually able to get away from the place, yet still felt that something might have been 'implanted in his head by the power which was drawing him on'.

As Size looked around in a state of frenzy, his eyes were attracted to nearby Armscliffe Cragg on the Eastern horizon (looking back towards the Otley direction). He gradually remembered his previous nights experience where 'a luminous cloud was hanging in the sky, which looked very like Pleiades, but singularly too low'.

Amongst the thousands of UFO reports and the handful of closer encounters with the supposed occupants of these craft that have emerged from the Ilkley Moor window area, some cases, like the one just described by Nicholas Size, merit more attention when we consider that the moorland may have been more than a window into the unknown, it may have been a portal between worlds. The West Rock encounter, which took place some 60 years after Sizes' experiences close by, includes aspects that mirror what happened to Size and more evidence that a portal (or vortex portals) exist in this part of Rombalds Moor, of which Ilkley Moor is the highest point.

The West Rock incident involved two teenager boys, one called Wayne and (other name withheld so we will call him Chris). Wayne began to describe to me in 1994, how he and his friend, who he kept on insisting would never 'go near those moors again', had traversed the steep slopes of the northern edge of Rombalds Moor for years. I began to form a picture of the particular sites he was mentioning. His Journey to the summit of West Rock, above the Ilkley Tarn and White Wells was one I had no problem recognising. I had walked the same track many times myself. As his route description reached the point where they had first observed a ball of light, hanging motionless in the air just above the gigantic rock outcrop that overlooks 'rocky valley', goose-pimples raised on the back of my neck. For, without my telling him, Wayne had no idea that the only thing now, stopping them from entering into the site of one of Britain's most unusual UFO epics, (the Ilkley Entity Photographic Case of December 1987) was the UFO itself, standing as if a sentinel between the fairly safe and normal, and the place where a group of green clad entities allegedly abducted an ex policeman. Unbeknown to them at the time, if Wayne and his terrified friend had carried on along their intended direction of travel without their passage being halted by the ball of light, then one wonders just what they would have been reporting to me, if anything at all?
From what had been established in my interviews, both witnesses agree that their encounter took place on 29th October, 1991, sometime between 4 00pm and 8.00pm. At this time of the year, even in fine weather conditions, the moors can quickly draw in the darkness as the evening arrives. On this day the weather was, to say the least, 'appalling',

certainly not a day for going out to enjoy a leisurely walk. Add to this, the fact that it was nearly Halloween, it would seem the night-time desolation of Ilkley Moor would be the last place to venture after daylight hours unless you were very brave. The walking journey to the top of the northern edge of the moor took about an hour and a half (due to carrying backpacks & wearing heavy wet clothes) and this is quite an uphill struggle normally. I checked the journey time when I went with Wayne to Ilkley Moor on Saturday 22nd October, 1994, and we reconstructed the same route that he took with his friend on the day of the experience. In all fairness I found that the journey could have been quicker, but factors like taking periodic rests, climbing across rocks in their path, leaving their intended route to look at moorland features, expanded the time by approximately thirty more minutes.

Wayne described the journey he and Chris took to get to West Rock in accurate detail but it soon became evident that he was not able to give the same accuracy in describing the 'chase back down the side of the moor.
After the encounter with the ball of light to the edge of the moor was without any recollected detail, only a vague impression from Wayne. I wondered why this should have been so? From the start, Wayne insisted that the return journey took what seemed to be only a matter of ten minutes!
A number of known & established factors surrounding the case, made this statement inconceivable, especially in retrospect, when Wayne stated correctly that the walk up to West Rock took approximately an hour and a half. We should remember that most of the return journey consisted of them both running in the dark in a terrified state and the track from the moor would have to be negotiated with utmost care over the slippery rain laden ground. This would have made it almost impossible to move at any kind of speed over the drenched bracken and muddy track ways. Also, the witness's unfamiliarity with that region in the dark, causing them to slow down & stop to re-assess their surroundings would have added time to the escape.
I soon began to realise in the investigation of that case, that a time anomaly may exist, but one which was very different from those that had previously been reported in the area where mostly it was cases of missing time during the event. Yet here we had what seemed to be a case of time being gained if anything during Wayne and his friends journey off that

moor!

If this is correct, then whatever happens during some close UFO experiences, seems to affect our perception of time and the way that we value or measure time. In the West Rock incident, we know that Wayne and Chris were actually chased back off the moor by the UFO low in the air behind them as if in pursuit. Both claimed that the ball of light, giving off a low electrical sound like a hum, followed them along the very same route they took and when they reached the moorland roadside, it hovered over a council signpost they hid under. It was later found that this signpost had been melted and the metal post bent over.

It might be reasonable to suggest that the two witnesses had interacted at some point (possibly at the site of West Rock) with the UFO, and that some kind of contact had been established between them both and the hovering object. Did time alter at this point?  We could speculate that time had been speeded up to such a rate that reality for the teenagers changed too. One minute they were being chased by something they feel was not of this planet and the next they were off the moors looking on as object sped back in a moment with no sound to its original position, hovering once more above that massive overhanging rock.

Another equally baffling case from this part of the moor concerns three friends, now in elderly age, who experienced this odd time anomaly. The location where this event took place overlooks an area of woodland called Netherwood - a place name with 'strange' connotations, between Ilkley & Addingham, on the Hebers Ghyll edge of Ilkley Moor. High above these woods on the north-western rocky outcrop can be found the ancient carving, the Swastika Stone. Just what the symbol on the carved rock represents, has left local historians pondering and suggest that it is so positioned there for no other reason than to signify the Universal Godhead of some arcane religion, incorporating the design of the cross and the wheel of creation. Archaeologists propose that it may be from the Bronze Age, but could also be two or more separate carvings in one, from different eras in history. Other cup & ring motifs found on the local moorlands seem to indicate that this was once a common practice by our early ancestors. Timothy Taylor of Bradford University says about the carving, " we don't know just what the art meant. It may have memorialised ancient magic places revered in the preceding Stone Age." George Annings was one of the three middle-aged visitors to the carved rock, who attended the outing organised by his spiritual church in nearby Leeds. The other two were both women in their late forties who had all become friends through their shared interest in spiritualism. George relates what happened to all three of them in 1983

"Our visit to the swastika stone was made sometime in the early autumn of that year. I arrived at the church in Leeds only to discover that our leader had been notified of several absences due to illness, and that there was only the three of us at the meeting. On the spur of the moment, it was decided that we would pay a visit to Ilkley Moor and for some unknown reason it was suggested we should go look at the Swastika Stone in particular. At about 7.00pm, I parked the car at the edge of the moors, then followed a track over two streams that were easy for us to step across at Hebers Ghyll. We reached the outcrop of rocks where the ancient carving can be found. It was still quite light in the evening about 7.15pm, when we all sat down at the site to meditate. I then fell asleep, and as far as I know, so did the other two women!

"None of us could remember why this had occurred or how long we had been asleep. We just woke up all together, in the darkness of a late night! Everywhere was completely dark and silent. We found it difficult to make out just where we were standing, just able to see each other if we got close up. This brought about panic from my two female friends, understandably, through not knowing what had taken place there and why everything around us had changed in what seemed like an instant of falling off to sleep.

"Then, some moments later we felt the air around us fill with what seemed like a static charge, we could all see a ball of bright light that appeared to the south and just hung in the sky near to our position. It was the only source of light we could see, apart from tiny street and house lights in the valley below. At first, I took this to be a rescuing helicopter that must have spotted us, but then we became puzzled because there was no sound coming from it and it was so near. The light coming down was not a beam, but more like a 'bubble of daylight', standing out dramatically within the darkness of the open moors like a spotlight. There was no way that it was the Moon, as the ball of light was seen (by all three of us) to be getting closer, too close, as we watched.

"The UFO remained at about rooftop height. I know it sounds peculiar, but we all began to feel safe with it being there even though we didn't know what it was, and so we decided to walk towards it. As we began to move cautiously in the dark, all sense of fear and being alone on the moor went away from me. The brightness that was being emitted from the light and onto the ground underneath it, kept a little ahead of our position, as if leading us further on to follow it like some kind of pied piper. I would still have to see a map of the region to find the exact direction we took earlier from the road to the Swastika Stone site, but the light moving ahead of us was leading back to where our car was parked!

"When we eventually got to the safety of the car, after having to cross the two streams in a disorientated state due to the bright light reflecting off the water and wet rocks, we soon realised that three hours had elapsed from the time we first fell asleep by the stone to us waking up with the arrival of the UFO. It was now 11pm and no matter how we tried to suggest a sensible reason for this loss of time to each other, there was no accounting for the whole experience by the Swastika Stone and we still have no idea where the missing time went."

Like many more window areas, Ilkley Moor has a long recorded history. The moor was once an ancient forest, hard to imagine today and all kinds of animals and wildlife, now long gone, featured at the place. The first Neolithic farmers of the area moved to the higher grounds of the moorland tops in order to find new grazing and escape the perils of the man-hunting beasts like wild boar in the depths of the forest below. Open to the skies on this high point of land and feeling more secure, early forms of religions began to appear surrounding the planets, stars, Moon and the Sun. On the high plateau of Rombalds Moor evidence of early man's appreciation of the wonders of the natural world around him, made headway for the construction of communities in the way of encampments and solar temples, standing stone circles, carved rocks, etc. Megalithic man made his mark forever on the highest parts of the moor.

Something else was happening at that time though and this connects with what we know about the migrations of Neolithic races across the continents and Europe around 1500BC. A project like none ever seen before was under way to mark out across the whole planet a system of marker points in stone which would form a grid pattern. We have evidence of these markers everywhere and none more so than on the high reaches of Ilkley Moor, where there are more ancient cup & ring carved rocks, standing stones, stone circles and other megaliths per square meter than anywhere in the the rest of the world. Something very important was being recognised in those early times by a peoples that we have been led to believe were ignorant of forward thinking in the modern sense.

I visited the 'place of horrors' on Ilkley Moor many times and gained a good understanding of the locality over twenty years between 1980 and 2000. One particular place mid way up the northern slopes of the moor, a small Victorian bath house and healing spa called White Wells, became something of a magnet for my investigations into the UFO phenomenon. The Ilkley register for August 1793, recorded a singular accident to a girl aged nine years old. She was drowned in one of the baths whilst attempting to bathe herself. In 1982 the babysitter to the owners of the Wells at that time, was terrified at the apparition she saw, a ghostly figure of a young girl weeping at the side of the building.

In the works Upper Wharfedale by Harry Speight, we learn of a curiously sculptured stone (which is now actually a part of the flooring) was found at Ilkley Parish Church. A plaster cast of it was made showing in relief a half-length human figure wearing some sort of skullcap. In each of the hands are held two serpent-like rods in an upright position.

Most scholars believe this to be a representation of the Goddess Verbia, Roman protector of the nearby River Wharfe and waters in the area. The site it was excavated from was part of an altar in days gone by and the inference may be drawn that the two serpent-like objects are intended to typify the bodies of two sacred streams entering the symbolised singular embodiment of the river itself. A number of Holy Wells, springs, etc., can be found throughout the whole of the llkley region and in retrospect, some have even suggested the goddess figure might even apply to the god of strength, Hercules, hero & conqueror of evil spirits, one in each of his colossal hands. There are such sacred streams around White Wells which run down the moor side into the River Wharfe. The Cow and Calf rocks, for centuries, were believed in tradition to be the 'home and domain of the local fairy folk'. Today, it is still known as the 'Fairy House'. This area in Victorian times was, if we are to believe all records, saturated with manifestations of small human-like entities.

The best known of all fairy encounters on Ilkley Moor, took place at White Wells, less than a quarter mile away in 1815.
Briefly, a certain William Butterfield, the respected keeper of the wells, went to open up the healing baths on mid-summer morning. To his amazement, as he tried to enter the large wooden door to the building he found that the key would not engage in the lock and simply 'melted' into it. However, the key was solid as ever when he took it out of the lock to inspect it. When he eventually opened the door, he couldn't believe his eyes,
'There was a strange humming and buzzing, and all around the bath, many small folk, dressed all in green, were hurrying and scurrying into and out of the water. Something seemed to indicate Butterfield's presence to the elemental horde, so they all scampered over the low walls of the building, back out into the oceans of the vast moorland'.

But why do so many odd things take place at this location and why over so many years? I applied dowsing, which is a physical extension of the psychic ability using tools like rods and pendulums' to try to find an answer to that question.
At the White Wells site, the ancient spring and well waters that feed the bath house, actually originate behind the white building that can be seen from the town. About fifty yards to the east and behind the Wells is what

appears to be a ten meter radius tumulus which has three trees situated on it in a triangular formation. These rise up out of the top of this mound, all around which are scattered formations of small rocks in clusters and larger single ones. The largest of these rocks (the Calf) guarding the entrance to the 'Fairy House' also known as the 'Fairies Kirk' in older times when the Saxons tried to build a church at the site, it is said that the fairies strongly resented this, distrusting and eventually driving the Saxons into the valley below.

Through dowsing experiments at White Wells and the 'Fairy House', I found that they are positioned geographically upon a 'line of energy' which follows the route of an underground stream. This runs north/south. When observed from the White Wells site, this 'line' runs down the length of Ilkley's Brook Street and continues through the site of the old Parish Church; the place of the goddess, Verbia, holding the serpents. Some dowsers like myself, state that they can perceive spiralling energies within and just above the surface of the ground which look like the vortexes of water that you find in the sink after letting the waste water out of it.

These vortexes are found in and around the sites of stone circles too. I found this effect quite prominent around the White Wells site, yet as far as I know, no standing-stones are to be found close by or ever have been. Using a hazel twig in the position that is described by the goddess Verbia and the serpents, I managed to get really strong indications at various positions around the White Wells building, to suggest that these underground vortexes of unseen energy accumulated at the site. At first, these were in no order and I seemed to be randomly plotting them all around the building, but through a period of over twenty separate visits to the place, I established markers in the landscape and on maps which indicated where the spiralling effects of the energy within the earth there connected to each other. These spirals were nearly always in a clockwise direction and some even passed through the building itself, as they were able to grow in size at certain times of the year.

It was whilst researching these vortexes and dowsing at White Wells, that I experienced at first hand, one of the most strangest events to ever happen to me around that time.

Although I didn't know it at the time, it had a direct bearing on the rest of my future life and the eventual work on Portals that I am now writing about in this book. It was March, 1982, I found myself searching out a particular book about the fairy encounters at White Wells which I knew was available in the Ilkley main library. I had flicked through this little book on a number of previous occasions and as it was an old and rare book, being for reference only, it should for all purposes have been still on the shelves but I could not find it anywhere.

The librarian insisted that the said book was on its particular shelf and in the correct place. She told me that she had seen it there only recently, so I returned to other books at a nearby table, frustrated, puzzled and disappointed that I could not find it. Maybe, I thought, the book had been taken away from the library and the librarian had got it mixed up with another book? Suddenly, I turned sharply to hear a woman's voice, gently saying, "Is this what you are looking for?"

She reached over my shoulder and took the old brown paper covered book from the shelf that I had searched over several times. I was in utter disbelief. The book was directly in front of my eyes in a place where it had not been situated before!

This experience quite shocked me at the time, and I swear to this day that I just couldn't have missed it. I now believe that I was witness to the actual materialisation of that book out of thin air.

Mrs, Hill was a kind old lady, unusual but in a nice way. On that first contact in the library, I felt that she was quite special. Something inwardly told me that this was no ordinary person. I was actually in awe of her presence, her old age was irrelevant, there was a beauty to her that transcended the physical form. Her soul was wonderful.

It became evident with time, that she was what is generally termed a psychic medium, but looking back now, god rest her soul, I tend to think Mrs Hill was a vessel for those who came before and await unseen to return to this world.

After explaining to me that she simply 'knew' just what I was looking for, the book and why she understood why I needed it so much in my work, she invited me to her nearby home to further discuss our obvious mutual interests in the lesser known about side of White Wells. Upon entering her home in Constable Road, Ilkley, an amazing sight befell my eyes. Paintings depicting all kinds of 'fairy folk', angels and light beings, many, many of them, spiralling out of and above White Wells into the skies of the moors. This extraordinary woman in her early sixties at that time, was obviously talented too in an artistic way. Or so I thought. She soon told me that her paintings were the result of trance-like states that she often found herself in at inappropriate times! I began to wonder if her lovely home-made wine may have helped a little in reaching such a state of unwitting consciousness....

Mrs. Hill was also a very knowledgeable person about the Ilkley Moor region and had lived there most of her life. I spent a number of evenings listening to her dialogue about the times gone by in Ilkley. When I dared to bring up and asked her about how she actually felt at the times of these trances, she explained how she would suddenly become disassociated with this reality and her surroundings, she'd not matter where she was and that it would seem to take only a very short time to conclude her paintings. I found this puzzling, giving to so much detail in the paintings, I would presume a lengthy period of time would be required to complete such. She once told me,

"If you happen to be present when I do my painting, I am sure that I would be half ignoring you, but I wouldn't mean to be rude."

In Jenny Randles' book, 'Alien Contact' she writes about UFO Contactee, Gaynor Sunderland and how in an almost 'day dreaming' state she could attain the paranormal experience and remember it afterwards. She writes, "You are aware of the environment about you and yet, you're wrapped up entirely in a sort of 'sphere of influence'."

Mrs. Hill died in 1988, but she did leave me with a happy reminder of not only her great artistic talent, but also an inner feeling she so greatly impressed upon me when she was living. It was a simple water colour that she gave me as a present on an early visit to her house, called 'Fairies at White Wells'. It depicts little elemental folk, fragile yet so strong in expression of all natural energy. They are in flight and in motion. They spiral up from the ground, passing through the Wells building, over a nearby hillock upon which stand three tall trees, then out and away into our tangible real world.

So what are these underground energy streams that form spirals at ancient sites and how was it possible for early man, responsible for the stone circles, to recognise these places of power?

I touched on the answer for this in my previous books, but feel that this needs to be examined further and explained in more detail. First, we have to consider planet Earth itself and the supposed world-wide energy grid that criss-crosses it from pole to pole.

Modern thinkers on the theory of inter-dimensional portals suggest that these are located at certain points around the globe at power centre points and in turn, these points make up a crystalline grid of unseen energy lines that join together like a living network. According to David Childress, "the energy fields across the world are stronger in some areas as compared to others, and in these areas they form sort of a Vortex, thereby making the energy more useful in its sense". The theory suggests that an Earth-Grid system of Earth Energy fields allows portals into other dimensions at the points where the geometrical patterns meet. These Vortex's have been in existence since the birth of the planet and are a natural part of its make-up.

Geometrics in all kinds of recognised shapes and symbols are inherent at all portal sites. They are often the visual concept of the portal that we can recognise at this time, created by a pattern of values or shaped designs.

The theory states that the planet Earth is a dodecahedron and the geometrics we recognise in it, is all that matter is composed of, including the Earth.

Of course within these energy grid points on the globe which cover hundreds of miles of land and sea, there are smaller areas which can be explained as Portals and then within those, we have smaller areas, sometimes only a matter of meters across, called vortices or vortexes. It is within these vortex areas that we find most of the spiralling underground influences of Earth Energy. Shirley MacLaine, who has studied portal energies states:

"Vortex. The word brings to mind a spiralling energy, such as a tornado or water going down a drain. But vortex earth energy is very different because the energy of a vortex is multifaceted. An earth energy vortex can be electrical, magnetic, or electromagnetic. And even those terms are a bit misleading. A magnetic vortex doesn't mean that the energy is literally a magnetic field, nor is an electrical vortex the carrier of electrical current. These names actually reflect the effect of the energy found at a specific vortex point. An electrical vortex is an energizing, activating location. A magnetic vortex attracts energy much as a magnet attracts iron filings. Electromagnetic vortexes combine the qualities of both types to provide an energy that attracts, activates and energizes."

Inter-dimensional portals are electromagnetic vortexes; they attract positive and negatively charged energies from many sources found on this planet (and off it) and these can be energised at the portal site in order to help activate them. Many portals found across the globe today are in a state of inactivation due to neglect, change and intended shut-down by certain parties of the human race. Other portals have always been in a fully charged state and energised to a point where they remain 'open' and others still await the energy boost needed to activate them again. Some have been shut-down for thousands of years.

Researcher Nigel Wright of Paranorth, theorises that portals are rifts or tears within the fabric of this reality and that these rifts can be measured by comparing the Electromagnetic Fields (E.M.F.'s) with normal background readings found around portal sites. He has noted that when certain types of UFO and associated phenomenon occur, then the EMF readings increase many times that of the normal background for the site. He speculates that this change is due to the placement of energy Ley lines which create portal vortexes where these meet or cross. He feels that it is no coincidence that portals are found where there are a high number of Leys and ancient sites which produce a high percentage of unexplained phenomena.

But, the question remains of course, is it the presence of energy lines in the landscape that cause these phenomenon to appear, or is it that the phenomenon is just being noticed at these places where Ley lines happen to be found by coincidence? At this stage in the research of portals, both theories seem to be as valid as each other. We should extend this question and also ask if portals are a static thing at the site and do not come into being, so to speak, that they have always been there as a natural part of the make up of this world and everywhere we understand . Does the phenomena that happens at the portals cause the background E.M.F readings at those sites, to change by there apparentness, or is it that the phenomena itself affects the E.M.F 's in order to allow us to know that it is/ they are, using the portal?

In 1989, through channelling information about the hidden whereabouts of a lost stone circle on Ilkley Moor (which is described in my book 'The

Circle & The Sword): *'Paul Bennett had asked me to help him find an ancient stone circle which had been known to the early Victorians, but somehow lost at the turn of the century. After much farming had cleared many relics from the moorlands. He had found a description in an old book which read,*

' There was a rude circle of rocks on the reach behind White Wells (place of horrors) fifty years ago, tumbled into such a confusion that you had to look once and again before you saw what lay under your eyes; the stones were very large and there was no trace of line about them, and this may have been a rude outpost of the tribe for the defence of the great living spring and also of Llecan (Ilkley) lying below.' Rev. Robert Collier 1885.

Within two weeks I had located that site of a double ring stone circle, quite a rare thing in this part of the country, through a combination of help from a celestial guide and dowsing over a map of the moors. The site was positioned next to the course of Backstone Beck (the great living spring?) which certainly feeds the township below before running its course into the River Wharfe.

I began to realise that the placement of such ancient sites played a major part in locating portals. Many people still find it difficult to understand that others like myself who obtain information like this from our Celestial guides, are also quite capable of using our own humanly acquired knowledge to investigate these places with the same approach taken by scientists and archaeologists. No matter where the aspects of locating the stone circle may have originated from, we still need to be able to work with that information in our own reality and that is exactly what I did back at the newly discovered Backstone Circle to better understand why I had been led to rediscover this very ancient site.

A number of people who visited Backstones during the early 1990s began to report strange phenomena directly above and close by the site. Most were of balls of light sightings and ghostly shapes that would weave in and out of the standing stones, similar to those described years before by Nicholas Size, yet the people who reported them, had never heard of 'the haunted moor'.

There was something in the re-discovery of the stone circle, that seemed to open up a gateway which began to let through these kinds of observed phenomena. The reports began to flood in over the next five years, while investigators working at the circle, speculated as to what it's form and design was really intended for. This site seemed for all intents and purposes, to be much more than a long lost religious temple or maybe a ritual alter of the moors early inhabitants. There was a sense of purpose with this place that was as valid today as it was, all of those thousands of years in the past. This place was filled with a kind of sacred, yet unseen, energy. A sort of living battery of inclusion within the stone circle pattern. It could not be overlooked that this feeling and sense of the sacred may have been due to the actual formation of the standing-stones themselves?

In 1994, I decided to map out Backstones and although there has been a published description of the supernatural events that took place there at that time in my other books, I have decided to include here for the first time the notes that I made during those initial investigations because I feel that it is important to show the reader that all avenues and possibilities are covered when we look for signs of portals at these ancient sites.

" The actual shape of the circle (s) is not a true ring, but consists of two ellipses with their pointed narrow ends to the south. Most of the outer circle stones, found to be partially underground, are also found on the southern most point of the circle, following the path of a single trench. This double ring aspect of the circle is unique to this part of Ilkley Moor, but there is another example, a larger stone circle remains close to Shipley Glen to the south, called the Soldier's Trench.

Immediately to the west of the site is found a dry stone wall which has been constructed as a sheep-fold built around 1900, now unused. There is also a larger oblong structure of stones, determined to be an old gunpowder store for the shooters on the moors in olden times and behind this is found a small quarry which shows signs of once being the site of an Bronze Age bell-pit. Land to the south-west of the site drops to the banks of Backstone Beck and become marsh about 500 meters away. To the east, across the beck, there is evidence of an encampment including a number of remains for dwelling places, of a similar age to the circle itself which has been dated at around 1500BC.

Looking closely at the arrangement of the stones in the two circles reveals a number of linear carved markings upon them. These seem to be of considerable age and may date back to pre-Roman times, with further evidence that Norse and Ogham inscriptions can be found on the edges of the main stones at the site. This indicates that the circle was known about during different periods of history and visited by several different cultures.

In the summer months of 1990, Peter Chattaway along with other members of the Yorkshire Earth Mysteries Group dowsed around the stones of the site using a device that Peter had invented, utilising micro-electronics, crystals and a touch of human dowsing ability. Just like I had done so previously at White Wells, he found higher than normal levels of earth energy between certain stones at the Backstones site. His findings suggested that a band of energy flowing above the ground close to these stones, moved away and out of the circle site in a westerly direction towards the bell pit and a cairn on the higher ground of the moorland. This line is significant, in that if we continue it in a straight direction across the moors, we pass through several ancient sites and end up at a place called Cowpers Cross. It was at Cowpers Cross, that Nicholas Size first encountered those ghostly phantoms, he described, on Ilkley Moor.

The Twelve Apostles is perhaps the most renowned and enigmatic stone circle on Ilkley Moor. It is situated 2.5 km from the nearest road and dates back to the Bronze Age at least. At first it appears to be a ring of stones, clearly recognizable and in good condition.

However, its appearance is deceptive because a survey carried out in 1929 states that the original site consisted of 20 stones with one at the centre and was oval as opposed to circular in shape. Written history aside, this circle also features in ufology, determining Ley lines and astronomical alignments across the ancient landscape of the moors which connect up with other sites, like Backstones Circle. One of these lines of earth energy runs eastward to a location which has made Ilkley famous in the lore of UFOs. Close to White Wells, a pit like crater within Barmishaw Holes on the higher ground above the Swastika Stone, became known about all over the world in the late 1980's. This was the place where a former police officer managed to take a photograph of a small green coloured entity, which he offered as proof for the alleged alien abduction experience he underwent at that site in December 1987.

Philip Spencer (pseudonym) lived in Ilkley. He had decided to take a walk over the tops of Ilkley Moor to visit his father-in-law's home at East Morton. So, he set off to climb the steep slopes beyond White Wells at about 7.15 am, a shorter route which took him by a stand of trees, clearly visible behind the old wells' building. He had taken his compass and camera with him on the journey as weather conditions on the moor at that time of year could change quickly and it was easy for even the most experienced ramblers to get lost in the moorland mists. Looking back over his shoulder, he saw how pleasant the view over Ilkley in the valley was and so decided to take some snap-shots of the town, once the morning light had improved. Eventually reaching the tall pine conifers by the left of the steep and rocky track-way, he was suddenly aware of a humming sound coming from above. He looked up at the cloudy sky, noting how a stiff wind had started blowing against him. Then, something caught his eye!

About 30 feet away, in the massive hollow to his right, (which is a huge crater scooped out of the hillside close to Barmishaws) a small green creature scuttled off into the depths of the hole. Philip shouted after the creature, "Hey!" The being stopped when it was about 50 feet from him and began to wave its long spindly arms, as if to ward off the former bobby. Reaching for his camera, Philip instinctively took one shot of the creature, just before it disappeared behind the rim of the hollow. Getting his wits back, he then gave chase and got an even bigger surprise. When he finally reached the hole of the pit in the ground, there in front of his eyes sitting at the base of the hollow was a strange object that looked like two giant silver saucers stuck together, edge to edge. On the top of this hovering UFO could be seen a box-like structure, that was slowly descending into the craft. The humming sound that Philip had heard earlier, returned, and as it reached a crescendo of sound, the UFO shot straight up into the cloudy sky.

Puzzled, alarmed and confused, Philip decided to return to the security of Ilkley, cutting short his journey to East Morton. As he entered the town he became once again utterly confused, for the town was a hive of activity. All of the shops were open for trading and people were busily going about their daily morning routines. Philip looked at the town hall clock. It was showing 10.00a.m. Yet it should have been no more than

8.15 a.m., no more than a hour could have elapsed since he started his journey. He was absolutely certain of that. He then remembered about the photograph he had taken of the strange small entity. There was a one-hour photo developing service at Keighley (this was in the days before digital cameras and instant photo's), so he decided to catch the next bus there from Ilkley and sure enough when the film was processed, Philip found the print he wanted amongst other views he had taken with his camera. The one showing the thing he had seen on the moors was there in his trembling hands.. The one that proved he wasn't going mad after all.

On 6 March 1983, Philip underwent regressive hypnosis conducted by Dr Jim Singleton, a consultant psychologist,in an attempt to establish what had really happened during his lost time on the moors. Although this type of case follow up exercise is now regarded as somewhat unreliable, back in the 1980's it seemed to be standard practice for many UFO abduction claims. Even so, it is interesting to note what Philip Spencer claimed under that regression:

Philip: "I'm walking along the moor. It's quite windy and there are a lot of clouds. Walking up to the trees I can see this little something, can't tell, but he's green, moving towards me. I still can't move... I'm stuck and everything's gone fuzzy. I'm... I'm floating along in the air. I want to get down, and this green thing is walking ahead of me and I don't like it. I still can't move.. I'm going round the corner and this green thing's in front of me. Oh God... want to get down.

Philip: "There's a ... there's a big silver saucer thing, and there's a door in it. I don't want to go in there... . Everything's gone black now. I can't see anything.... Now there's a bright light, can't see where it's coming from. I'm in a funny sort of room. I can hear this voice saying don't be afraid. I don't feel afraid any more. I can still see this green thing but I'm not frightened of it now.

Philip: "I'm being put onto a table. I can move now if I want to but I don't feel frightened. And there's a beam-like pole. It's above me. It's moving up towards me. It's got a light in it, like a fluorescent tube. It's coming up from my feet. I can hear that voice again, saying we don't mean to harm you and don't be afraid. Makes me feel warm as it's moving up to me. It's coming up over my stomach, towards my head. Close my eyes, I don't want to look at it in case it hurts my eyes. It's gone.... There's something... my nose feels uncomfortable.

Philip: "... It's time to go. Everything has gone black. I'm walking up near some trees. Some movement. I can see something, a green creature. I've shouted to it. It's turned round. I don't know what it is. I'll photograph it. It's turned round now."

Extensive investigation of the Philip Spencer case & photograph, by Ufologists' Jenny Randles, Peter Hough and Arthur Tomlinson, concluded that whatever it was, the 'entity' depicted in the print had really been at the site and was not the end product of any faked processing on the negative. This does not mean that the entity as observed, is surely an alien entity or ET. In fact, it could be any number of things. Only the witness should know, but even this has never been fully established. We just do not know 'what' it is, yet it is there for all to see in one of Ufology's most famous and startling photographs. The entity appears to have a long body, with short legs and quite large ears at the side of the head. The arms are very thin and long, left arm seemingly longer than the right, as it is reaching down to the ground, resting on the grass. Under hypnosis, Philip Spencer gave additional details about the entity description, indicating that it was about four feet tall.

Examination of the actual photograph suggests it's height as being between four feet and four feet six inches tall. It had large pointed ears, big dark eyes, no nose and a very tiny mouth. The hands were very large with three large fingers like 'big sausages' and it's feet were V-shaped with two large toes on which it 'shuffled along' rather than walked in the normal manner. Also, during the hypnotic regression sessions, Philip Spencer recalled how 'the creatures seemed part of a team'. They weren't acting as individuals, but more like bees, as if they were doing what they were programmed to do. He had the feeling that they were 'good' and would not harm anybody. In retrospect, he claimed to have actually liked the entities. An unusual attitude considering his experience, but one which seems to be common to a number of unsuspecting UFO abductees once they start to come to terms with the encounter.

For the reasons of this book the aforementioned UFO experiences from within the same region on Ilkley Moor, highlight the fact that something highly unusual has happened and continues to happen at this portal. Again, the evidence for this area being a portal is found not only within the amazing and inexplicable detail of such cases, but also from what we can learn about the actual positioning of the portals within the landscape. A study of the Barmishaw Holes region of Ilkley Moor gives a good indication that it shares certain geographical and geophysical attributes found in other window areas.

I wrote back in 1997, 'The location where the event took place has been the subject of an on-going investigatory study since 1990. We have already noted how the area surrounding it (from White Wells to the north, and West Rock Ridge to the east, from Addingham Moorside to the west, and the Twelve Apostles' circle due South-East) encompasses this region of UFO and other paranormal occurrences. We may ask why this should be so? The physical make-up of the land has been changed a number of times throughout its history since the great glacial disruptions of the last Ice Age. Decades of natural weathering and man-made alterations to the land, have formed the moors into its latest aspect, remaining dramatic and eye-catching with its huge rocky outcrops along the fault-line ridges that dissect it. The many hole-pocked indentations in the northern slopes of the moor, a hollow of which is claimed as the site of the landed UFO and its occupants in 1987.'

What is this 'hole' where the green creature emerged from? For here we have an enigma with its own merits, one which cannot be ignored if we are to establish any kind of answer to the mysteries of the moors. That this site (a huge oval over 30 feet deep with a smaller 30 feet diameter crater within its northern perimeter), is as enigmatic as any other place where UFO encounters have happened in the world. Is it, as some claim, the place where a badly aimed German bomb landed and exploded during the last World War, or is it the remains of one of the smaller (now disused) quarries of the kind that can be found behind the Cow and Calf Rocks? The smaller hole where Spencer says the UFO touched down, is now frequented by campers. It has become a perfect site to pitch a tent surrounded on all sides by an outer-wall, provided by nature's grassy arena, only accessible by the same track way taken by Philip Spencer in his pursuit of the small green entity.

In the past 30 years, I have made dozens of visits to the site of the 'hole' and it never fails to astound me. It is, if anything, a special place. There seems to be a kind of disassociation with everything else that exists outside the hollow. You enter into a sense of another realm in there. Weather conditions become meaningless as soon as one scrambles into the midst of the hole. Due to the vastness of open farmland surrounding the Wharfe Valley, even on the calmest of days the wind can play havoc along the northern ridge of the moors. Sometimes you can literally sense the change in these conditions as you begin to walk through the unseen gateway of the crater, leaving the gusts of wind behind as if they never really existed. Quietness and a discomforting calmness reigns above all else within the confines of that very strange place.

It is very probable that the 30ft crater is what remains of an ancient Iron Age bell-pit, now filled in and overgrown with small rocks, moorland grasses and bracken. The site has been frequented by New Age & occult groups over the years, obviously regarded as a 'special' place, mystical symbols being positioned and carved onto rocks within the centre of the hole. One of these, a simple swastika motif was found at the site during the summer of 1994. Psychic medium Lyn, from Nottingham was asked to look at a photograph of the site in 1993 and remarked, even though she had never visited it or knew anything about its UFO connections and when I read her remarks I could not help but think about what Nicholas Size had written all of those years ago,

" I sense it is a place where small beings visited many times in the past, and so it held an aura of negative energy as they drew upon it to appear in this world. It is also a place of ritual gatherings of small childlike beings. I can see these dancing around open fires at the site."

When viewed from the Ilkley township below the moors, the northern rim of the hole can be made out along the skyline to the west of White Wells. Its position depicts a dramatic break in the landscape, where a rise of some 10 to 15 ft high and 40 ft across, points out where the smaller crater is hidden from view. This raised ground is only found on the northern edge of the hole site. The remainder of the bowl having a naturally formed perimeter which runs south away from this higher ridge. It is as if this extra formation has been forcefully raised up from within the smaller crater. Could it be the result of removed earth during the Iron Age excavations or made by something else? Upon viewing the site several times this does not seem to be a satisfactory answer, the formation is reminiscent of the way lunar craters had been formed on the Moon when a projectile such as a meteorite enters the surface at an acute angle. The ground around the projectile (travelling at immense speed when it hits) is moved forwards and upwards out of the hole, in the opposite direction of the impact. This creates a higher level to the rim of the crater. One thing for certain is that the moorland crater inherits perfect stealth attributes due to this effect of the raised ground on the northern rim. Standing inside the area of the small crater it would be quite possible for a vehicle of some 20ft high (and hovering above the base of the hole) to remain concealed from view on all sides. At this position it would be totally undetectable by ground and air-based radar, being below the natural level of the higher-ground.

The object would, to some extent,still be able to operate above actual ground-level (i.e. would not have to touch down), advantageous to anything with the desire to move off at speed. This may be highly significant with regards to the 1987 case and opens up speculations about the way some UFO's covertly operate in our airspace. If I were a Ufonaut about some secret mission on Ilkley Moor, then this would be the site I would choose for its almost perfect stealth within the landscape. I would send out 'helpers' upon touchdown, to clamber and shuffle amongst the grassy slopes of the northern rim, to observe the surrounding countryside, the odd looking top secret NSA listening base to the north,and its townships below. They could report back how Menwith Hill on the opposite side of the valley, failed yet again to detect or even understand what was taking place right under their very noses!

One of the most puzzling aspects of the Ilkley Alien Photograph was the strange square-shaped 'blob' of diffused light that is found on the right-hand side of the print. This was first noticed by Peter Hough, the Manchester-based Ufologist who worked on the case from the start. This blob coincided exactly with the same spot where Philip Spencer had explained observing a box-like structure moving down into the craft in the hollow. It seems odd then, that little emphasis had previously been given to examining this part of the photograph, in view of the highly unusual nature of this extreme coincidence. In 1990, a year after the initial investigation, Yorkshire-based UFO investigators for the Independent UFO Network, Philip Mantle and Andy Roberts decided to visit the site in order to evaluate its findings for themselves. They hoped to discover what the blob had really been and whether it had been anything other than a photographic flaw in the processing system? Their finds at the site concluded that the blob was due to a natural feature: a flat rock half way up the northern rim of the crater. This rock was supposed to have given off a diffused light reflection (i.e. a glare) in the right weather conditions, from overhead sunlight. This led Roberts to believe that Philip Spencer saw the blob in one photograph, but kept quiet about it until the investigators pointed it out, coinciding with his story about the box-structure entering the landed UFO in the crater.

But there are several points of disagreement here with the their finds, and certainly the supposed replica photographs they took themselves to establish the way the blob was formed, leave a lot to be desired as they had been taken from angles which were not the same as Spencer's. It seems that attitudes as to exactly what this blob-image was, changed somewhat in 1993. When I began a re-evaluation of the information learned from the Ilkley Alien Photographic case and the photograph itself, which could now be examined with home based Personal Computer imaging software, Peter Hough had now taken the line that, "there was no mystery regarding the blob. It was caused by reflective light (not from any rock this time) but off the ground itself" Peter proposed that moisture-content and ideal lighting conditions, like those conditions found on the morning of the actual encounter,had made parts of the moorland terrain reflective to sunlight. This had been caught by the camera used by Spencer when he took the shot of the entity.

Again, this seemed a fine and sensible solution, but needed to be replicated exactly, if it was to become anything more than an obvious attempt to rationalise the blob-image. So, again I visited the site in June and October of 1993, in order to take comparative photographs in as near the same way that Philip Spencer had done so in 1987. During the later October visit, the weather conditions were quite similar and the fauna in the area had already changed in preparation for the winter months ahead. It was quite obvious that all of the 'highlighted' areas of the landscape, as seen in the original print, (both in the foreground and background) were not due to this change in the colorations of the moorland grasses from summer green to a creamy-buff that showed up very light on the photo's taken by myself. There was no evidence of anything that would cause fauna-coloration or reflective & diffused light at the position where the blob can be seen in the Spencer photograph. All other areas can be easily recognised in both sets of photographs and concurrent with the original panoramic view taken by Spencer. We know that Spencer was shooting towards the west with the sun directly behind him and it is possible that this is where the reflection theory arose from. If so, then 'something' had to be in the position to cause a reflection in the first place if we are ruling out the 'soggy ground' and 'wet rocks' ideas. If the surprising and unexpected presence of the blob, alongside what was supposed to be evidence of an actual alien being was not enough, the late Arthur Tomlinson and the late David Barclay, both regional UFO investigators at the time, discovered an even deeper mystery surrounding the photograph. Within the box-image, which seems to be transparent in colour, there can be found what looks like a face with features including an oval head, eyes,and mouth. This face seems to be looking down at the alien entity standing to the left of the box (blob) in the original Spencer photograph, and David Barclay believed,

" The entity was looking back over its shoulder towards the angelic, almost cherubic face in the box. There is no doubt about it, that the face holds the answer to the whole mystery surrounding Spencer's claims that day in December."

Thinking about the Ilkley case now in 2013, I reflect upon what investigator Peter Hough once said, "It is strange but true that if Philip Spencer had not produced a photograph of his alleged abductor, then the case would have been more easily accepted as a genuine abduction experience. The introduction of the photograph into the equation means there are only two possible answers: the affair is a hoax, or, the case demonstrates the physical reality of UFO Entities. As you will see, with time and hindsight there may be a third possible answer which has more to do with demonstrating that what happened with Philip Spencer on Ilkley Moor, fits well with what we know about UFO entities today and the ever growing possibility that they might originate in other none physical realities.

In 1991, Margaret Goodhall found herself contemplative and overwhelmed by a powerful impression that she believed came from the stones of Backstones Circle itself and was affecting her thoughts. She later described,

' Sitting in the circle and admiring the scenery, wondering how long the stones had been there, my attention kept being drawn to the largest of them. I knew it was studying us all. I find it hard to describe what happened next, I suddenly became a part of the circle itself, as if it was a living thing. I had no sense of everyday things any more, but the stones had a physical sense within them and they knew we were there.

I felt as though I had always been a part of those moors and that I had never know change or the concept of time. I felt as timeless as the moors.'

Then, as if to throw everything into utter confusion, Margaret claims that the stones of the site began to communicate with her,

'You wondered how old we are. We have existed since the world first reformed, yet what has never existed? We who stand here have never been changed by your civilisations, our awareness is changeless, timeless. We work to a pattern and are, at this time, once again silent. All forms do this. Our realm is inter-mingled with all earth-forms. Our form is the Earth and that is how we can touch you, your awareness of us in your being, yet your human awareness has been deluded by change, birth and death in the line of time. You once knew this. Remember it!

'For this was the knowledge of the first peoples. Some seek change in this world and other realms, but know it to be here also (Margaret points to her forehead) - it is within the Earth here, and it is with you. It is the Earth knowledge. It is life.'

Experimenting with a copy of the Philip Spencer image in 1996, I realised that the dimensions of the surrounding landscape and the width of the track that the creature stood on, were too wide and not of normal size. This was very puzzling. What had made the photograph look like this? I found that when the photograph was shrunk and compressed in a computer software, the image of the green creature shrank, changed and morphed into a typical 'grey' looking entity! I was astounded at this transformation back then. Was this nothing more than a bizarre coincidence, or was I actually looking at the true form of these beings? I had changed the whole landscape in the photograph and in doing so, had I managed to expose the true identity of these Greys? By altering that single photograph back then, I propelled myself along a train of thought that maybe E.T '.s are here, but hidden in view as something else. If they are able to morph themselves to meet the visual aspects of their surroundings, then maybe they are the shape-shifters?

Above: Angels or something else? In the story of Jacobs Ladder we find much allegory concerning ancient stones and entities that do not appear to be human.

CHAPTER THREE

Shape-shifters

'Up the airy mountain, Down the rushing glen,
We daren't go a-hunting, For fear of little men;
Wee folk, Good folk, Trooping all together;
Green jacket, Red cap, And White Owl's feather!'

I have suggested in previous chapters that everything that is connected with portals is energy in one shape and form or another and that we are all a part of that universal energy too. In affect, we are the portals and the portals are a part of us. The difference is that whatever gives us the actual appreciation, as to what we can comprehend as a portal, takes form from our limited knowledge concerning the matter. It is in a way, like trying to fully understand what other planets look like which are at a vast distance from us, for example. We can base what they might look like (maybe a very good guess based on present and past knowledge of known planets) or we can speculate to some degree about their make-up and actuality. Again, the latter choice is solely dependant on our knowledge in the past and at the present time. But, without actually visiting the planet or gaining better actual knowledge about it in some other way, we cannot say for certain that the planet is like anything we are aware of. The same reasoning applies to the portals.

All we can really do at this time in our evolution, is to decide to do two things which may help or hinder our understanding of portals and the energies that travel through them in many different forms. One of these, is to speculate as to what portals may be – which isn't very scientific and will probably only lead us to the conclusions we want to reach anyway, and the second, is to admit to our selves that we do not know all that is yet to be learned with regards to ourselves, never mind the question of the portals, and then look for evidence in as many ways as is creatively possible in the human mind. We need to search within, for a point where we begin to find actuality reason and fact overriding the speculation as to what these portals are.

In later chapters, I have laid bare the evidence which my wife and I found at the Settle Sun Dial Portal in North Yorkshire, England, in all its glory. The underlying fact remains, no matter how you look at what happened at that particular portal, it involved much more than UFO sightings. So many different kinds of diverse phenomena were recorded at that particular site, that no single conclusion could be reached about the origins of these different phenomena. It was impossible to state whether these were produced by ET, inter-dimensional beings, human spirits or a mixture of all of them. At the point I write this book in 2013, there does seem to be a pattern emerging, but to say any more than that at this stage, certainly would be speculation on my part.

The fact remains though, backed up by some excellent and interesting evidence (photographic, video, sensory and witness based), that some kind of supernatural phenomenon takes place at and close to portal sites. This is without a shadow of doubt. An underlying factor with all of these different kinds of phenomena, is that they seem to be intelligent (in the human sense of the word because they seem to move and act in an intelligent way) and are able to shape-shift into different visual forms.

The notion that other worldly entities have the ability to be shape-shifters, is a very ancient one. The ability to change their mass and there appearance is the key factor which gives whatever shape-shifters are, the sense of being intelligently elusive to human beings. They take away the control of the elements that mankind so desperately clings on to, being able to project the illusion that they lead man into situations and not the other way around. The shape-shifters are the boss in the world of the unknown and man grasps at the fringes of reason in order to understand their merry dance! And in doing so, the shape-shifters not only bring out into the open the inner fears of mankind, a fear of being alone in a world that he cannot fully understand, a fear of being alone in a reality that will not show him its full potential.....yet.

Who are the shape-shifters? We do not know. They are as real as you and me. They represent something that we can acknowledge, and maybe something many of us may fear, but that is all we can say. The only thing we can do at this present time is to consider who or what is shape-shifting, speculate as to the reasons why, for how long they have been here doing this and why, if at all, this is important to us.

Most of the kinds of entities and phenomena that have been observed at the portal sites are of a none fully physical nature and look like phantoms or ghosts, ethereal, etc. There is a reason for this which will be explained later, but for now we will go on the evidence we have and this is the most reported state of the shape-shifters. Modern science tells us that most physically solid shapes cannot change shape without some kind of force imposed upon them. This is due to how the atoms that make up those forms being very tightly bound together, are unlike loose atoms we find in liquids and gases. Solids, liquids and gases have their properties of liquidity or movement due to the types of bonds that atoms share. Of course man can manipulate solids quite easily at certain levels of liquidity. It is child's play to recognise that some solids like dough can be 'manipulated' by the hands to give it 'another' form. In fact, many solids can be altered in this way by moulding, tearing, squeezing, folding, cutting, stretching, twisting, bending, squashing, filling, scrunching, and threading. What I am showing here is that we can easily change the form and shape of something, even if it had a different physical form before being manipulated. It really is child's play. In all of these procedures, energy is the force, which when imposed upon the solid, allows its physical structure to be changed and we can as easily comprehend this in a visual way.

If we take a piece of flat paper and make a flying paper plane from it, we impose energy force on to it, by folding, cutting, etc. to get the required shape. In affect, we have controlled a situation with the human intelligence and knowledge of how to make a paper plane, which is really just us changing the shape of the solid paper to make another recognisable form. Taking this a step further, we have actually created on the visual level something which is now 3D out of a 2D piece of flat paper. We have given the piece of paper another form. It has shape-shifted, not by magic or the supernatural, but by the known principles of science!

Let us speculate that an intelligence superior to mankind in many ways, has achieved the ability to change its own solid form by manipulating the energy that it is made from and is able to do this at will. That sounds fantastic to us at this point in our evolution, but not impossible. The paper plane example shows us that, albeit a far reach from that to actually changing the form of a living being, but, look around you, how many solid things do we see in our world today which started off as something and was changed into something else. Even that paper plane was once a tree and before that something else. Everything in our world of solids is shape-shifting by the hand of man and even nature to a lesser degree. Even the seemingly visual solids of our own bodies change with time and in doing so, science dictates that we are in fact shape-shifters too! The concept is not that strange now, is it. The concept is nothing to fear.

The conceptual offerings of shape-shifters in traditional folklore from many countries include the legendary creatures to have this ability, which is represented in a full body transformation. This enables the 'creature' to trick, deceive, hunt, and kill humans in most accounts. Throughout history many murder sprees have been attributed to the presence of these beings. The most famous of these of course are the Vampires and Werewolves. In more modern times there are no less than six different definitions of what a human shape-shifter is. Taken from the Urban Dictionary it states:

1. Someone who morphs their life to match the person they happen to be dating or living with.

2. A weak-minded individual who bends their personality in order to befriend certain people.

3. A human who can take on other shapes usually in the animal family, like dogs, wolves, tigers, etc.

4. A female that appears initially to be attractive, but when seen from different angles or on different occasions, looks to be ugly or mediocre.

5. A person who can alter their shape into a form of an animal. Usual shape-shifters can change into only one animal, but sometimes they can change into multiple forms at will. Silver

cannot harm shape-shifters, nor can items of religion. The usual animal form is a very large wolf, and shape-shifters usually get mistaken for werewolves.

6. Shape-shifting is a common theme in mythology and folklore as well as in science fiction and fantasy. In its broadest sense, it is when a being has the ability to alter its physical appearance.

The cross-over between the physical and the none-physical attributes as to what determines a shape-shifting human is quite clear here. The term can be used to describe someone who morphs into something or someone who is not themselves in the normal state. This makes no difference if this is implied as a state of mind or an actual belief that someone can physically become something else. It is interesting to note however that even if the shape-shifter changes, it is usually into something that is often lesser then themselves in the natural state, for example, morphing into a 'weak-minded' individual or a female who's attractive looks change to something less appealing. It is almost implied that whatever change takes place, it results in a lesser being or species, like an animal. I think that this has much more to do with mankind's own instinctive fears concerning change in many ways. Change in himself and what he may become, change in his world and what perils might lay ahead in his uncertain reality. The shape-shifters of tradition and fantasy tell us much more about ourselves and our fears, than they do about the ET shape-shifter's who use the portals.

At this time there is no certainty in our human understanding who these entities are, so we have to give them our own identities to recognise them when they appear at the portals. Some of these same entities appear at different portals all over the world, some are only found at certain types of portal sites, the answer is diverse. The majority of entity types that use these portals are of a humanoid – ET hybrid kind, sometimes accompanied by other ET types like the Greys and Elemental beings. Human spirits are also found at these portal sites which seem to be connected with the history of the place the portal is situated at.
In his book 'Passport to Magonia', the late Jacques Vallee considered Elemental beings as shape-shifters which were able to manifest

themselves into recognisable creatures:

The bodies of the Elementals are "of an elastic semi-material essence, ethereal enough so as not to be detected by the physical sight, and they may change their forms according to certain laws."

'Shape-shifters do not seem to be physical in the same way we are. They can de-materialise and walk through walls, travel back in time, levitate, move objects with their minds, appear to us in an etheric state without their physical bodies, talk to us telepathically, enter our dreams, and become invisible. These are powers that come with being 'ethereal', and indeed they are highly advanced because they live in a higher dimension inter-penetrating ours. To enter our world, higher dimensional beings must focus themselves into a narrow range of vibration to intersect our dimension, otherwise they remain invisible to us. We are like fish unaware of being watched by people outside the aquarium, people who can choose to make their presence known by tapping on the glass or sticking their fingers in the water.'

Whether all of these entity types are able to truly shape-shift with intent is not known, as some, like the human spirit forms never actually reach complete solid states when they appear and only seem to shape-shift when they de-manifest from this reality. Other kinds, like the humanoid -ET hybrids, seem to project themselves or are able to manipulate energy in their surroundings in order to change the shapes and forms of themselves and natural objects & life forms (plants/animals) in a way that is intended by them. The purpose for this is often unknown at the time of the actual event, but sometimes on rare occasions psychic messages and channelling's are received which give tentative clues as to the hidden reason behind the occurrence.

There is a local story that close to the Settle portal at the top of School Hill, roams a demonic dog which stopped travellers in the past from continuing on their journeys to Malham. Interestingly, this phantom dog would sit guard at the point where three tracks met and climbed the hills out of Settle. As in many other such accounts of the Barguest, Padfoot, or Guytrash, as it is known in the north of the country, this particular shape shifter had gleaming headlight-like red eyes. It is said that a Barguest is said to roam the snickle-ways and side roads of York and to witness this nocturnal apparition is said to be a warning of impending doom. In my thirty years of researching the paranormal I began to see a pattern emerging as to where these Black Dogs were appearing and without a shadow of doubt, there were correlations between the physical locations in the landscape and where the phenomena occurs. In nearly all cases, I would find historical evidence of other strange apparitions close by and in modern times UFO sightings had been also reported not far from where the Black Dog would hang out. There seems to be a good reason why all of these supernatural phenomena take place in these clusters which we will examine in due course.

Appearing from time to time alongside Guytrash at the Settle portal are strange ghost-like owls, but these seem to be a modern development based upon the previous encounters with the Black Dogs. Something links these two animal forms in age old tradition and that is the notion that they are harbingers of death.

Some native American traditions consider the owl as a symbol of death and in others, the *'superstition refers to the idea that the presence of a white owl carries mystical or supernatural meaning. Those people who are near the white owl are said to be near death. The white owl has also been associated with bad luck. Those near the white owl will bear unhappy events.* '

It is also said that to hear an owl screeching at night could result in bad luck, as if the screech is a warning of this impending doom. It gets worse, if a baby hears the screech of the owl, then the young child is destined to become an unhappy person in later life or possibly that they would become a witch. Should the owl be heard screeching in cold weather then a storm was coming and it was said that owls were the only creatures that could live with ghosts. One folk tale about owls that may have a deeper meaning, is that if you see one in a tree and you walk around and around the tree, the owl will turn its head to follow you, never taking its eyes off you, until it wrings its own neck! The reality is, of course, that no normal owl is able to turn its head all the way around.

However in other cultures, the white owl is a sign of good luck. An Afghanistan legend states that it was a white owl with supernatural powers which brought mankind the knowledge of flints and iron so they could make fire. In exchange, man gave owls feathers to enable them to fly. In other parts of the world, the owl was seen as the sign of a wise woman, bringer of good harvests, a symbol of guidance and help. The owl was identified with the night and the underworld in Meso-American traditions as well. The image of the Green Owl was used in Teotihuacan on mirrors. The mirrors were symbolic of supernatural caves or passageways thus linking the owl to entrances to the underworld. This links importantly with the tunnel systems found close to the Settle portal in Yorkshire and the numerous ghost owl sightings made there.

So, although reports of ghost owl sightings at portal areas seem to be increasing, it is obvious that there once was a long held tradition connecting these birds with the supernatural in a variety of different ways depending on the culture and period in time. There is something unusual & sad in the fact that as these reports grow, the actual numbers of real owls are diminishing worldwide. Before you simply put the ghost owl down to fantasy, folklore and legend, consider the sudden increase in UFO related events where owls are involved in the reports. Judy Carroll who lives in Australia writes about her own encounters with E.T 's and her owl sightings in her book, 'Looking through eyes of wisdom'. The book cover depicts an owl looking out at the reader. She claims direct UFO contact for the past 50 years, in particular the Gray types, or as she calls them, the Zetas. Judy believes that these are not ghost owls, but real ones that are being controlled by the E.T 's who use the birds to look through their eyes in a kind of telepathic manner.

Interestingly she states, ' *the Zetas are expert 'shape-shifters' and can easily appear as a very real owl, or whatever, if they need to. They seem to prefer animals that resemble themselves, that is, ones with large eyes or at least good night vision eyes.'* Others who have experienced the owl phenomenon in connection with ET visitations the world over, seem to be repeating the same accounts. They suggest that some of these owls may be a kind of window into our world and some other force could be using those great big eyes as a tool to observe this reality. It seems that their eyes are like video cameras and linked straight into this world. Whitley Strieber, the writer of his best selling book Communion, was one of the first of the modern ET Experiencers to note the owl connection. He thinks that the Greys come in groups of three and appear as owls.

Every culture in the world has its own shape-shifter lore as we have seen with the transforming owls. Legends of creatures who can transform themselves into animals or other men abound. Usually, the animal involved in the transformation is indigenous to or has lived for ages in the area from which the story derives. Let us look at some of the more well known shape-shifter legends: (I have not included Werewolves or Vampires in this section as they are not reflective of the shape-shifter energy that is associated with either ancient sites and portals in particular.)

Selkies are creatures found in Faeroe, Icelandic, Irish, and Scottish mythology. They have the ability to transform themselves from seal to human form. Selkies are able to shape-shift by shedding their seal skin, a risky endeavour because they must reapply the same skin in order to return to seal form. Stories surrounding these creatures are usually romantic tragedies. They are allowed to make contact with humans for only a short amount of time before they must return to the sea. In many cases humans have unknowingly fallen in love with Selkies. Other times, humans have hidden the skin of the Selkie, thus preventing it from returning to seal form. Male Selkies are very handsome in their human form, and have great seduction powers over women. If a man finds and steals a female Selkie's skin then she will be under his control and is often times forced to become his wife. The creatures have been known to lure humans into the sea, by creating illusions and a false sense of reality.

In Japanese folklore the **Kitsune** is an intelligent and magical being. The creature's strength increases with age, wisdom, and life experience. Kitsune is a Japanese fox. They have the ability to assume human form and are great tricksters. The creatures are noted for having as many as nine tails. A Kitsune may take human form when it reaches a certain age, usually 100 years. They prefer to assume the shape of a beautiful woman, young girl, or elderly man. The creatures have the ability to clone the appearance of an individual. Kitsune have a fear and hatred of dogs. They can willingly manifest themselves in people's dreams and create illusions so elaborate that they are perceived as reality. The Kitsune can fly, become invisible, and often times generate fire or lightning. In some regions of the world the creatures can bend time, space, and drive people mad.

The **púca** is a legendary creature of Celtic folklore, most notably in Ireland, the West of Scotland, and Wales. The púca is a mythological fairy and ultimate shape-shifter. The creatures are capable of assuming a variety of terrifying forms, including a horse, rabbit, goat, goblin, or dog. No matter what shape the Púca takes, its fur is always dark. They are most commonly seen as a black horse with a flowing mane and luminescent orange eyes. Púcas have the power to use human speech and although they are known for giving good advice, they also enjoy confusing and terrifying humans. Púcas have a fondness for riddles and are sociable creatures. They love to gather and play pranks on unsuspecting people and children. In many regions of the world the Púca is seen as a creature of the mountains and hills. They are incredibly respected and if treated nicely will help humans. If a human is enticed onto a Púca's back, it has been known to give them a wild ride, though unlike a Kelpie, which will take its rider and dive into the nearest stream or lake to drown and devour him/her, the Púca will do its rider no real harm. The Púca has the power of human speech, and has been known to give advice and lead people away from harm.

The **Wendigo** is a creature appearing in the mythology of the Algonquian people. Descriptions of the Wendigo vary across culture, but they are generally described as a large alien-like canine beast. They are malevolent and cannibalistic creatures. Wendigos are strongly associated with the winter, the north, and coldness. Human beings will transform into Wendigos if they perform cannibalism. The person will become possessed by the demonic spirit of the beast, usually in a dream. Once transformed, the individual will become violent and obsessed with eating human flesh. These monsters are the embodiments of gluttony, greed, and excess. They are never satisfied with killing and consuming one person. Wendigos are constantly searching for new victims. They have been classified as giants and upon transformation the human will grow considerably in size. They populate rural and highly forested, mountainous regions. Recently the Wendigo has become a horror entity, much like the vampire, werewolf, or zombie. Among certain native tribes, cannibalism, even to save one's own life, was viewed as a serious taboo; the proper response to famine was suicide or resignation to death. On one level, the Wendigo myth thus worked as a deterrent and a warning against resorting to cannibalism; those who did would become Wendigo monsters themselves.

Of course there are numerous accounts from all over the world concerning the little people and the elementals, as we have seen at Ilkley Moor's White Wells who were said to be able to change shape and appearance. Fairies, witches, and wizards were all noted for their shape-shifting ability. Not all fairies could shape-shift, and some were limited to changing their size, as with the **Spriggans**, and others, to a few forms and other fairies might have only the appearance of shape-shifting, through their power, called "glamour," to create illusions. But others, such as the **Hedley Kow,** could change to many forms, and both human and supernatural wizards were capable of both such changes, and inflicting them on others through transmogrification spells. Witches could turn into hares and in that form steal milk and butter or fly across the landscape as a bat or an owl. Significantly, these kinds of shape-shifters have been recorded at different times in history at or near to the Settle Sun Dial Portal, so it assumed that there is a connection between the portal site and the entity that is said to be shape-shifting there. The crossover between the occult and modern day Ufology seems as apparent as ever at certain portal sites that record a long held tradition of UFO & Alien sightings being made alongside other strange happenings and mysterious going ons. One such place which was a very active window area during the 1980's and 90's is Woodside, in Bradford, Yorkshire.

Waves of UFO sightings were nothing new to the rural regions of Yorkshire, but in 1981 the small community of Woodside Estate, near Bradford, experienced something that was quite extraordinary in terms of a UFO flap. Over flights of multi-coloured UFOs were observed and reported, often photographed for weeks on end which seemed to herald the beginnings of other equally strange visitations alongside inexplicable disappearances of pet dogs within the local woodlands. In the late 1970's, UFO investigator & author Arthur Shuttlewood highlighted the Woodside UFO connection in his best-selling book, *The Flying Saucerers.* In it he wrote of how upon a visit he made to this part of Yorkshire in the 1970's, he came across the following report from Wyke Woods (another name for a part of Judy Woods):

'From Wyke Woods, Bradford, Mrs G. Cassons tells us "two things moved at terrific speed across the sky. They were almost identical in shape and size, both were saucer- shaped. One had a revolving top half, the second a revolving lower half. The lighting was bright yellow in a whitish glow that was dazzling.

This particular area of woodlands have always been thought of as places where strange things happen. Accounts of UFO experiences are not uncommon with many reports to be found in the local newspapers. Woodside is a small council-run housing estate which became the focus for a wave of UFO sightings in the latter autumn months of 1981. Meandering multi-coloured lights were observed in the skies over Judy Woods and by the start of the New Year, such was the concern as to what was actually going on in the area, that the locals summoned the help of the scientific community and the West Yorkshire Police force to find out what was happening. Initially, no answers were forthcoming and the situation was put down to hype and imagined mass hysteria. Even when photographic evidence of the Woodside phenomenon was presented, showing marble-like globes of light seen to drop and emerge from the tree-top canopy of Judy Woods, plus weekly reports to the Bradford press of closer encounters with the phenomenon, little was done to re-assure the concerned residents living close to the woods. It was only when a spate of pet dogs going missing from homes around the area, and a connection being made with the UFO activity timings, that researchers began to explore the facts surrounding an utterly bizarre mystery.

Most of the background evidence for UFO visitations to Woodside were written up by UFO investigator, Jenny Randles in 1983, when she gave a whole chapter of her book, **The Pennine UFO Mystery**, to the happenings there. She echoed local investigators thoughts about the mainstream sightings and unusual events occurring there, but even at that time we felt that something much weirder than just UFO sightings were an underlying factor in the whole mystery. Significantly, Paul Bennett noted how UFO waves usually begin with peculiar weather conditions and this had been the case at Woodside. He wrote at the time,

"What seems to happen is that before a wave occurs, the entire sky gets lit up, only for a second or two, but definitely bright enough to read by.

Then the burst of energy instantly dies and perhaps a few minutes later another flash of the whole sky will take place; its nature echoing the first or previous one."

These 'energy-flashes' are quite different from lightening and can even occur in good weather conditions and clear skies, so there seems to be something else happening here. Possibly a kind of supernatural signalling effect proclaiming to someone, somewhere, that the onset of UFO activity is about to begin. By the 20th October, 1981, more strange flashes of light were observed over the treetops of Judy Woods and resident hairdresser Rafael Nobile began to log and photograph the first wave of UFOs as they entered into the woods by the cover of night and low clouds. His mother who was a strict Roman Catholic, didn't believe her son's initial claims. That was until she actually saw the UFOs for herself from her house in Fenwick Drive, Woodside which overlook an expanse of the woodland.

These were reminiscent of the reports being made to the local newspapers by other witnesses. Headlines like, *'UFOs Start Star Trek to Estate '* & *'Still More UFOs of the Woodside Kind',* amongst others, became almost common-place in Bradford's *Telegraph & Argus* throughout October and November of 1981.

Rafael's mother described them as likened to glistening marbles of many colours, ranging in size from star-like to the full-moon, silently manoeuvring above the woods, sometimes speeding off into the heights of space. When I found out about Rafaele's photographic evidence and the ensuing major wave of UFO encounters, I could see parallels with what I thought was a previous and seemingly isolated case concerning a Keith Theakstone (an amateur astronomer from the Woodside estate) and in his report he states,

"I arrived at Woodside never expecting to see anything like this, but shortly before 1300 hrs I was amazed to see a trio of lights in a line formation low in the sky.

Then suddenly, there was a whole lot more of them, each with dozens of smaller sparkling lights around the main object. As I watched these smaller lights, they blinked out and the formation was engulfed in a bright flash of light that covered the whole sky. When I looked again, a single illuminated disc, different to any astronomical thing I know of,

hung motionless and silent over the woods..... "
During the course of the Woodside sightings doubt began to raise its head. Were these real UFOs or just simply a case for mass-delusion as things became more confused when the Nobile family started to claim identifying a light-aircraft that seemingly made the impossible manoeuvre of taking -off into the night skies from beneath the trees in the woods! For, in truth there would be no possible area within the woods where any kind of small aircraft (other than a model) could have moved around on the ground, let alone take-off from any makeshift runway. But this kind of mystery is not uncommon in UFO lore; John Keel, who's own investigations during the 1960's and 70's, described many cases where UFOs seemed to have the ability to secretively cloak themselves into the forms of familiar everyday objects, but these often then performed impossible tasks attributed to them.

Not all of the close encounters of the Woodside Kind were made at a distance. One particular case made in the middle of the wave, by three local schoolchildren, brought about a sinister angle which added to the concern already shown. The children were on their way home from Wyke Middle School and had decided to take a short cut through Judy Woods. At about 1630 hrs they noticed a strange odd glow above the trees ahead of their route. This started to pulsate as they watched. One of the boys alerted the other children to the fact that quite suddenly all of the birds in the woods had stopped singing, all was silent and not as they knew it should have been at that time of the day. With a cracking noise that shattered the previous ghostly silence, a white spherical object floated towards the edge of the woods at tree-top level. All around its rim were red and green lights that twinkled and flickered on and off, before turning to green as the UFO stood motionless above a nearby farmhouse that overlooked the Woodside estate. The children fled towards their homes, very scared! One poor boy could not reach his own house, so he banged on the door of a friends and as he did so, his friend's mother watched in awe as the object hung directly over the boy's head, seemingly having chased him there. The object vanished in front of her eyes and like in so many other cases we were to discover at Woodside, the children were then instructed to never again wander into the nearby woods alone.

During the 1981 wave, there were rumours of Alien Abductions associated with the lights being observed in the woods and several accounts are on record involving the sudden and mysterious disappearances of pet dogs from the local housing estate.

Many of the houses back onto fields that are adjacent to the woods and as these are away from the busy roads they were the preferred places for the local children to play. Of course there were still natural aspects of the environment that may have caused danger to some of the more adventurous children, like the man-made reservoir and electrical pylons that dissected the region between the houses and the woods. When mysterious things first began to happen, these open expanses became strictly out-of-bounds to the children, so some of them ventured into the woods to play, away from parental eyes. Rumours began to circulate in November 1981 of dogs from Woodside being kidnapped. It was true, there had been a spate of missing pets reported to the Bradford Police, but little firm supportive evidence pointed to anything other than the unfortunate mishaps like traffic accidents and natural causes for their deaths amongst the odd normal theft. Certainly, for a while no bodies of the missing dogs were found, even though the official police line was as that the missing dogs most probably had been killed in road accidents. A clue to the disappearances came about at the end of the year. On one particular visit to investigate this aspect, I was about to enter the woodland, when I got talking to two local teenagers and they made me aware that the mysterious lights and the pet-abductions were quite definitely linked. They told me how,

" They had been playing with their pet dog Rex, throwing a stick for it to fetch in the fields. In the direction of Judy Woods, an invisible rushing wind like a tornado, came towards them and one of the young men thought he saw a glowing ball of light about the size of a football where the energy could be felt.
In a terrified panic, leaping into the air, the dog bolted into the woods - and with it, the unseen presence dissipated!"

After a week-long search around the Bradford rural countryside by their father, the unfortunate pet was eventually found, dead. Even more bizarre, was the fact that its head had been removed from its body, the torso now positioned in a watery gully in the heart of the woods known as 'the beck'.. Rex, was not the only dog to befall victim of the Woodside

Thing. Paul Bennett wrote his inventory notes at the time: *"I discovered that the highly-strange action of impaling one-half of a dog's skull on an Oak tree, was found to appear extensively throughout the woodland during the 81 JASON (July to November) UFO flap. Whatever was going on in those woods, it involved much more than bloody spacemen..."*

As the months rolled into the winter of 1982, more decapitated dogs were being discovered within the woods, their skulls like Rex's, being impaled onto the trunks of Oak trees. This looked to be more of a case for satanic witchcraft being practised in Judy Woods and little to do with the UFO sightings being made throughout that time, but this in itself prompted others to state correlations with known occult lore, concerning two avenues of historical legend. One, which confirmed the practice of decapitation and the impaling of animal skulls (particularly dogs) onto tree-trunks in the Seventeenth Century in those very same woods, and two, of a much earlier reference in occult practice; which involved a demonic- force called the Bruculaco - often described as a vampire-entity, unseen, yet able to exist by draining the life-force energy from its victims. The only known form of protection from this vampire presence was to impale a severed animal's head onto the tree where the Bruculaco was said to be resident. Within Judy Woods, it seemed that the Bruculaco was being held at bay by this bizarre practice for the last 300 years at least! So we now had a theory to work on, and as the winter months of 1982 brought a covering of snow to the Woodside estate, Paul Bennett & I searched out the woodland in the hope of finding a clue which would bring together this legend and the seemingly modern-day UFO sightings and abductions. It was not long before we found the location of Judy Marsden's cottage. Now, no more than a trace of stones in the brambles and undergrowth where four woodland paths meet at the point her home once stood. This had once been the domain of a recluse and claimed seventeenth century witch, after whom the woods had taken its name, Judy Woods.

Local tales tell of how Judy used her natural potions and charms for protection against evil spirits. Was she aware, we wondered, of one evil in particular, the Bruculaco Entity? For both Paul Bennett and I could not believe our eyes when we found impaled upon the only Oak tree outside her cottage remains, the aged and weathered skull of a cat or a small dog!

Amongst all the living creatures including Man, on this planet, dogs are often reputed to be the most intuitive and psychic, so it seemed obvious that this unfortunate creature would become quarry for those practising occult rituals of protection in those vampire infested woods. Furthermore, occultism and in particular with connection to the Bruculaco Entity, the action of cutting open the cranium was said to 'enable the release of the life-force (i.e.- the soul) from the animal after it had been possessed by the vampire.' With this operation. a certain amount of energy would have escaped too. Was this observed by the locals of Woodside in the form of balls of light, maybe UFOs? The idea is not as far-fetched as it might seem at first. I have spoken to a number of nurses in hospitals which care for the sick and dying, and they have reported to have observed luminous lights emerging from the dead person up to an hour after their demise. Often, they said, these multi-coloured lights would ascend upwards, through the glass of the hospital ward windows, and high into the skies above.

We cannot suggest for one moment, that there really existed an entity called the Bruculaco in Judy Woods, for there are no actual reports or records of any kind of vampire activity being witnessed during the 1981-2 flap. But other circumstantial evidence does point to the possibility that certain locations within the wood seem to hold a presence which although unseen, can sometimes be felt and acknowledged. I have been a dowser for several years now, and often try to use this gift as an accessory in my UFO & Portals investigation methods. In particular it is useful at reported UFO landing site locations, where the dowsing pendulum often 'picks-up' clues that normal investigatory techniques do not, and provides a way of tuning into the environment where the experience has taken place. A group of local boys from the nearby village of Wyke had been playing a game of hide & seek, when two of them came across a great hole in the ground within the northern reaches of Judy Woods. It was 1977, the year when the UK became host to one of the largest wave of UFO sightings since 1947. As we have seen, UFO activity had been noted by Arthur Shuttleworth at Woodside, so it seems a safe bet that this region played its part in the overall national flap. The 'crater' had not been there the previous time that the boys were playing in the woods. It had appeared it seemed, out of nowhere. The curious group began to explore the crater, descending into it, but almost as quickly climbed straight back out again covering their noses and mouths with their hands as a sulphurous stench began to emanate and render the air foul all around the hole. Different from the usual stench of rotting vegetation found in other natural hollows in the woodland. Interestingly, their pet dog as it neared the same crater, began to 'go mad' and this was highly unusual because it was normally a very placid and gentle animal. It ran around in circles at the mouth of the crater, foaming at its mouth and giving out loud barks, as if in pain. The dog seemed to fear something unseen, its eyes glaring into mid-air. Then it did a very curious thing. Picking up small stones in its mouth, the dog began throwing them with some force in the direction of the terrified children.

The crater in Judy Woods looked almost artificial as I stepped closer to its edge. There were no trees close to its circumference and those a little distance away had been burnt as if they had been torched sometime in the past. Something was odd about the way all the branches were leaning outwards away from the crater's rim, broken and decayed. Plant life near to this site was struggling to survive. But why was this so?

"Why not try some dowsing here?" asked Paul Bennett. So I took a forked-branch of hazel in my hands and began to walk around the crater at a steady pace. Every so often, it would twitch downwards indicating a reaction to an energy there. I began to feel a tingling sensation as I repeated over and over in my mind the thoughts, ' has this crater any connection with the Woodside UFO sightings?'. I also noticed how following a pull on the dowsing rod was moving me accordingly towards the centre of the crater and down into the bottom of it. Here the force of the energies I picked-up became extremely strong. The dowsing rods nearly being pulled out of my hands with some force.

The greenwood has always been a place where strange & mysterious things have happened; a gateway between our real world and the beyond. Another place like Woodside, is Clapham Woods in the South Downs of England. There are a number of comparisons with Judy Woods, stunted tree-growth, unseen energies, UFO sightings, etc., and it even has its own mysterious crater believed to have been made by a wartime bomb or maybe a falling meteorite. Whatever the truth, it is said that nothing will grow in that crater and that there is a noticeable smell of sulphur at that part of Clapham Woods. This 'rotten egg' like stench has long been associated with evil or negative manifestations and satanic ritual. More importantly, the same smell has also been noted in several UFO close encounter experiences. One startling discovery came in October/November 1972, when a young schoolboy and his friend were playing around with a Ouija board and it began to spell out the name of the woods. It also told the boys that Clapham was being used as an Alien base & these beings had landed recently in the woods, just as they would in other woodlands in the coming years.

Ufologist and Internet Radio presenter Russell Kellett, believes that he has experienced the strange going's on in Judy Woods and feels, like Paul Bennett and myself, that occultism is (and was) being practised there. In 1997, he was with friends camping adjacent to the woods and heard a strange sound coming from the south, through the trees. As he looked in the direction of the noise, he saw a glowing source of light, red in colour, manoeuvring through the woodland at close to ground level. Investigating the area later, he found a great circular expanse, devoid of trees or plant life that had been marked-out by 'ticker-tape' running from tree to tree trunk on the outer expanses of the area. To all ends and purposes, the site had been marked by a human presence (possibly the Police), one which Russell thinks was there, when the lighted object and eerie sound was observed the night before. Was there a covert group of people using Judy Woods to enable some magical ritual intended on suppressing the vampire-like energy of the Bruculaco? If so, who were they, and where did they come from?

There is little doubt that something really unusual was occurring in the woodlands of south Bradford during the early part of the 1980 's. I am absolutely convinced that a real Ariel phenomenon was being witnessed by the locals of Woodside as there were plenty of good photographs of these objects to show that this was the case. I thought it would be interesting to re-visit the Woodside area again for myself in 1997 and to try re-establish contact with some of the original witnesses to find out if there had been any more changes or further sightings. One of the prime witnesses was Keith Theakstone. He still lived at Low Moor in the Woodside area and was forty years old when I met him for the second time. In April, 1998, he told me,

"People keep seeing things over those woods. It hasn't really changed. I know the thing I saw back in '81 was something not of this world, but I do try to remain open-minded about it all. I know what I saw, and it was not like anything normally observed in the sky. "

Rafaele Nobile still discusses the Woodside events with his family and his mother remembers well the multi-coloured lights they photographed in 1981. In all, over fifty separate pictures were secured during the first few months of the UFO wave and digital cameras hadn't been invented then.

During the first two weeks of February 1998, a further string of unusual sightings took place across northern Britain and many of these reports involved a pair of large white lights that were observed across the Yorkshire countryside. In particular, claims of the same object came from the Leeds and Bradford areas, typically close to the locations where events had occurred during the 1977 & 1981 flaps. The UFO had been well-documented and described by several witnesses as being the same configuration. It had even been video-recorded as it passed over the suburbs of Leeds by a security officer, and later appeared on the television news. What Keith Theakstone told me, in a conversation I had with him on 5th April, 1998, left me gob-smacked to say the least,

"I had another UFO encounter on the 2nd Feb. this year (98), in which I watched this object coming over Judy Woods, above a place called Royds Hall. There were two very bright objects which looked like the stars in Orion's Belt, and they seemed to be joined together by a darker object. It came from the west and headed towards Leeds at about 17.30 hrs. As it passed over the estate, all of the dogs started to howl.... "

Shortly before the Settle portal was discovered in 2010, I had my very own experience in sighting one of the ghost owls. I had observed a UFO that was chased by military jets in the skies above the portal site just before the owl episode happened. In hindsight, I now believe that the two incidents on separate days were connected with the ET visitations that began shortly afterwards in the same locality. I wrote about observing what looked like a giant owl in my previous book, but it was in the way that it stared at me, looked ghostly in appearance and eventually vanished from sight, that I realised this was no ordinary owl. Apart from that, it was over a meter tall too!

In the ongoing paranormal investigations at the portal site, a place we call the 'horseshoe trees', we have seen and photographed the ghost owl on a number of occasions. This has happened at Rendlesham Forest too in the south of England, where some believe a similar portal exists. The forest on the edge of RAF Bentwaters in Suffolk, is close to the Sutton Hoo ancient burial site. It became famous in December 1980 for an alleged UFO encounter involving military from the nearby base. Much has been written about the landed UFO and supposed occupants communicated with at that time, but there has also been further on-going investigations by Brenda Butler and Dot Street in the forests where it happened up until today. They believe and have collected a mountain of evidence to suggest that like the Sun Dial Portal at Settle, parts of Rendlesham Forest allow energy vortexes to appear in amongst the trees which are being used by ETs to journey into and out of this world. Investigator Derek Savory has encountered the ghost owl there on a number of visits to the Rendlesham Forest portal and has also captured its image on camera.

So, to summarise, we find different kinds of shape-shifting entities at portal sites which use the inherent natural energy of the place to manifest into our own reality. Other types of entity use actual living physical life forms in this dimension like animals, owls, etc., as hosts for their own monitoring & surveillance means. In both cases it seems that these higher dimensional beings are able to manifest their own energy to morph into our world at portal sites, but our perceptions of this happening, does not seem to last for very long. It is thought that the Greys are designed to operate in our reality while being controlled through a mind to mind instruction directed from the dimension they came from. Others, like the Reptilians manifest in a similar way, but are able to bring their own mind awareness (a kind of consciousness) with them into this reality. In all cases, there are advantages and disadvantages for any of the beings that visit our world in this ethereal state. They cannot stay for long in this dimension because the energy to allow them this, is not stable or powerful enough to bring about a full manifestation into the physical. This is as much to do with the conditions of the actual portal sites on this planet as it is to do with the amount of transference in energy needed to bring them through at these sites. One advantage they do have is that their ethereal forms are four dimensional and able to operate outside our concept of time, so these shape-shifters can see and manipulate our possible past, present, and future realities simultaneously. They are capable of engineering very complicated manipulations like changing the past in little ways to affect the choices you are likely to make in the present. Negative entities don't know which choice we will make, and they cannot change the choices we have already made, but they can see and change everything else. Shortly after we discovered the Settle Sun Dial Portal, I was confronted by one such being, who appeared to me at the horse shoe trees. He claimed that his name was Jeremiah and that he was a human spirit from the 17th Century. He looked like a ghostly manifestation and kept moving in and out of our reality, but was able to communicate with me through the mind. After a short while, he turned quite nasty with me and told me that I would get ill if I did not stop working at the portal. He told me that I would 'malfunction'. Soon after threatening me with a kind of curse, I realised that this was something else, his use of the word malfunction giving him away to be a negative entity. As stated here, Jeremiah was quite capable of cursing me with the illness that I was destined to have, but he certainly was not responsible for it happening.

A disadvantage they have is that they are not able to violate your free will or override your choices as they operate outside of this dimension. Forcing someone to do something is only possible in this physical reality. The best they can do is to tweak the situations and the circumstances surrounding those choices, to try pressure you into choosing something which may be more beneficial to themselves. It is by tweaking the past to create difficulties in the present, by looking ahead to see what you might do, by telepathically manipulating the weakest minds of those around you, that they can create negative and artificial synchronisations. Remember not all entities are negative in these actions and many use the same tweaks to bring about positive outcomes for us all, for themselves and for the planet too.

Above: *The Author, Nigel Mortimer at Cleatop, near Settle. Once the site of a large and impressive stone circle, now little trace of it can be found.*

CHAPTER FOUR

Inter-dimensional Entities

Who are these visitors that seemingly travel through dimensions and visit our recognisable reality? Do they use a technology that we cannot comprehend to achieve this, do they manipulate time and space and do they understand the concepts of the mind in the same way that we do? In order to better understand these questions, we need to take a descriptive look at the types of inter-dimensional entities that have been recorded throughout history as travelling through the veil of the gates unseen. Some of these have been described as looking like us, some looking very different and some likened to something from the farthest reaches of the imagination. In no particular order, may I present:

The Blue People

From the biblical texts we find legends of beings described as Angels but there are other ancient books that describe such spiritual beings. And they are depicted as having a blue tint to their skin. In the Bhagavad-gita , evidence again supports a very ancient race of blue skinned entities through the stories of Lord Krishna. Instead of being an Angel, Krishna was described like that of an 'avatar', god or demi-god. He was a teacher of the workings of creation, the understanding of a self-realised soul and he taught his people the science of yoga and meditation in all their forms, known as the path of work, the path of knowledge, the path of mysticism, the path of devotion. Even so he was different from humans. He was always depicted with 'blue skin'. Shiva is also a 'dark blue' skinned being.

Another accounted race of blue skinned beings can be found with the Ainu, who were an indigenous people living in Japan. Cherokee Indians

talk of blue skinned people that lived on the land before the Cherokee (in fact they openly state that the Cherokee wiped them out) and that the blue people did not live on the land, but underground. As the sunlight was too harsh for their large eyes, the blue people only came out of the caves at night to tend to crops and garden, returning by dawn into the inner earth. The Cherokee called them 'Moon People'.
Mark S. Miller writes,

' As a student of anthropology some 30 years ago, I stumbled across reference to a former race of humanoids who were blue. Once, in addition to the four known races of mankind, there was a fifth race that dwell on an unknown continent in the middle of the ocean between Asia and Europe (i.e., North America). This race, the most ancient of all, was called the Blue Moovians. They were very tall, about seven feet, and very thin, and had extremely large heads. They possessed all manners of powers of the mind: teleportation, telekinesis, ESP.
One day, in response to a stimulus known only to them, they conveyed to regular humans that they had, through their powers of astral projection, located a planet more suitable to their needs in a far distant solar system or galaxy, and all at once they each and every one disappeared from the face of the earth and teleported themselves there, never to be seen or heard from again. This supposedly occurred about 60,000 BC.'

There are accounts of these blue 'people' from all over the world. The Picts were an early race of Scotsmen who fought naked and painted themselves blue with woad. They were known as the blue people. Merlin and possibly Guinevere of the King Arthur legends were said to be of this blue race of Picts who held the supernatural hidden knowledge of another world. From Ancient Egypt we recognise that the colour of something was a clue to the substance or heart of the matter. When it was said that one could not know the colour of the gods, it meant that they themselves were unknowing, and could never be completely understood. In Egyptian art, colours were clues to the nature of the beings depicted in the work. For instance, when Amon was portrayed with blue skin, it alluded to his cosmic aspect, the sky and water. blue took on the meaning of life and re-birth. It was identified as the colour of creation. Amon was often shown with a blue face to symbolise his role in the creation of the world, and by extension the Pharaohs were sometimes shown with blue faces too. Thoth, the Architect of the Universe and the keeper of wisdom and the truth, was often symbolised by a blue bird or a baboon with a blue face. In UFO lore, there have been a number of beings that have been described as having the colour blue associated with them. On February 17th, 1996, Paul Green had an experience with Blue coloured beings who attempted to abduct him. He relates,

'I woke up suddenly at dawn and immediately felt a distinct presence in the bedroom. I had heard it come into the bedroom (and round to my side of the bed) and I first thought it was our daughter. Outside, dawn was just breaking. Finally, puzzled at why my daughter had come into the bedroom so early in the morning, I actually opened my eyes.

I looked over to my wife's side of the bed and was quite surprised to discover an unknown entity standing by the bedside. It was standing in front of the wardrobe, nearly facing us. Its entire body was giving off a soft dull bluish white glow.

This entity curiously had more human proportions than those found in typical Greys. A small head with a distinctly pointed chin, a bald domed head and a very thin neck. The "Blue Man" also had a barrel shaped body, and very thin flexible arms which it was waving around very slowly in a fashion that reminded you of Tao Chi movements. The glow it gave off may have made picking out any facial characteristics impossible. The entity was not menacing in any way, on the contrary it seemed to exude an aura of peace. I am surprised that I did not freak out. The entity seemed to be glancing in the direction of my daughters' bedroom (which is across the corridor), when I first saw it. Almost as soon as I consciously registered its existence, the entity suddenly reacted, turning its head slightly towards me and then smoothly stretching out a hand in my direction, fingers widespread.

A pale yellow ball of light, not unlike a miniature Sun sphere complete with minuscule solar prominence all around it, leaped from the palm of its hand straight towards me in slow motion. It hit me in the face, square between the eyes, and that was the last thing I saw. Suddenly, it was broad daylight, and the entity was gone. It was as if time jumped forwards.

I don't know what the entity (whom I have dubbed "Blue Man") was, but I was not scared in any way, only surprised, and unbelievably calm. Whatever it was, it wasn't anything I have read about or seen in any book or magazine. However, I am curious; what was it doing in our bedroom? ' The following night strange things began to take place again in the Green's household,

' I slept very badly. I was worried that the entity might come back. I was now quite scared. I spent the whole night clinging to my wife. I have this irrational fear that they might take me away and not let me come back. I spent the night huddled under the blankets, scared of looking up to see the entity looking at me again. This may sound incredible or ridiculous, but I felt a presence waiting in the bedroom all night. Around 05:35 am, I heard bird song outside. Tired of clinging to my wife, I turned over and lay on my back, all the while keeping my eyes closed. I had just turned over on my back when something or someone grabbed my left arm or hand in a vice. Almost simultaneously, I felt a familiar buzzing, a vibration assault my hand, starting from my finger tips, travelling slowly up my arm and then begin to creep across my body. The vibration was familiar, except it was ten times stronger than usual, feeling more like a strong electric current, and it hurt me. In my line of vision, I caught a glimpse of a pair of eyes looking intently into mine. The entire image was again bathed in a pale blue glow, the same glow I saw before. All I saw were the eyes. They looked vaguely human, and curiously female. The eyes seemed to convey concern, worry. There was a distinct iris, and eyelashes.

Somehow, I managed to tear myself away from its intense stare, roll over, and grab my wife in a blind panic. There was the most horrid pain in my left arm. She of course woke up to find me almost frantically clinging to her. I told her what had happened. Interestingly when she looked around there was nothing in the room to see. As soon as I managed to calm down, I tried to get back to sleep. No sooner had I closed my eyes, when I received a clear telepathic message, a definite mental impression. I say telepathic, because I perceived the following words quite clearly in my head, and I quote: "Your daughter and yourself are precisely the same". There was something about the way the message was put across, it sounded like the source of these words did not seem to have a perfect command of English, and even the sentence did not sound right, indeed I had no doubts that the source was alien to the English language. It also seemed the entity relaying this message was almost mocking me. I initially thought this message was in reference to my daughter.

Nine months and a few days after the "Blueman Incident," we had an addition to the family. A baby girl. Today she is 2 years old, and way beyond her years as far as intelligence is concerned. This child is also telepathic, and she does odd things I used to do as a child, which the older daughter doesn't. The blue beings were right. "We are precisely the same, but not in an ordinary sense, but it is something we both have.'

A number of religious icons have manifested at portal locations including 'visions' of the Blessed Virgin Mary & Mary Magdalene, who seem to be older representations of modern sightings of the 'Blue Lady'. Perhaps one of the most enigmatic and well documented cases of these 'blue lady' apparitions took place at Fatima, Portugal from May to October 1917. Involving three children, Lucia, Jacinta and Francisco, more than 70,000 people of all walks of life saw the sun, contrary to cosmic laws, twirl in the sky, throw off colours and descend to the earth. The children predicted that this would happen after communing with the vision of the Blessed Virgin who appeared by a tree in the same field. Although I have included the visions of Mary, also known to the children as 'the Queen of the Universe', she is strictly not an entity in blue, as all of the sightings of her (and of an Angel) at Fatima, were of a being that looked female within a dazzling white light. Illustrations of the visions from a religious point of view have given the Virgin Mary blue and white garments with the sacred heart and rosary additions. I still feel that it is right to include 'her' here in this section as the case typifies the kinds of human-like entities which appear in similar ways, but are then recognised later as religious icons. With that in mind, lets look at an overview of the Fatima case and what actually took place there. *'In 1917, three shepherd children living just outside Fatima, Portugal had a series of visions of a lovely lady in a cloud. The anticlerical government in the region wished to squelch the Church, yet further reports of religious experiences become cause for serious concern. Even so, the children stand by their story, and the message of peace from war and hope the Lady brings. In the last vision, attended by thousands of people, the Lady proves her reality with a spectacular miracle that is seen by everyone present, the dance of the Sun.'*

The Blue Lady has been seen at many other religious sites and places of worship like Fatima, but 'she' has also been sighted at none-religious places too in more recent times and although the icon looks more or less the same, having similar dress and acting in a saintly manner, modern reports do not always include any one particular view that the entity is a Christian character. For example, I myself have witnessed such a Blue Lady on two separate occasions at the woods of Rosslyn and at the woodlands of the Settle portal. I must admit that when I first saw her appear and float between the trees, I thought that she was indeed, the virgin Mary. However, I have since learnt that she represents something else to me more closely linked with a certain kind of Extraterrestrial being, but I am still unable to decide whether this ET is able to manifest as Mary of the bible or if the Virgin is a messenger from God, who takes on other forms like E.T.'s? In both cases, the entity is able to appear mainly dressed in blue religious looking garments that are surrounded by a white vibrant glow, she is able to communicate words to the mind and can levitate off the ground. Most sightings of this form of the Blue Lady are short lived up to several seconds.

The Greys (Zetas)

Not strictly portal travellers, the large headed, almond eyed and thin bodied greys have been sighted near to and around portal sites. These entities are said to be responsible for other sighted creatures that appear to be watching over the portal entrances, especially in woodlands, like the phantom or ghost owls. At the Settle portal two types of greys have been reported and captured on photographs, one being a smaller (or possibly child) typical iconic type and another being of an orange and gold colour, which seems taller (about the size of a tall human male 5'10" - 6.00') with a broad head and rounder eyes. There have been no reported abductions made by these greys from ancient site portals as far as we know, but cases do exist of abductions (which these types seem to be most connected with according to reports) from buildings close to natural portals. The possibility that portals exist within the buildings cannot be ruled out of course, through which greys may be able to travel.

The Pleiadians

Included in this classification are the more human-looking entities and we could include the 'Blue people' as there seems to be some evidence that the 'Blue Lady', often sighted at portal sites within woodlands and groves, has stated that she is of the Pleiadian race and that although they use space vehicles to manoeuvre in our own universe, they are also capable of inter-dimensional and time travel through portals. Mostly associated with the classic Eduard Billy Meir encounters during the 1970's in Switzerland, Pleiadian Beings were supposed to have contacted him, informed him about the planet that they came from and the space technology they use to travel to this world. The Pleiades Star Cluster in the Constellation Taurus is their home. Although remaining highly controversial today, his claimed encounters (he had several and was able to take numerous photographs) with one particular female called Semjase, has a feel of the my own visitations from the Blue Lady, who I know, through my own channelling with her, to be of the Pleiadian origins. The Pleiadians state that they are here to raise the human awareness of its own spirituality at this time of need and there are Special Pleiadian Forces residing at a very high frequency that is lighter than what we know now.

The Space Brothers, Spirit Beings & Angels

The most celebrated contactee of the 1950's was George Adamski. Due to the 'too good to be true' evidence that he put forward for his own contacts in the Californian deserts with what he called the 'Space Brothers' -an intergalactic family of different types of mainly human looking beings - Adamski's claims have been sidelined by most of Ufology. One of his claims that was unproven at the time due to man's only recent adventures into space, was that he said one of the beings he met and talked with using the mind and sign-language, was from the planet Venus. Science has a problem with this 'outrageous' statement as we all know now that Venus is a world that could not possibly sustain life in the human form as we know it. However, even though in Adamski's

101

time, the possibility of other dimensional worlds and beings existing in them, was something unrelated to the subject of flying saucers, there were other contactees who came forwards to claim that advanced human-like entities came from places called Inner Worlds, more or less the same as the dimensional states that we describe today. The possibility remains that Adamski's Space Brothers may have been travellers using dimensional gateways in space and time and who knows which planet Venus they really came from if he was telling the truth?

Celestial Beings may cross over into a number of these categories listed which may be down to either the way witnesses describe them without full knowledge of who or what they are, or that they become so advanced in their true form that they are able to take on the appearance of other types of beings. What some people may describe as an Angel may well have been a highly advanced spirit of human or none human origins.

The RODs and Energy Beings

This is a fairly recent phenomenon which may have been overlooked by mainstream Ufology in past years. Jose Escamilla, who claims to have been the first to film Rods on March 19, 1994 at Roswell, New Mexico, while sighting a UFO (which in my opinion is not too surprising as the two phenomena possibly have a common source) highlighted the fact that dimensional entities come in all shapes and sizes, even minute.
It was interesting that sceptics claimed that on August 8th, 2005,

'China Central Television aired a two-part documentary about flying rods in China. Surveillance cameras in the facility's compound captured video footage of flying rods identical to those shown in Jose Escamilla's video. Getting no satisfactory answer to the phenomenon, curious scientists at the facility decided that they would try to solve the mystery by attempting to catch these airborne creatures. Huge nets were set up and the same surveillance cameras then captured images of rods flying into the trap. When the nets were inspected, the "rods" were no more than regular moths and other ordinary flying insects'.

It was deduced that all flying Rods were no more than optical illusions created by the slower camera recording speed. Without quite knowing it though, the same sceptics might have stumbled across something here with the speed of the camera recording the event of Rods flying about, that leads towards actually proving this to be a genuine phenomenon.

What has become known as the Chilli Pepper footage, concerns a video which I took soon after the Horseshoe Trees vortex at the Settle portal had been located in 2012. Aiming the camcorder towards a corner of the field adjacent to the site, where I inwardly felt that something was trying to come through the dimensional gateway there (which gave me a sense of pressure of the air around me being sucked away by something unseen), I initially felt like two large eyes were looking at me from quite close to the rock strewn ground in front of dry stone walling. Almost out of nowhere there seemed to be a kind of wind suddenly blow up in the place I stood, whereas it had been a calm day. Just as I zoomed in with the lens and back out again to try fill the picture with the area where I felt the presence, an odd blue energy burst into view (I was looking at the video playback screen in live recording mode and not directly at the place where this happened), once, then again larger this time, and then smaller and fainter. The blue of what looked like flat circles of lighted mist on the playback screen, looked much fainter than I recall, once viewing them later on download to the computer.

For some reason, which I do not recall, I decided one day after the visit to the portal to slow the video footage down (slow motion), maybe I thought that this would make the appearance on video of the blue bursts of light more dramatic for the viewer? I was amazed to find, that by slowing the footage down by 200 times normal recorded speed, another object appeared in the footage which could not be seen with the naked eye beforehand. A strange orange-brown shape that looked like an elongated chilli pepper appears from a tree off to the right of the frame at a height of about 15ft and then travels across the air, 20-30ft towards the right in a downward motion (in the foreground) , and through the exact position where the blue mists would have been, but were now nowhere to be seen in the speeded up video.

Looking at the recorded object in stills taken from the video frames it seems as if the object changes shape and almost wriggles through the air like an eel, but a much shorter length. It looks to have an almost translucent orange lighted body with two fin-like appendages near to the front and a silver or grey coloured area just behind these on its top part. Whatever it is, it certainly looks to be aero-dynamic in shape, like a torpedo. It was absolutely silent to the human ear.

Maybe this is the same kind of phenomena as is being reported by those who see and photograph Rods? Could it be that whatever Rods are, they move at such speeds that even though our cameras fail to show them, they are really still there. This would mean that they travel at tremendous speeds, but if true, in doing so, this may be one of the reasons that they are able to traverse the unseen corridors of portals?

The Giant Beings

Looking at the local myths and legends that are related from areas which later prove to be portals due to the many kinds of paranormal events happening there, time and again accounts of people having encounters with very tall or even gigantic beings are not uncommon. We have seen already that the presence of giants were said to be roaming the Earth in early biblical times, but the concept of such beings living amongst mankind in the modern era is much more difficult to comprehend. Yet, there are reports of gigantic entities that have been seen at portal sites in existence; the one discovered in a cave close to the Settle portal which I described in my previous book.

I do not think it is coincidence that legends (especially here in England) of traditional giants, like the story of Rombald, the Giant of Ilkley Moor, who are often situated at places which have later become recognised with enough research as potential portals. It was not uncommon that in the early 19th Century, tales about the giant Rombald (the area is now called Rombalds Moor) included his wanderings in the middle of the night, flitting from one sacred site to another, maybe from the Cow and Calf Rocks to one of the ancient stone circles or cairns on the higher moorland, with flaming red eyes that shone like two fiery stars in the night skies.

The depictions of these giants with demonic looking red eyes again makes the crossover with other entity types observed at the portals like the Black Dogs and Shape-shifters. Expert on all things monstrously weird from the UFO world, Nick Redfern gives the account of a similar case, involving the Schwab family, who was then living in the English city of Bath. Late one weekend night in mid March 1978, while they were driving past Stonehenge at around 11.00 p.m., they were shocked by the unbelievable sight of a "twelve-foot-tall thing, like a giant man," standing in the middle of the road.

Slamming on the brakes, Mr. Schwab brought the car to a rapid, screeching halt, and he, his wife and son watched amazed as a bright light from above suddenly enveloped the mighty being, and they could see it was almost human like, but twice as tall and in a silver suit and two big eyes."

The Shadow Entities

Reports of shadowy entities are becoming more and more frequent close to and at ancient portal sites. It is open to speculation whether the Shadow People are human spirit forms or some other kind of none human entity. Heidi Hollis brought the public attention to the modern beliefs in shadow people, relating how witnesses described them as dark silhouettes with human shapes and profiles that flicker in and out of peripheral vision, and claimed that people had reported the figures attempting to "jump on their chest and choke them". She believes they can be repelled by invoking "the name of Jesus".

This is very interesting as I am witness to this unnerving episode, which happened to me sometime in the mid 1990s when I lived then at Menston, near to Ilkley Moor in Yorkshire. I had been laying in bed trying to fall off to sleep, when I heard the audible sound of something which sounded like a large dog coming bounding across the hall outside the bedroom door. I closed my eyes as I felt the pressure of the room drop as if something unseen was taking up all the air in it and I glimpsed an odd looking dark shadow in the shape of what looked like a wolf that pounced through mid air and landed on me in the bed. I could feel the weight of this 'shadow' creature pinning me down and the heaviness on my chest area became so uncomfortable that I thought I was going to die! What seemed like minutes of sheer terror and panic passed by and then I don't know why, as I was not particularly religious at that time, I started to pray to God to help me overcome whatever it was that had attacked me. Over and over I repeated the prayer-like plea, maybe as some kind of last resort for help, and then suddenly and without any warning or sensation of movement the creature was gone. At the time I told my ex-wife about the incident the following day, but she laughed it off as me probably having had a bad dream which I thought had been real. No more was said about it in any serious way until that following evening, when she screamed at me from her side of the bed, panting for breath and describing exactly what had happened to me the previous night.....it seemed the shadow-wolf was back!

Not all witnesses have had negative encounters with these Shadow Entities. Some see them as having even good, helpful or neutral intentions and that at least some of them may be an energy form that originates from other dimensions. Due to the vague nature of their appearance it would be wrong to exclude Shadow's from other types of entities observed at portals as witnesses believe them to be ghosts, time travellers, or something else. In the past, it was always thought that Shadow People were only seen from 'the corner of the eye' and that if direct visual contact was made with them they would vanish from sight. This does not seem to be the case any more, as there have been reported experiences where witnesses have observed these entities appearing and moving at close quarters and the Shadow's do not move away when confronted. Some of these entities have red glowing eyes, which seems to put them in the phantom category like Black Dogs, Hell Hounds, and the like. The dark countenance and malevolent feelings that are often reported in association with these creatures has led some researchers to speculate that they may be demonic in nature. If they are demons, we have to wonder what their purpose or intent is in letting themselves be seen in this manner. Is it merely to frighten people or is there some other greater plan at play?

The Elementals

Mainly due to portals occupying land, sea and air that is ancient and sacred in one form or another, they are associated with the natural elements and as such elemental beings which are said to either inhabit the actual location in a semi-physical form, or to use the portals (as many other entity types do) to travel between their realm and ours. Folklore and human traditions are steeped with tales about the encounters with the 'little folk', faeries, elves and gnomes which happen at these places often named as fairy rings, fairy hills and houses (tumulus), fairy track-ways (Leys) and fairy groves (trees).

To date, only one particular entity type of this classification has been photographed, but not actually sighted with the naked eye at the Horseshoe Trees vortex. My wife Helen was sounding in the ring of rocks that we had constructed at the site, using drums and chants, and suddenly declared that she felt that there was an elemental presence in the portal ring with her. As she said that, I picked up the camera and took a number of photographs of where she continued to dance and chant at the centre of the circle. Both of us, although making a thorough inspection of the ground and bushes all around the site, found nothing in a clearly visual way, to indicate anything unusual had made itself known to us. We both agreed later that a strange imagined spiralling cone of energy came to both of our attentions while at the ring which left us feeling a little dizzy and slightly off balance.

The results of that experience can be seen in the photograph that accompanies this section of the book, for right in the bottom of the left hand corner of just one such picture can be clearly seen something that should not be there. Looking like a small elemental gnome wearing what looks to be some kind of pointed hat and dark sunglasses, I like to call this little guy, 'the blues brother'.

Whether or not these elemental entities are real physical beings or not, or possibly some kind of projected manifestation from a different life-form at the portal (or elsewhere for that matter, as these beings have been seen all over the place, all over the world) is open to speculation. Knowing how higher life-forms that have made themselves known to us at the portal site in the past two years, can change shape, project shapes and influence the environment, I think it would be foolish to underestimate a phenomenon that can do this, with the limited (but ever growing) knowledge that we have now about them.

The Time Travellers

At a time when the internet is abound with videos claiming to show actual time travellers from the present day at important events in history and others talking on mobile phones decades before they were invented, the question as to whether portals allow humans and other intelligent beings to move through passages of time, is more important than ever. Even if it turns out that a good majority of these alleged videos to be faked (and I suspect that this may be the case, if only for the reason that what we may call time, the measurement of things happening in a linear order, will probably be shown, in time, to be something we cannot imagine at this time in our evolution. What is important is the fact that we are embracing something which until very recently remained in the realms of fantasy and science fiction and the very notion of time travel being something that science would look at, at all, brings the parallel worlds of quantum physics and the paranormal ever closer.

The concept of a time travel tunnel is a reality if we are to believe news in May 2013 from GuiZhou China. The tunnel is over 400 metres long, built years ago, but if you journey through it, the time on your cell phone (and this only works on cell phones which seems likely that something else is at play here) loses one hour. When investigators personally tested the tunnel, they reported that the phenomenon happened about eighty percent of the time and gave an indication on how it works. Say you enter the time tunnel at 9.00am and exit the other side of the tunnel at 9.05am. Mysteriously, the time on your cell phone will display only 8.05am. We are told that after travelling away down the road for a while your cell phone time will eventually return to normal.

To date, there has been no scientific explanation been offered as to how or why this is happening, but the local Chinese have asked the question, 'would repeatedly travelling in and out of the tunnel make a person younger?' It has been proposed that the phones are being effected by an unusually active magnetic field, or maybe simple interference or a problem with the cell towers, but nothing definite. It does lead us to other pressing questions though. What would happen if you entered the tunnel from the other side? Does time speed up?

To discount the possibility that some higher life-forms have been able at some point in their own evolution to have understood what we term 'time' is like modern man agreeing with our stone age ancestors that there will never be anything more technically advanced than rubbing two sticks together to create fire. To state that we know all there is to know concerning time is more a question of the state of the human ego, than anything else. To be able to project a sense of the Self over the expanse that we call time will not be measured with clocks, but maybe by the advanced minds of those who truly appreciate worlds that allow all considerations to be correct or even incorrect at the same moment, no black or white, no absolutes, but rather a world of willpower and creativity, for even up to this point in our own evolution we have only got to where we are, by recognising the fact that we are much more capable than we are ever given credit for.

The Jinn

More and more people who visit portals are beginning to state that they are being influenced by the presence of the Jinn, but mostly overlooked by other than those who study the occult, these particular entities may have closer relationships with portal energies than we can imagine.

The Jinn are supernatural creatures from Islamic mythology as well as pre-Islamic Arabian mythology. They are mentioned frequently in the Holy Ku'ran and other Islamic texts, inhabitants of an unseen world in dimensions beyond the visible universe of humans. Having free will, the Jinn can act in good and evil ways and everything in between, they can be male called 'jinni' (where the word Genie comes from) and females 'jinniya', and they seem to be at some level Elementals like the fairies of the western world, being formed from 'holy fire' energy.

There have been modern day encounters with the Jinn. One incident was reported in Egypt by a certain Hank Wessleman PhD.,

'This Jinn was encountered in a shrine at the great mortuary temple of Medinat Habu near the Valley of the Kings. After my initial encounter in the temple on Dec. 7, 2009, I returned to the shrine through my shamanic journey-work on Dec. 8 where the Jinn and I then had a most

unusual conversation. Let me say in advance that this dialogue did not occur in English nor in Arabic but rather in the non-verbal communication modality that I conceive of as 'think-feeling.'

According to Wessleman the Jinn appeared to him as a manifestation at first as two disembodied eyeballs, but it then carefully chose to reveal itself as a smoky humanoid form that flickered at the edges, shifting back and forth from one vague shape to another in pastel hues of orange, yellows and greens, with deeper core areas of more brilliant light as its mood shifted in response to the dialogue between the Jinn and Wessleman. Oddly enough, once Wessleman had informed the Jinn why he wished to make communion with it (to enhance his own spiritual journey), the Jinn agreed to assist him in a respectful way once Wessleman had tricked the Jinn by offering a thought-form of a pot of honey in exchange for the Jinn's name.

Although Jinn can become mischievous, they are willing to barter their services to humanity. They regard us as 'creators', while they understand themselves as being 'affectors' and can only manipulate events to a degree in order to bring about the desired outcomes. For example, Jinn encounter accounts have shown that they are capable of casting spells and illness on people in the work of their human masters. At the Settle portal my first encounter with a none human entity (who tried to present itself as a human being from the 17th Century called Jeremiah, to me) was possibly of this Jinn type, It threatened me with illness and a curse before letting its guard down and revealing itself by using inappropriate words in the dialogue I had with it, words which did not exist in the time period it pretended to have come from.

Jinn are fully aware that other types of life forms and higher level energies exist in many dimensions and seem close to those they call 'the masters, or the watchers'. When Wessleman asked his Jinn if he could make someone ill, the Jinn replied that there was only so much it could do to affect a situation stating, *'Who can say what is written on another person's soul? We cannot purposefully influence their destiny without tampering with their agreement'.*

Guardians and Gateway Keepers

Modern day Master shaman and portal gatekeeper John Lipscomb, has worked with portals to both access the spirit world of humans and other dimensional entities, but he believes that portals that have been created by man and naturally occurring gateways are very different. He states,

'Entities on the other-side can use a variety of different ways to communicate with us and just as we use electrical energy to provide us with useful machines to help us do many things including communication, those entities do the same with their own types of energy sources.'

John has built a device which he claims enhances the energies at a portal so that he is able to 'see' and photograph images or reflections of spirit entities that have been projected onto a screen. He uses a circuit of connected DC and AC current battery cells to surround the screen frame around it and above it, in order to create a field that can be 'used' by the entities at the portal to manifest their essence onto the black screen. I had similar information given to me by my Celestial guide, before I ever saw John's device, concerning the way the Ark of the Covenant 'operated and operates' and the principles that he gives here, although understandably somewhat simpler in construction seem to point towards what I was given in a channelled way by higher intelligences. We may speculate, that by John building his device and using it in connection with his deeper understanding of ancient portal lore, he is in affect a guardian of the gateway. Gateway keepers seem to be something quite different.

Once a dimensional portal has been found and there is enough evidence obtained from the placement of the portal for its reality, a great responsibility comes upon those who wish to interact with it. For thousands of years in all cultures across the globe, sacred openings and hidden gateways to other realms have been at the heart of spiritual and religious understanding. They are the places where this world's inhabitants meet with others of another, or maybe a passageway from which the human living energy passes once the physical body is no longer able or needed to operate functionally. Like all journeys, there are usually well established road maps and it is the role of the Gatekeeper to make the considered decision as to whether an entity is able or worthy to move between different worlds, depending on their purpose and intentions. Some people with deep understanding of the hidden knowledge concerning portals, are able to, through degrees of attainment, reach a level where they can obtain 'Keys'. These keys in a metaphysical sense 'allow' hidden doors to be opened, but not all keys fit all locks -again it depends on the intentions of the entity or person's quest, whether or not they are successful in gaining entrance to other worlds. This can get quite deep for us to understand, as it is not always the case that what we might view as 'negative actions' that might stop someone from moving between dimensions, either physically or spiritually. For, as in many cases, what someone does or doesn't do is not always a reflection of their intentions and mistakes can happen along the way. If bad or wrong things are caused with intention however, it would be the role of the Gatekeeper to understand why this has happened and only allow such an energy to traverse the realms after reading their life-map (past, present and future), and in doing so, protect the portals from misuse.

Not all portals have Guardians or Gatekeepers from this world. Some are left unrecognised and simply forgotten about due to the passage of time and if in an 'inactive state' then this is OK to a degree, but should somebody decide to dabble with the energies at portal sites 'for their own gain maybe' then there are energies waiting in the ether of the portal environment that may try to take advantage of such naivety and use tricks and misdirection to use the portal for its own agendas. Once a portal has been activated by recognition (thought forms), ritual practice and meditations, and the pure will of the person to use the gateway, then it should become almost as important as looking after your own child for the opener of portals should be wise enough to realise that he or she holds the golden key to one of the greatest secrets the human race has ever known about.

PHOTOGRAPHIC EVIDENCE:

THE SETTLE PORTAL

Working between 2011 and 2014, the following photograph's were obtained from the site of the Sun Dial Portal at Settle and the surrounding area within 3 miles of the Horseshoe Trees vortex. All photographs have been classified as genuine phenomena (images that have not been faked, photo-shop, manipulated by humans with intent to fool anyone and have been witnessed by one or more people at the portal site.), although of course there is only independent witness testimony to these photographs and events. What we have found at the Settle portal seems to be similar to other types of phenomena from portal sites all over the world. We present our findings here, so that others working at portals may come to recognise some of them for themselves.

1.Above: *Orb phenomenon – typical of the orbs that have been photographed numerous times at the site, but unseen with the naked eye at the time, this sequence shot shows an orb that has moved a distance of 1 meter in 3 seconds from right to left. Although skeptics have stated that these orbs may be camera flash effects or lens flares, moving insects, etc., this does not account for the seemingly intelligent abilities the portal orbs possess, maneuvering around trees and appearing upon request.*

2.Right: *This orb was actually witnessed by the photographer, appearing and then moving into the stomach area of the person by the tree. Its glow was much brighter than most orbs that have been seen at the portal up until now and this object left a trail of white light behind it as it moved closer to him. At a steady pace.*
The person in the photograph felt no pain as it moved through him and emerging in a second out of his back, the only feelings he remembers is that he thought that someone was standing near him, but he could not see them.

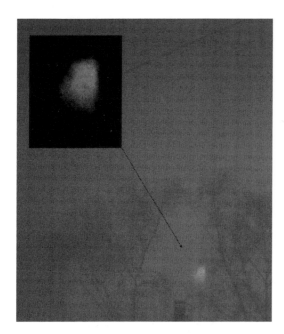

3. Left: *Plasma type UFOs are not uncommon sights over the Settle township. These orange coloured balls of light are one of the most common kinds to be reported by witnesses.*
They may be connected to changes in the electro-magnetic fields at certain times of the year, possibly influenced by astronomical alignments too.
These plasma types are seen close to ley lines and energy sites close to the portal. When sighted they look to be almost alive, as if there is some kind of internal energy (which does look electrical in nature as it hisses and buzzes), but unlike ball-lightening, they have been seen to change into different kinds of objects in mid air.

4. Left: *The author could see this orb in front of him, but the photographer could not. He was instructed to take the photograph anyway. The orb was moving in mid air as if it was juggling between the hands of the author. Lasting for about 3 seconds duration with no sounds, the orb vanished before his eyes. By using a kind of mind to mind request to the orb energy, the author believes that the intelligence presenting itself as a ball of light, is able to follow simple commands. By asking and recognising that the orbs are real, it seems they are happy to assist*

5. Above: *Not all orbs appear within the vortex of the portal. This image shows a giant orb that appeared above the Freemasons Lodge at Castleberg, less than 500 meters from the vortex in the evening hours of spring 2013.*

6. Left: *Bursts of light in mid air have been witnessed at the portal site that can move around in the atmosphere. Unlike natural phenomena such as ball-lightening, these light-forms seem to be under intelligent control. This light was photographed as it maneuvered around the trees in the foreground. Photograph taken between Settle and Langcliffe on the High Road*

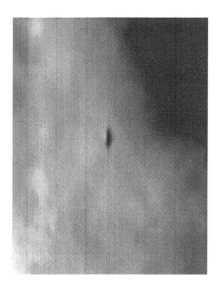

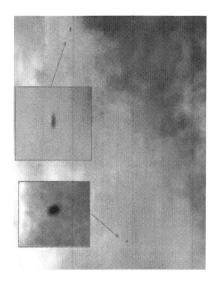

7. Above : *Two objects at cloud height over the portal at Giggleswick. Both were observed by the author in May 2013 at mid afternoon, moving in and out of the cloud cover at speed. These seem to be a structured object and look to the naked eye to be made of a metallic substance? Although these particular objects are the classic 'saucer-shape', other sightings made in the same area, depict triangular and oblong structured UFOs.*

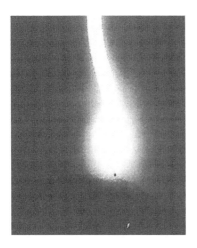 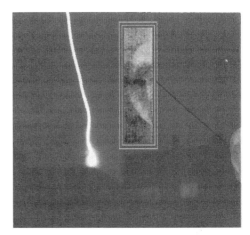

8. Above: *This photograph was taken by a local garage worker one early morning in the summer of 2010. The camera picked up an object that descended from the sky and illuminated the top of Castleberg at the site of the Sun Dial Portal. Closer inspection of the photograph revealed that two small objects could be seen in the glow; a dark round object and further down the hillside, a white plasma looking object. The white colored object was positioned at the spot where the horseshoe trees vortex is situated in the portal. When the photograph was lightened to show more detail in a computer enhancing software, a strange image appeared on the right side of it which was not seen originally with the naked eye. What looks like the face of an Grey type being, seems to be peering around the edge of the photograph, but it has been suggested that this may be an affect of brightening the image. At first, it was suggested that the face might have been a thumbprint on the emulsion of the photo, but on closer inspection, it was found that the image of this 'face' was under the surface of the print.*

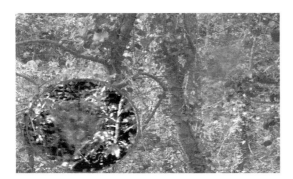

9. Left: *When a rustling sound was heard in the bushes near to the Horseshoe Trees Vortex in 2014, the author decided to take a photograph in that direction although he did not see anything unusual at the time.*

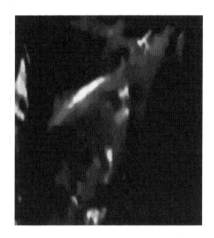

10. Above: *Still frame image from video taken at the Settle portal vortex site in 2012, which became known as the 'Chili Pepper' footage.*
After the author captured a strange blue flash of light on film, he slowed it down and there appeared this odd looking vivid orange object moving fast across the frame. Nothing like this was seen at the time and it is thought that the object moved too fast for the naked eye to catch its movement.

11. Left: *The author's wife Helen in this photograph, was channeling at the horseshoe vortex of the Sun Dial Portal. In her mind, she imagined there being small elemental like entities with her. This photo shows what looks to be an Elf like head wearing a pointed hat, blue in color and unlike anything else observed at the site. Interestingly, the image of the 'Elf' appeared right in the bottom left corner of the photo, as if looking into it!*

12. Right *This apparition of what looks like an owl perched on the fence has been observed a number of times in the Sun Dial portal region. Some investigators regard it as a kind of elemental guardian watching over the portal.*

Other owl shape-shifters of this nature, have been seen at the Rendlesham Forest Portal in Suffolk. This photograph showing a very similar ghost owl with dark eyes, taken by investigator Derek Savory **(Below).**

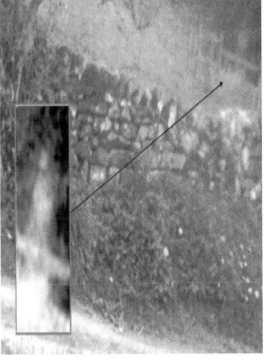

13. Below: *The author watched and photographed a mist that rose from the ground in the vortex of the Sun Dial portal in 2012. Forming at first into a column of fog, details began to emerge in it and faces began to appear for a few moments before vanishing back into the mist.*
This photo shows what looks like the face of a dark skin colored person looking left; with white eyes and lips. Another being to its right, which looked like a kind of reptilian, is seen as its' form starts to dissipate into the mist it appeared out of.

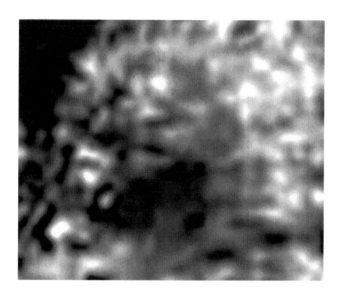

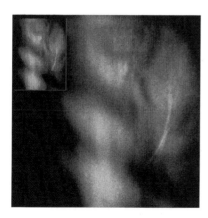

14. Left: *Two heads of beings that appeared in the portal area in 2013. Both are recognisable as types of beings that have been reported before this photo was taken. The grey blue being is a Grey type and the brown being looking right (in profile) has the appearance of the beings that Mike Oram encountered in his book 'Does it rain in other dimensions?'*

15. Right: *A rare photograph taken by the author of ET beings appearing behind his wife Helen. A tall pale skinned being with domed head was accompanied by smaller Grey types. The author asked, through channeled messages between himself and the tall being, if it would be possible to get their image on camera.*

16. Right: *This photo taken in the summer months of 2013 at the portal vortex on Castleberg, shows a small Grey entity which is hidden behind the tree trunk. In the skies close to its position, a small airborne object appeared. The author channeled this Grey and discovered that it was of a young age, only 1400 years old, and had been left as a guardian of the portal by older beings. After the photo had been taken, independent investigators inspected the area by the tree and nothing was found there which could account for the image in the photo.*

17. Above: *In this interesting photograph, which was produced when the author and his wife Helen meditated and asked permission to gain evidence from any entities at the Settle portal. There are two recognisable forms appearing at both sides of the pathway through the woods (circled).*

18. Above: *What looks to be a typical iconic Grey entities face was photographed by the author in early 2014. Many photographs of this kind, seem to show images of alien beings that are popular in culture of the time. Are the Inter-dimensional beings reading our minds in able to present themselves as something that we recognise, because the are in the true sense very different to us?*

CHAPTER FIVE

The Chapel On The Hill

A PORTAL THAT COULD NOT BE BUILT IN STONE

One of the most enigmatic of buildings local to Settle, North Yorkshire, is Giggleswick Chapel. In my previous book 'Isaac Newton & The Secret Sun Dial', I explained how this chapel had been built on a previous ancient site that was in my opinion, one of the secret place-holders for an inter dimensional portal at nearby Castleberg, Settle.

The actual placement of this chapel is so important to understanding why it may hold one of the worlds' biggest secrets. It was not placed where it stands today purely for ascetic reasons alone, but because in my view, it had to be located upon a rocky knoll that overlooks the village in order to fulfil its builders vision.

Just why the chapel was constructed with an almost eastern religious outlook, presenting itself with a copper dome instead of any Christian spire, is a puzzle in itself, and why should we find within this place of worship alongside Gothic influences, pagan symbolism & the swastika motif of solar worship? Indeed, Giggleswick Chapel is a place of unique function for it is a portal energy balancer built in stone.

"Much folklore and legend has grown up about this building. It has at various times been described as a mosque, a library and an observatory , as if some felt the need to attribute to this strangely beautiful building a strange and unique function."

Giggleswick Chapel was built in 1897 to commemorate Queen Victoria's

Diamond Jubilee and was a present to Giggleswick School by Walter Morrison M.P. Who lived in Malham Tarn House. The chapel was designed and built to very fine and specific measures by Sir T.G. Jackson who included only certain types of stone and marble for its wonderful mosaics which were said to have been brought to the chapel site from all over the country in order to include a greater range of stone colouring to the interior. Sitting on the knoll in the landscape to the west of Settle, the chapel stands out like a sore thumb, beckoning any enquiring mind to enter through its vast wooden doors and seek out the mysteries within.

Before we examine how the chapel itself and its position within the landscape is essential to enforcing the reality of the Castleberg Portal, lets have a closer look at the man behind its construction Walter Morrison M.P., to find out if he had any as yet unknown reasons for placing the chapel exactly at a geographical point situated on the Settle energy grid. Walter Morrison M.P. is still known as the man who 'had his fingers in many different pies'. He was involved in many different projects and aspects of local social life including the political scene around his beloved Malhamdale.

He was born in 1836 the son of a wealthy and large family, being educated at Eaton and Balliol College, Oxford, after which Walter took off on a Grand Tour of the world. It was probably on this tour overseas that he began to take in the eastern influences that we find incorporated in the Chapel today, travelling to Egypt, Syria and the Middle East. In Palestine he took to ancient archaeology and became Hon. Treasurer of the Palestine Exploration Fund from the year following its formation in 1865, remaining a member of the governing body right through until 1919. Returning to Yorkshire and a liberal turned conservative political life, Walter eventually inherited in 1857 the Malham estate which had been bought by his father James. Walter lived in Malham Tarn House and developed it to include an east wing, veranda and Italianate bell tower; a magnificent spectacle overlooking the sparkling waters of the tarn for any walker passing by.

An almost endless stream of visitors and guests to Walters home included Charles Kingsley (and his letters from Tarn House still exist), author of 'The Water Babies'. It is said that Kingsley was so impressed with Malham Cove with it's dark craggy outcrops of rock, swirling pools and natural beauty that it inspired him on the spot to write the novel. Other notable worthies included John Ruskin and Charles Darwin. Another was Thomas Hughes, the author of Tom Brown's Schooldays.

Some of the tenant-farmers on the Malham estate included those who were direct descendants of the once rich and powerful landowner families from the portal region around Settle and Langcliffe such as Stephen Carr who resided at Park House and later at Lee Gate. Walter Morrison M.P. had a good working relationship with many of his tenants and would often 'call by' unannounced just to pay a visit. He was a keen walker even in older age, seen striding around his estate, through the Ribblesdale vales and up the steepest of slopes in Settle. He spent much of his time either joining or organising different groups and clubs including membership to the Settle Cave Exploration Society. In 1975, an amazing discovery was made. A pothole was found under a paving stone in the kitchen of Darnbrook Farm, Malham Moor which was over a mile long. Exploration by David Hodgson revealed a chamber where seven names and dates were scratched on the wall including Walter Morrison 1867, he having been there over 100 years before!

His business interests are the main focus of this book and how this may have involved him in the deeper secrets revealed later, concerning the Sun Dial portal. Of course he had always been a wealthy man and held ownership of hundreds of different kinds of commercial ventures all over the world. Nearer home, he became Chairman of the Craven Bank.

Settle and the Craven district had its own independent Bank for many years with other well known local family names of Birkbeck and Alcock amongst its first directors. Walter had been a director himself, but then became the Chairman, in fact the last ever Chairman of the Bank in 1905, after which the Craven Bank amalgamated with the Bank of

Liverpool which in itself became Martins Bank.

Through his many diverse business ventures Walter Morrison M.P. accumulated a great deal of wealth on top of that which he had been born into, but he maintained a modest standard of living most of his life and became a generous benefactor for many worthy causes. Indeed he was a man of standing, but never one to gloat about his wealth and disliked being in the limelight, preferring a simpler life out amongst the natural wonders of the Yorkshire countryside. Equally, he was very passionate about education and was totally responsible for building two schools, Kirby Malham United School in 1874 and a smaller school at Malham Tarn, being personally involved with organising Christmas parties at the schools for the local children. One of these benefactors closer to the portal mystery would be Giggleswick School.

'Giggleswick's famous School occupies an admirable site beneath the wooded grit-stone hill (Mill Hill). The present fine building is the fourth house since it was founded by James Carr in 1507, the first school being a plain looking structure without any architectural adornment. The ornate building near the Parish Church (Alkelda) was the third. Few schools have enjoyed a more progressively successful history, due in no small measure to the distinguished masters who have served there.'

Local historians state that the Governors (of which Walter Morrison was one at this time) and the Headmaster were trying to decide what they could do to celebrate the up and coming Diamond Jubilee of the Queen and were failing with ideas, when Walter Morrison suggested that he would present the school with a new chapel. In fact, he went on to provide a new gatehouse into the site of the chapel and a building which became a cricket pavilion adjacent to the knoll on which the new chapel would stand, with no expense spared! The specific site of where the chapel was to be built was not within the existing grounds of Giggleswick School at the time, but over the road, to the south of the main school building and atop a hilly knoll; rugged terrain encompassed by a small woodland of trees. I have outlined in my previous book why I think that this particular site was chosen for the situation of the east facing chapel and the explanation that this was once a very ancient site, possibly that of a previous stone circle and embankment of which remains can be found.

We know that Walter Morrison wanted his chapel to be built to exact dimensions and only include the finest of building materials, even though he wished the building to become a part of the local landscape, blending in with the countryside around the portal area. So he engaged the services of the architect T.G. Jackson.

Gothic architecture, to which Jackson excelled and incorporated within his works including the chapel at Giggleswick, has very justly been called 'the architecture of the Freemasons'.

Interestingly, Jackson fell in line easily with Walter Morrison's wishes that this Christian Chapel should hold within its design an accent of Gothic and eastern flavours because he himself asserted that ' Gothic architecture was not exclusively connected with the system of the Christian Church, nor intended by its forms to symbolise Christian doctrine'. In fact, he believed that Gothic architecture was not the creation of any religious creed or doctrine but it was the offspring of modern Europe and was only seen as Christian because modern Europe was Christianised.'

This is interesting in that Jackson was saying in a matter of fact way, that no matter what religion was current in its form at any particular place and time, Gothic architecture transcends that religion in its own uniqueness. This sounds very much like the known concepts and ideals of Freemasonry which itself proclaims that it is separate from all religions , although it does incorporate within those ideals scriptures and knowledge from many of the worlds religions and a bias at this present time towards Christian morals & values.

It took four years for the building of the Chapel to be completed in 1901 and construction work was virtually none stop without interruption. Walter Morrison paid a total of £70,000 from his own pocket, which enabled him to have brought to the site Cedar wood imported from Argentina, different types of marbles from Greece, Italy, Belgium & Ireland. Every part of the building was to his very own specification, so much so, that it was said that no-one at any future date would need to add anything to which Walter would not approve. All of the ideas, the symbols and the layout of the Chapel were to a certain degree, those of Walter Morrison M.P. and no other person. There might have been very good reason overlooked until now, as to why he should take total control of the project, apart from the accepted view that this was simply because he had paid for it. For such a generous man, that just does not seem to fit?

With the idea that Walter Morrison M.P. may have instructed Jackson to incorporate Gothic influenced Masonic symbolism within the structure of the Chapel, my wife Helen and I set out to travel the short distance from Settle to Giggleswick, a matter of less than a mile and easily within walking distance from the portal at Castleberg, situated on the opposite side of the dissecting River Ribble.

Normally the chapel itself is closed to the public apart from special occasions, maybe a local celebratory service, or the once a year open day granted by the National Heritage. We decided to take advantage of such an open day planned in the late summer of 2012, our mission to seek out any symbolism within the building itself that would indicate anything unusual about its purpose other than a place of worship. The day began wet and miserable, but by the time we climbed the roadway from the village to the once ancient mound on which the chapel rested, the sun had broken through darken clouds in rays of anticipation. Walking up to the giant wooden west facing doors of the chapel, I caught a glimpse of the original foundation stone, nothing spectacular, but engraved tellingly with the round outline of the solar disk.

We walked into this amazing chapel with reverence and dignity, both silent in our approach to the inner sanctuary from the wind and rain we had left outside. Looking rather odd and out of place, at each side of the door entrance stood two smartly dressed men. They looked like the kind you see in the Vatican or maybe spy films, shades on each, to complete their dark suited attire. As we passed by them, neither looked at us but straight ahead, almost standing guard in military fashion. A written sign on a white board had been pinned to the back of the door, 'No Cameras'. It didn't take us long to realise that this chapel was much more than a place of religious worship. It was a time capsule, a gateway in itself to the past, but also like a portal it held clues to an as yet unforeseen future too. The magnificence of its' interior upon my first ever viewing, brought a gasp of wonderment which was shared by Helen by the expression on her face as she glanced back at me. My hand held firmly, the digital camera that I had secreted into my jacket pocket!

There had been local rumours that Giggleswick Chapel was constructed with a room cut out of the bedrock upon which it stands and something 'unusual' was kept in this room. Whether this is true or not I have yet to fully establish, but what happened that day when Helen and I visited the chapel, led me to wonder about this. Also, a friend in Settle gave me some tantalising information about this and said that not only was there a secret room underneath it, but that clandestine meetings of the 'Old Giggleswickians' (a Freemason group associated with older members and masters of the ancient Giggleswick School) took place in that very room. Living nearby, he told me that he could see lights coming from under the ground right next to the chapel foundations and hearing odd chants that came from that direction.

If such a room did exist under this chapel, maybe it was purely a tomb or crypt and there was no great mystery surrounding it. But, there was something we became aware of that afternoon, in the upper floor levels of the chapel that amazed me more, indicating that this place of worship may hold deeper mysteries surrounding portals and other dimensions.

In my previous book *'Isaac Newton & the Secret Sun Dial'* , I suggested that portals were known about in ancient times and Neolithic shamans marked out the position of these gateways with standing stones and stone circles upon the sacred landscape. The line of megaliths at nearby Settle on the hillsides of Castleberg facing Giggleswick Chapel in line of sight, indicated to me that a portal once existed and was well known about there. This became known as the Settle Sun Dial.

Obviously, the portal in this instance was associated with the Sun (as many other megalithic solar temples are all over the world), yet we were still utterly gob-smacked to find the symbol of the Solar Wheel of the Sun in all its' glory, tiled into the mosaic flooring of Giggleswick Chapel directly under its magnificent dome! I asked myself, what the heck is an ancient eastern swastika doing here in a Christian chapel in North Yorkshire? As I looked on at it, my mind delved for deeper mysteries within that place. I had seen this exact motif elsewhere in the local landscape before, twice before in fact, once at the site of the Swastika Stone (an ancient carving pre-dating the Bronze Age) at Ilkley Moor, and again carved into the foundation stones of Bolton Abbey.

Why was the swastika symbol so important to those masons from earliest to moderately recent times, for them to have been a central focus point within local buildings like the chapel and for what purpose did Walter Morrison ensure that the swastika was included in his gift to the school at Giggleswick? I felt that the answer to this, may lie within the chapel itself, if not to be found on the windy and often desolate slopes of Ilkley Moor in this modern era.

I took the camera out of my pocket and snapped a couple of photo's of the swastika image, looking over my shoulder towards the doorway where the two 'guards' stood. I was lucky on this occasion, they were busying themselves with showing other people details of the doorway arch, not looking in my direction. Then I caught a glimpse of something in one of the stained-glass windows on the southern side of the chapels' exterior wall that stood out like a sore thumb amongst all of the other symbols.

The window image shows Walter Morrison in the garb of a master of the school at Giggleswick, holding a model of the chapel. His right arm is supporting the model and his finger points to the underside of the building exactly at the point where the swastika symbol is inlaid into the floor underneath the dome. There is something rather odd about the stone built frame behind Morrison, with its red coloured stones that look to be darker the more you look into it, maybe representing a tunnel with a stone built archway. It is my own contention that Morrison is literally 'pointing to the fact that a tunnel to a secret room exists underneath the chapel building' somewhere in the vicinity of the foundations underneath the swastika symbol. Could we speculate that Morrison was aware of unseen doorways, portals to other places, other realities, and he wanted those who had eyes to see, to understand, that his chapel was no more than a modern day marker on the landscape, signifying that at this place worlds unseen possibly do connect?

The sun began to break through the clouds outside and shine through the stained-glass windows of the chapel. I started to inspect a corner of the nave close to where an ornate pillar covered in foliage and leaves stood. It was on its own, not a pair as one might usually find, but it reminded me of a much simpler version of the pillars found in Roslyn Chapel near to Edinburgh. Behind the pillar the northern-side wall of the building opened up to form a stairwell entrance. Looking back to my security friends still stood on guard at the main entrance as before, I winked at Helen and quickly took the chance to descend those stony steps. I noticed a sudden chill in the air as I rounded the first corner of what seemed to be a short spiral into the depths of the ground on which the chapel stood. Ahead of me I looked into a very small closet, filled with brushes and cleaning equipment and nothing more. Modern plastered & white washed walls accompanied me down about a dozen more steps until I rounded the last of them and found myself facing east at an old wooden door which was locked with an old heavy padlock that had seen some use over time. There were very small cracks in the wood panels of this door, but the light was too dark down there to see through them, and it felt to me as I tried, that beyond that door lay a space almost equal the size of the chapel above.

It seems quite credible that Walter Morrison had some kind of prior occult knowledge about the local portal in the region, but of course much better evidence for this was needed to confirm any involvement he may have had in secreting such knowledge within or under the chapel structure. A visit to the home of Morrison at Malham Tarn House, some six miles from the chapel, was undertaken by Helen and myself in the summer of 2013. We were astounded at what we chanced to find there!
Malham Tarn is a glacial lake, some 1,237ft above sea level, making it the highest natural lake in England. As mentioned earlier, Morrison's house, grand and overlooking this splendid lake, was passed down to his son before changing hands eventually to be leased to the Fields Study Council of the National Trust as it is today. It was on the occasion of an National Trust open day, that we decided to take the opportunity to look around the grounds and inside the house itself.

Upon entering the old but magnificent house, the first thing that struck me was the inlaid tiling that ran throughout the main corridor between the ground floor rooms. A mosaic of swastikas, repeated along the length of this passageway, quite reminiscent of the one found in Morrison's domed chapel at Giggleswick.
There grew a sense of excitement between us both, almost like this was some kind of sign given to us from the past, but much more 'evidence' was to come. After walking into the large and imposing lounge which looked out onto the western shores of the lake and included a single old photograph of Walter Morrison hanging over a splendid fireplace, I felt

the sudden urge to go upstairs. This was going to be tricky, as the staircase had been cordoned off with a barrier tape like that found at police crime scenes, but the impulse grew in me to dodge around this at the earliest opportunity and ascend that spiralling staircase.

Helen at first remained with my son Warren downstairs in the hallway. I took my chance to speed up one flight of about twelve steps and turned a rounded corner. I stood dead in my tracks! I could not believe what I was seeing right in front of my eyes. There on the wall at the top of the next flight, on its own with no other pictures around it, framed in the same manner I had seen it before at the Freemasons Hall in Settle, was a depiction of the Sun Dial Portal; the same one commissioned by the government in the 1700's. What was this doing in the family house of Walter Morrison?

Left: On a *previous visit to the Freemasons Lodge at Castleberg, Settle, Helen & Nigel discovered a framed print of the Sun Dial Portal. The exact same print was discovered on the upper floor landing of Walter Morrison's House at Malham Tarn. Coincidence?*

A link began to form in my mind between Morrison, the chapel he built to his strict planning at Giggleswick and the Sun Dial Portal at Settle. All seemed to be connected together with a thread that was not only elusive to most in the locality, but had been so for hundreds of years. If anything was to be found out further concerning this mystery and whether or not Morrison was privy to some arcane knowledge about portals, then it seemed logical to suppose that knowledge might be found within the very design of the chapel, itself.

By the time my book ' *Isaac Newton & The Secret Sun Dial*' had been published in October 2012, there had been a covert, but intense objection to it from some of the locals in Settle. I noted that most of these people were either associated in some way to the council or the Freemason's who held lodge in the same area. From trying to get the book banned to having it taken out of the town's library for no good reason, it became obvious that the content of the portal mystery within it, did not sit right with certain individuals and groups.

I realised soon, that I would have to use similar tactics if I was to find out anything else about the chapel and Morrison's involvement in hiding the truth about the Sun Dial Portal from the public, secreting his knowledge about it, only for those who were deemed worthy to understand its implications.

I wrote a 'white lies' kind of letter to Giggleswick School asking the history department if they had any old pictures or drawings of the plans concerning the chapel. I told them that I was writing a book about Chapels in the North of the Country (which in a way I was) and Giggleswick Chapel would form a part of that works. I did not hear anything for two weeks and was about to give up on my clandestine approach, when I

received an email which I never ever expected! This included a number of digital copies of hand-drawn plans, elevations of the building, interior notes about the design of the chapel and above all else, the actual underground plans for the foundations. I shook with anticipation as I scrolled through a number of pages on the computer screen, each one revealing more detail than I could ever have dreamed of.

There, right in front of me, I was looking on at the actual original plans for the chapel, thought up and designed by Walter Morrison himself!

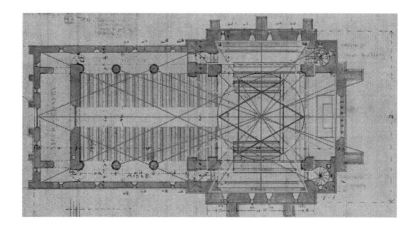

Above: *Part of the actual original plans drawn up by Walter Morrison's architect to the same sacred dimensions of those found in Solomon's Temple; incorporating the Solar Circle, the Templar Cross, the Masonic Square, & the Star Of David Hexagram.*

Three questions raced through my mind as I looked on at the plans. Did Morrison intentionally design this chapel as something more than a religious place of worship in the traditional sense, had he knowledge that geometric design could induce portal energies within buildings and in the landscape, and did he have prior knowledge about something important concerning the subterranean strata the chapel had been built upon?

As you pass through the village of Giggleswick there is a carving incorporated into a wall on the main road towards Settle. To some extent it looks quite out of place and doesn't seem to belong there. The carving shows what looks like an angel kneeling down and holding something. The angel seems to be positioned in the entrance to a tunnel or portal archway. The face of this angel has been obliterated for some unknown reason.

The archway is made up from nine individual stones held together in the traditional way by a Key Stone at the top. We could speculate, rather than holding something which seems to be resting on the ground anyway, the angel is lifting a cover from the floor within the tunnel to reveal something unseen. The significance of this carving will become apparent.

Underground passageways leading to portals and other dimensions are a common theme in the wilds of the Yorkshire Dales. Stories abound of unsuspecting travellers in these parts sometimes stumble upon hidden and secret stone entrances which reveal to them a hidden route to another mystical landscape, not unlike our own, but different all the same. In his excellent book *'The Lost World Of Agharti – The Mystery of Vril Power'*

Allec MacLellan, this local writer and adventurer of the Yorkshire Dales tells how he first came across a network of tunnels close to Kettlewell and in one of these he saw a bright green UFO-like ball of light that shot out of a cave entrance into the skies above him. Daring to inspect the tunnel closer, he heard strange rumbling sounds that seemed to be coming from way down in the depths of the earth itself. This led him to believe that he had discovered one of the many secret entrances to a lost and forgotten world in the inner earth. Nearer to the portal site at Settle there are rumours of secret underground tunnel systems, none more-so than the one found concerning the demolished house at Town Head.

Town Head Estate was bought from a local doctor Edgar's widow in 1949 and included a striking Victorian mansion called Town Head House. The owner at that time was Tot Lord (1899 -1965) who became something of a celebratory in Settle for his wondrous archaeological finds. The house was demolished in the 1970's to make way for local authority housing, but a puzzle remains as to why such an enigmatic building & its' ornate grounds should have been obliterated with no attempts to preserve it.

It seems that Tot Lord was another character of some importance from the Settle district who, like Morrison of Malham, was connected in some covert way with the Sun Dial Portal. In the Tot Lord Town Trail publication it states:

' In 1963 the Guardian newspaper interviewed Tot, who expressed his concerns about local mill closures, the consequence of building the Settle by-pass – fewer visitors – and Beeching's proposals to pull up the Settle Carlisle line. Tot suggested that the old sun dial, the biggest in the world, should be restored, and that at night it should be flood lit along with the rest of Castleberg. Tot felt that this would help put Settle on the map, and encourage crowds of visitors to the town.'

Is there any firm evidence that underground secret tunnels ever existed at Town Head House? Well, yes there is.

The building was once entered through double doors, to the right of which was a stoned up tunnel. This tunnel once led under the high road between the house and the woodlands of the Castleberg plantation and evidence still exists today for it. Directly above this tunnel there was a music room in the house, but due to ongoing bumps in the night, it became known as the 'ghost room'. We even have written historic evidence that subterranean rooms and passageways were built into the foundations of Town Head. Behind the arched door of Dr. Edgar's surgery was a barrel-vaulted passage with stone pillars leading to long cellars and rooms, with features not unlike those found in a Norman Crypt. It is said that Settles' most ancient man-made feature, whatever that may be, may still exist behind this tunnel door!

Without a shadow of doubt Town Head once held a number of mysteries which have not been totally forgotten about today. Local Settle resident Danny White (pseudonym), who knew Tot well and would drive him miles to look for flints said,

" *I never managed to go into those secret tunnels (at Townhead) as they were always locked up. Now they are walled up at bottom of the garden steps which led to the kitchen gardens back then. It is a shame, I will never know what lurked down in those cellars?*"

Denis Lord a direct descendent of Tot Lord stated,

" *Yes there were tunnels under Town Head. When we used to visit uncle Tot & auntie Maggie, we used to explore one tunnel that exited in the lower front garden, the entrance of which can still be seen when coming up the steps from the back of the houses there now. I'm not sure that it was so much a secret tunnel as just an access to the lower garden, though we always used to imagine it was .*"

The significance of tunnel systems and portals being connected is one which seems to allow a covert journey to and from the unseen entrances of this world to another. My suspicions concerning a tunnel running from Town Head into the Castleberg woodlands (plantation) were now valid, but something more gnawed at me and I realised what that was, once I had visited the location of the tunnel in the summer months of

2013. My intention to inspect the Town Head tunnel came about after I found a copy of an old drawing dated 1847 which showed the house and grounds in some detail, but also confirmed the route of the tunnel mentioned running under the High Street road to Langcliffe. I decided to tackle this tunnel problem from three angles. a): I would use dowsing with a pendulum on the 1847 map to see where the route of the tunnel ran into Castleberg, b: I would visit the actual place and inspect it visually and use dowsing to establish the same route of the tunnel I might find through the prior map dowsing attempts, and c: I would consider all of this information in line with the actual position of the Sun Dial Portal on that same hillside slope, What I found, utterly amazed me!

First of all, having previously located the Sun Dial Portal site (which we named the 'Horseshoe Trees' due to the shape of trees that surrounded it, I could see that this position was already known about (certainly to the originator of the 1847 map) as it was marked as a circle of tree's exactly where the portal can now be found. Tracks and woodland paths are drawn on that map too and the scale is large enough to determine some of them that are still in use today. Townhead House is also drawn in with the known tunnel that runs under the road at High Street into Castleberg woods. Dowsing on the map in April 2013 with the intention to find the course of this tunnel after it emerged on the woodland side of the road, I marked out a route which took its path in the very direction of the portal site. Some would state that this may have been due to the fact that I was already aware about the site of the portal on the map and I unconsciously or maybe consciously took this option for the tunnel route?

What was needed was confirmation at the actual tunnel site that this was the correct line of the tunnel which I felt continued its path underground and into the steeply ascending hillside, so later that month Helen and I visited Townhead tunnel to investigate this possibility further. Visual and on-site dowsing confirmed that the tunnel which is now filled in, but leaves a trace of its route in the vegetation growth about a meter and a half wide, certainly does run for some distance towards the portal.

We have already looked at the possibility that the biblical Moses might have acquired a device that may have been a portable portal creator, but what about the place where that device was supposedly eventually housed, the Temple of Solomon. If the builders of the chapel at

Giggleswick had been aware of the Settle Sun Dial Portal and had tried to construct secret tunnels in the area in order to move secretively between its site at Castleberg and the chapel, then this would actually be mimicking the layout we find at the site of Solomon's Temple. I think with that in mind, we can speculate that the designers of both the chapel and the original temple, had a similar purpose in mind and if this turns out to be the case, then who knows what amazing finds may lay at the end of the portal tunnel at Settle? From the written evidence, from the evidence we find in the landscape of both locations in England and in Jerusalem and from the paranormal evidence, we have a good case to explore this link further and can postulate that the Temple of Solomon was once an active inter-dimensional portal site.

What we regard as the Temple today is actually the third such building to occupy the same site or very close to the site on which the Dome of the Rock sits. Important as centres of religious worship for both Christian and Muslims alike, the dome hides secrets which go to the very roots of the portal mysteries. Before we look at the layout of the second Temple, that which was built under the influence of King Solomon and one which must have held some significance in its proportions, as it is often found in Gothic buildings of worship even today, we should concern ourselves with its actual position within the landscape in Jerusalem.

In the bible we learn that King David sought out a place which could be the focal point for all of the fighting and quarrelling tribes and sections of Israel so that all would feel equal in the face of God, so he made a compromise and chose Salem, the Jesuit Canaanite city that he called Jerusalem. This place we are told, had existed for centuries and was roughly situated between the two former kingdoms of Hebron & Shechem which had been one of the Ark sanctuaries. It was also strategically situated on a hill, easily defended and away from the major trade routes, so as to escape any tax levies that might have been impounded on the building of a Temple at that time. Not long after Jerusalem had been established, the Ark was installed in the tent of the Tabernacle on the site because God did not want David to take 'him' into a man made building due to all of the wars and killing that David had been involved in. This is odd, but may have some relevance as we shall see. As far as the God that dwelt within the Ark (the portable portal

138

device) was concerned, he preferred to live outside of stone built buildings, in the natural surroundings of the rocky landscapes and within the thin walls of a tent! Could it be that this was an important but much overlooked point being made here? Does this indicate that this Ark (whatever it was) operated much better if it was not surrounded by the thick stone walls of buildings, or maybe that it needed to be positioned at a particular spot in the landscape that was not polluted by the construction of man.

We know that buildings often hold the energies of past events and 'memories'. Maybe in some long lost and half forgotten way, we were once told that in order for the portal devices to work and stay activated, they need to be well away from any man-made buildings or constructions that could inadvertently mess up the way the device operated? When I first formulated this notion from that simple piece of biblical text, I felt a shiver run down my spine. Of course! This may be why we have places of worship (buildings like temples and churches) made of stone that often tell the story of the secret portals and hold vital clues to them, but such portal devices (like the Ark) are seldom, if ever, are actually found within these sacred buildings in any physical sense. It just might be, such buildings are the very last places a working model could operate!

Evidence for the site at Jerusalem being much older than the Bronze Age in which David found himself fighting Goliath and building temples and palaces to house god driven devices which did not want to live therein, has been found close to the Temple of Solomon. Back to the Stone Age and the important Neolithic era that connects with the shamanic knowledge of the Portals surrounding the standing stone markers that these peoples positioned in the ancient landscape, we find evidence that a kind of religious practice that was pagan was conducted by the Natufians; whose culture flourished in the region slightly before the creation of figurines found there, lived by hunting and gathering. Animal bones recovered from this time period show that gazelle were probably the Natufian hunters´ main prey, in addition to deer, aurochs and wild boar. According to research, the Natufian communities were the precursors to the first Neolithic settlements of the region and probably the world. Some evidence points to the cultivation of wild cereals, that would have been made possible by a worldwide climate change shift that occurred around 10,000 years ago. This race, although from the pre-Neolithic period seem to have led extraordinary lives and certainly knew about the concepts of life and death. The skeleton of a 12,000 year-old Natufian Shaman was discovered in northern Israel by archaeologists at the Hebrew University of Jerusalem.

'The burial is described as being accompanied by "exceptional" grave offerings - including 50 complete tortoise shells, the pelvis of a leopard and a human foot. The shaman burial is thought to be one of the earliest known from the archaeological record and the only shaman grave in the whole region'.(Dr. Leore Grosman of the Institute of Archaeology).

Remembering back to what I had written in my previous book about the Settle Sun Dial Portal being a megalithic stone structure that had been purposefully taken away from the landscape in an attempt to hide from history its true purpose, we find that this kind of thing may have also taken place in the Middle East during the Neolithic era. There is certain evidence in the history of the region to suggest that the use of standing stones by stone aged farmers in central Europe, derived from the Middle East about 3000 years ago, but the practice of forming stone circle structures could date back as far as 9,000 years around Turkey, Syria, Israel and Jordan. Recently a number of strange wheel like stone structures which can only be seen from 100ft in the air , were found in the lava landscapes of Azraq Oasis, east of Amman in Jordan. These look similar to the Nazca lines of Peru and have baffled archaeologists as to what they might represent. The best solution they can come up with is that they are burial cairns, but have not found anything close to them in the way of human remains to support this theory and when it is considered that some of these wheel circles are up to 230ft across, then that would have to be a very big tomb indeed! What has been established about them is that the local Bedouin call them the *'works of the old men'.*

A few years ago, an awesome archaeological discovery was made in southern Turkey, just north of the border with Syria. Three megalithic stone circles that were deliberately buried thousands of years ago on a hilltop were located at Göbekli Tepe. What is astounding is the dates for these megalithic stone circles have been given as several thousand years older than the first stone circle built at Stonehenge, and they were built by a hunter-gatherer society. Yet, the ability to design and lay out these stone structures was with these people, or had at least been given over to these people at a time when such feats seem out of place. Most of the stones (called pillars) at Göbekli Tepe weigh 10 to 20 tons, the largest are 50 tons. The stone T-shaped monoliths are 3 metres high, although the one in the centre of each circle is taller than the outer stones. The largest pillar is 9 metres high and was found unfinished in the nearby quarry.

The Gobeklo Tepe site has been associated with the biblical Garden of Eden, even though a look at the region today would not seem to support this speculative theory at best. With thousands of years, the climate and geographical conditions have changed quite dramatically and what looks today like a dry and dusty wasteland, was once fertile ground that was capable of sustaining a variety of plants and livestock. Archaeology in Syria and Turkey has established that this region later known as the 'fertile crescent' was very lush immediately after the last Ice Age ended. The environment was exceptionally rich, herds of wild animals were huge, and plants and food were easily obtained.

Indeed, English researcher Andrew Collins identifies Eden in his writings as a large region encompassing Upper Mesopotamia (South-east Turkey, Northern Syria and Northern Iraq). He believes that the Biblical Garden of Eden in the Old Testament is a memory passed down that persisted throughout the ancient cultures of Mesopotamia. This memory of the extremely lush environment of this region of the fertile crescent immediately after the Upper Palaeolithic ended and the glaciers retreated north, may have been deliberately and carefully preserved by the priesthoods of Sumner, Egypt, Babylon and Assyria. What we see at places like Gobekli Tepe might also indicate that something else far more significant than just a luxurious garden of abundance once existed there and these amazing standing stones we find today, although dusty and grey with time, shout out to us that at this place (and other sites like it all over the world) the veil between this dimension and the place the ancients called the domain of the gods, is less than a thought away.

In ancient Palestine, standing stones were called 'massebot' (singular: 'masseba') and were well known objects. They were often mentioned in the Old Testament as we have seen. Jacob erected his pillow-stone as a masseba at Bethel (Gen. 28:18) and Moses set up twelve massebot at Sinai before the altar at the ratification of the covenant, possibly in a stone circle formation. (Ex. 24:4). The significance of the word 'pillar' and 'pillow', both objects being described as standing stones or massebot cannot be pure coincidence. At a later time in the Bible we learn that these pillars of stone were denounced with some violence attached to their destruction and removal from the landscape, much in the way that remaining standing stones were removed from the Christian landscapes of Europe in the period between the 1600's and the 1800's. King Josiah led a reformation in which these standing stones were destroyed from all the "high places" (II Kings 23).

The masseba was literally a stone that was 'set up' (standing on the ground) and we are told by Carl F. Graesser, author of *Standing Stones in Ancient Palestine*, in this position it served as a marker, jogging the memory. This is exactly the purpose given by the First Peoples to the early human farmers during the Neolithic period in Europe, that the standing stones were markers and indicated where the sacred ground of the portals were positioned in the landscape. The standing stone would arrest the attention of the on-looker because it stood in a position it would not take naturally from gravity alone; only purposeful human activity could accomplish such "setting up." The study of massebot, therefore, is the study of those purposes that led to that "setting up."

As a rule the types of stone that became massabot (standing stones) were ones that were unmarked and unworked natural slabs of rock. In ancient Palestine they were called 'plain stones'. Although plain (and it has been determined that such stones were without inscription with purpose by those who erected them during the Bronze and Iron Ages in the East) the masseba held the same kind of supernatural essence that European & Americans man has attributed to standing stones found in their countries. However, a difference in that megaliths from all over Europe were known during the 19th Century as Rude Stones, due to connotations that the pagan element of the upright and often pointed stones resembled the male phallus, no such connection seems to have been made with the massabot of Palestine and Syria. Many scholars regard them as 'sacred stones'.; the abode of some animistic spirit, either of a deity, demon, or dead man. Animism has fallen into disfavour and the sacredness inhering in a masseba is described today in terms more similar to some kind of 'vessel'. The stone is conceived as a medium of power, as charged with a concentration of the divine power operative in the whole sacred area. In other words, the standing stone marks the area where some kind of spirit energy is held in a sacred space, maybe within the stone itself.

Depending where you find standing stones around the world, they seem to perform four known functions. Memorial - to mark the memory of a dead person, Legal - to mark the legal relationship between two or more people, Commemorative - to celebrate an event or honour an individual, and Cultic - to mark the sacred area where a deity might be found or to perform worship and sacrifice. A fifth element might be as a Marker, as suggested for the purpose behind the massabot of Palestine and although all four functions have been known to be correctively attributed to standing stones at different historical time periods, I suggest that the marker theory is one which is attached to the original purpose for standing the stones in the first place. Jacob set up the classic cultic masseba at Bethel to mark the presence of Yahweh there who appeared in the dream. "Surely Yahweh is in this place, how fearful is this place. This is the very house of God; this is the gate of heaven" (Gen. 28:16-17). Here we see that according to the biblical story of Jacob, he has a dream (which we will explore further) in which he observes the presence of God. When he awakes, he sets up a standing stone in order to say to others, "hey...this is the spot where I had my communion with God and this location is special because at this place, where I stood the stone as a marker, God can be found here!"

In the bible we read that Jacob stated, "This stone, which I have set up as a masseba, will be a house of God" (Gen. 28:22). "House of God" is the usual term for "temple." Just how far are we to press this term in understanding massebot? In some way this stone symbolized or was a temple in miniature. Here we have a direct link between standing stones and the ancient temples of the biblical era. The story of Jacobs Ladder is one which is set in a time (possibly Bronze Age) in which the practice of setting up standing stones was the norm for the priesthood of the day.

"Now Jacob went out from Beersheba and went toward Haran. "So he came to a certain place and stayed there all night, because the sun had set. And he took one of the stones of that place and put it at his head, and he lay down in that place to sleep. "Then he dreamed, and behold, a ladder was set up on the earth, and its top reached to heaven; and there the angels of 'the creator' were ascending and descending on it. "And behold, the eternal creator stood above it and said: "I am 'the eternal creator' of Abraham your father and the creator of Isaac; the land on which you lie I will give to you and your descendants. "Also your descendants shall be as the dust of the earth; you shall spread abroad to the west and the east, to the north and the south; and in you and in your seed all the families of the earth shall be blessed. "Behold, I am with you and will keep you wherever you go, and will bring you back to this land; for I will not leave you until I have done what I have spoken to you."

"Then Jacob awoke from his sleep and said, 'Surely 'the eternal creator' is in this place, and I did not know it.' "And he was afraid and said, "How awesome is this place! This is none other than the house of the creator, and this is the gate of heaven!' "Then Jacob rose early in the morning, and took the stone that he had put at his head, set it up as a pillar, and poured oil on top of it. "And he called the name of that place Bethel; but the name of that city had been Luz previously. "Then Jacob made a vow, saying, 'If 'the creator' will be with me, and keep me in this way that I am going, and give me bread to eat and clothing to put on, "so that I come back to my father's house in peace, then 'the eternal creator' shall be my 'creator'. "And this stone which I have set as a pillar shall be the 'creator's' house, and of all that You give me I will surely give a tenth to You." (Gen. 28:10-22)

We have established that in the historical record this Jacobs pillow was probably a massaba and that after his dream of the ladder between the earth and heaven, he set it up at the sacred site as a marker. We read in the bible that after some years, Jacob returned to that same sacred site and here, he 'wrestled' with an entity that proclaimed itself as a man, but then revealed itself to Jacob after the fight to be the essence of God. Most theologians accept that this description of the wrestling 'man' was probably an Angel. It was at this time that God changed Jacobs name to Israel; and Israel again set up and dedicated as a monument of witness the stone pillar which he had dedicated as "God's house." Its sacred character was now firmly established. The story of the Stone of Destiny then moves on and there is evidence (as we have seen) that it was uprooted and moved around the area at a later date, both with Jacobs son

Joseph (at which time it was called the Shepherd Stone) and even later with Moses. God instructed Moses, "I will stand before thee there upon the rock in Horeb; and thou shalt smite the rock, and there shall come water out of it, that the people may drink"; thus they were saved from death. This miracle was repeated later, but this time Moses was instructed merely to speak to the rock, not strike it; because Moses disobeyed God and hit the rock in a grand display before the people, he was not allowed to enter the Promised Land. In due course of time, we read that after Joshua had conquered the Promised Land and divided it among the 12 Tribes, he reminded them that they must ever be loyal to God, and he set up a stone as a monument of witness to this warning; the Hebrew says he took "the stone of greatness", which seems to be nothing other but the stone which was "God's house".

After the fall of the Temple of Solomon, the sacred stone then made its way to Ireland (where, we are told there was another Israelite tribe established which may have been the ancestors of the 'sons of Dan or the Tuatha Dé Danann, they are often referred to simply as the Tuatha Dé, a phrase also used to refer to the Israelites in early Irish Christian texts); a passage secured for it by Jeremiah and the daughters of the last King of Judah, Zedekiah. We learn that with Jeremiah went Baruch, his scribe, and the king's daughter; and with the princess, he would also certainly take the hidden Stone upon which the later Irish kings were crowned. The ancient Irish record the coming of 'the Great Prophet,' "Brugh" his scribe (obviously Baruch), and the daughter of a king, about 583 B.C., which would be the correct date; and that with them they brought the "Wonderful Stone," or "Stone of Destiny.

The stone, called Lia Fail was kept at the capital city of Tara for some three centuries, and all the kings, descendants of Eochaidh and Tea Tephi, were crowned on it. Then, about 350 B.C., it was sent to Scotland for the coronation of Fergus, King of Scots, who was a descendant of the Milesian kings of Ireland with due respect for the founders of both great nations, Scota (Pharaoh Akhenaten's daughter 'Meritaten'. There is a tradition that when Jeremiah brought Scota to Spain, he also brought the 'stone' upon which Jacob laid his head at Bethel when he had the vision of a ladder extending to heaven (Gen. 28: 12-19). This was the 'stone' used as a Coronation Stone in Solomon's Temple. Second Kings 11: 11-

14 tells of the anointing of a king, after which all the men around the king 'clapped their hands' and said, 'God save the King' while 'the king stood by a pillar, as the manner was, and the princes and the trumpeters by the kin.'). It remained in Scotland, and all Scottish kings were crowned on it, until 1297 A.D. when King Edward I of England invaded Scotland and captured the Stone, which he took to England, where it was placed in Westminster Abbey. It was built into the Coronation Chair, the oldest piece of furniture in England still serving its original purpose and all English kings and queens bar one, have been crowned on it ever since. Historically, there seems to be be little doubt about the stone having connections with the near east. Its origin was well known during the entire time it has been in the British Isles, and from practically the earliest times it was called 'Jacob's Stone.' William of Rislanger, writing in the 13th century, records the coronation of John de Baliol as King of Scotland in the year 1292 ' the stone upon which Jacob placed his head.'

Jacob's Stone was also know as the Stone of Scone, apparently named after a monastery at Scone in Scotland where it eventually came to rest, but there is a problem with this assumption in that a record of the Stone of Scone is to be found in the Holy Scriptures, and the word "Scone" itself is found in the Scriptures no less than 66 times in the Hebrew text. The meaning of Scone, Sh Ko N in Hebrew, and written Sh-K-N, means dwelling, and sometimes dwell. So the Stone of Scone is the Stone of Dwelling. This fits in with what we already know about the original stone of Jacob being a massaba and held as a marker for the 'house of God' or the dwelling entity within its marked sacred site. It is more likely that the monastery at Scone got its name from the stone when it was housed there.

Indeed, there is evidence to suggest that the ancient area around Scone Palace (where a replica of the 'stone of destiny' sits in the gardens) had Neolithic and Druidic origins. A stone circle known as Scone Wood Circle, originally stood in New Scone until excavated in 1961 prior to the housing development it is now in the midst of close to a recreation park at Sandy Road. Seven stones were recovered. The diameter of the circle is about 16-17 feet, graded with the largest stones on the W-SW arc. As in all mysteries, the case deepens and what we know of the Stone of Destiny today (the red/yellow sandstone block currently housed in Edinburgh), may be no more the massaba of Jacob than any other of the thousands of similar stones found throughout the world. There is one such standing stone, however, that remains in Ireland which may be a better contender for Jacob's pillar.

As we have stated, the Lia Fáil is reputed to have been brought from the east by the Tuatha Dé Danaan, and was originally situated in front of "Dúmha na nGiall", or Mound of the Hostages at Tara. Today, an upright 'stone of destiny' can be found close to Dunshaughlin and is a wonderfully simple standing stone. It was transplanted to its present location to mark the mass grave of the United Irish insurgents who fell at the battle of Tara on May 26th, 1798. Given it's position and similarity to a marker stone as found in the east, this stone is as good a bet as any to be the actual stone that Jacob rested his head upon in the account from the bible.

It seems from all of the biblical references we have looked at so far, there seems to be an underlying theme which involves standing stones from the Neolithic era and later, that are associated with amazingly mysterious meetings with a god-force or spiritual energy at the sites where these stones are to be found. In all of these accounts the most striking for me was the one in which Jacob recognises, after his ladder dream, that the place is a 'Gateway to heaven'. What is a portal if not a gateway to another realm, another place where celestial entities reign and hold a knowledge that transcends the abilities of human understanding in those early times. All of the elements are there and it seems without doubt that the Old Testament patriarch's like Jacob, Joseph & Moses, were all able to not only recognise where these pagan cultic sites of worship had been, but also retained the secret knowledge within their lineage to be able to 'operate' such gateways and enable them to commune with entities they took to be deity's and Gods.

CHAPTER SIX

SKINWALKER RANCH - A COMPARATIVE PORTAL STUDY

How do you study objectively, something which until very recently remained in the realms of science-fiction. How do you evaluate different kinds of unexplained phenomena that take place in such portals as can be found at two major sites; one in the UK and another in the USA. How do we even start to consider if these gateways into other worlds unseen, might be as real as you and me and the planet that we all live on?

I t has always been the endeavour of mankind to try make sense of that which, for now, makes no sense at all. We must resolve ourselves to the recognition that we are on a journey of revelation. Our own realisation concerning who we are and what we are is the key to understanding that which we do not yet know. So, let us study those things which we do not fully understand in the best way possible. Let us be brave enough to put one foot into the murky depths of the unknown; the pool of hidden knowledge where all answers might be sought. Let us look within, and let us consider.

This study, conducted in the summer to winter months of 2013 at the Sun Dial Portal at Settle, North Yorkshire, was something that I thought necessary if we are to try to better understand what might actually be happening there? This study will look at several key factors which are known about this particular portal site and other factors which remain on the verges of speculation, yet cannot be ignored. To study one portal site in isolation is not enough if we are to attempt such a qualification of the substantiating factors that make up the 'reality' of the phenomenon that has been witnessed at such places. For this reason, we can compare our findings with the well documented events that have taken place at the Skinwalker Ranch in Utah in the United States.

Background to the Skinwalker Ranch Story:

When I first read about the paranormal events that had taken place at the Skinwalker Ranch in Utah, it did not take me long to realise that a number of seemingly valid comparisons lay between what Helen and I had found at the Settle portal here in the UK and what had been happening over in the States. Many examples of UFO, Shape-shifters, and Orb experiences were so similar that it would not take too much a stretch of the imagination to place such under a common origin of classification.

Until the release of the Skinwalker movie in 2014, it would be true to say that not many people and even those studying the UFO phenomenon in the UK, had ever heard of the ranch or indeed knew just what a Skinwalker was supposed to be. There have been several good books written about the investigations that took place at and around the ranch since and before the film, which offer so much in the way of detail and evidence for something highly unusual happening there, that I would like to offer here some striking information which may support the Utah Basin as being yet another area where portal openings between worlds may exist. Before we examine these comparisons we need to look at the modern day account of what took place at the Sherman Ranch (named after the family who lived there), in order to get a feel for the area in question.

The Skinwalker Ranch consists of up to 500 plus acres of desert-like farmland located in south-east Utah, south of US Interstate 40, which enters Utah from north-western Colorado. Bordering the Uintah-Ouray Indian Reservation, east of the Duchesne/ Uintah County border, the nearest land mark is Bottle Hollow Reservoir, directly north of the Ranch. As we will see, this body of water seems to be a focus for paranormal activity, consistent with Malham tarn near to Settle here in the UK. To the north of the ranch property can be found a great escarpment of elevated rocky strewn land, consisting of ancient Indian burial grounds, carved rocks and cave systems. Records show that the area was known to be the haunted domain of ghosts and spirits. The local Indians have tribal accounts of spirits haunting the area that go back for generations. Although it is known that the previous occupants of the Ranch dating back to the 1930's, did report sporadic unexplainable events, these grew in intensity after the ranch was bought, lived in and worked on by the Shermans in 1994. Terry and Gwen Sherman moved in and began life there with their two children, seemingly taking up the idyllic lifestyle that they had always dreamed of. Prior to that, Terry Sherman was raising cattle upon various plots of land he was renting, while Gwen was employed by a local bank. Shortly after settling into their new home, Terry began to tend to the labours of the farm work that would be their livelihood. Moving his cattle livestock onto the ranch, Terry began to notice that strange geometrical shapes started to appear in the fields. These were not crop circles as such, but depressions up to a foot deep, like 8ft basins, as if something heavy and circular had sat itself down on the ground. Then there began a run of the cattle dying off from what seemed to be unnatural causes, often strange cuts and markings to the eyes, and blood drained carcasses were discovered, typical symptoms associated with these very strange and unexplainable cattle mutilations.

Later that year, a run of UFO sightings started to take place over the ranch, accompanied by odd sounds, screeches and mysterious floating balls of light that could be seen above the skyline escarpment night after night by the puzzled Shermans. After that, the property was plagued by the appearance of baseball-sized spheres of blue light that would both emerge from and disappear into orange coloured portals. It seemed to them, that these blue orbs were being controlled by some kind of unseen intelligence, having the ability to hover for short periods of time in one place or moving off at immense speeds. Some of the UFOs were said to be gigantic objects, metallic looking and the size of football fields! Other people, neighbours, began to come forward with their own sighting reports from nearby farms, so it seemed that the Sherman family was not alone in being witness to the Skinwalker encounters.

After an amazing, but very disturbing run of paranormal events at very close quarters, the Shermans decided to sell the ranch. We will look at some of these experiences in closer detail later in our comparisons with the Settle portal as they show many similarities. The family had had enough of something which they not only found difficult to explain or rationalise, but had realised after only two years in residence, that it had had a true and direct impact on their attempts at a blissful life rearing cattle. Prize animal stock was being systematically destroyed in ways and methods that seemed straight out of science fiction. The next buyer of the ranch was Robert T. Bigelow - a former member of MUFON (Mutual UFO Network) and NIDS (National Institute for Discovery Science), the owner and developer of the Budget Suite Hotel chain and Bigelow Aerospace. There is much much more to the Skinwalker story than can be included here and a number of excellent books have been written about this subject including 'Hunt for the Skinwalker' by Colm A. Kelleher, Ph.D., and George Knapp. For our portal comparisons we need not venture too deep into that particular rabbit hole, but I would advise the reader to do more research into this fascinating account. By now, the burning question is however, 'what or who is a Skinwalker and why was the Sherman ranch named such' ?

'In some Native American legends, a skin-walker is a person with the supernatural ability to turn into any animal he or she desires. To be able to transform, legend sometimes requires that the skin-walker wears a pelt of the animal.'

In other words, it seems the Skinwalker, a supernatural manifestation of what most Native Indian tribesmen regard as being wholly evil and has been around since very ancient times, is intent, a Shape-shifter, about which we discussed in a previous chapter. However, we need to look more closely at the phenomena and attributes associated with this particular shape-shifting entity, be it of original human form or not.

The Navajo Indians described the Skinwalker as a human witch who takes on the form of an animal. They state that this witch is evil and that they can shift into animal shape through spells and incantations. It is generally believed they take the form of a wolf, coyote, crow, fox or owl, but can also take any other animal form they desire. What I find interesting is the mention of two particular kinds of animal gets a mention -the wolf (or maybe a large dog breed) and the owl - both of which we know are prime shape-shifters found in other encounters in portal areas around the globe. Although it seems bizarre to suggest that the belief concerning the wearing of animal pelts like those of a wolf or coyote to assist a human witch's transformation into the Skinwalker, it must seem utterly off the scale to imagine anyone trying to cloak themselves in the tiny feathery skins of owls or small rodents maybe!

Although there are many second and third party accounts describing how the evil witch changes from human to Skinwalker, there are no actual descriptions that I have been able to find to suggest anyone has been around to actually witness first hand this happening. I am not suggesting that some kind of shape-shifting entity does not exist here, but having had first hand experience of seeing a shape-shifting owl over a meter tall at the Settle portal, I personally feel more inclined that whatever is the original entity, it may not be human in origin and therefore, probably possesses the ability to change its form without the need to acquire animal skins to wear during the process. I certainly did not find any trace of an owl pelt after the 'ghost owl' disappeared. This got me to wondering. Maybe the old tales of the shape-shifting Navajo Indian witches could have been memories or copycat enactments of something that they did not fully understand and that they were projecting themselves onto a phenomenon which they knew was around them, but seen as a kind of supernatural force that they wished to harness for themselves?

Skinwalker Ranch Phenomena:

Most modern day writers on the subject, agree to some extent in the ancient Indian legends of there being places in the landscape where this reality meets another, reflecting the portals we have been discussing so far. The Utah basin is a good example of such. During the period of the Sherman occupancy of the ranch, there were several independent sightings made of what looked like giant orange disks of light in the skies, which would take on the form of openings or portals. Researcher of the paranormal Brian Allan states,

'The people who have seen them state that the portals (which are flat discs several feet across apparently suspended vertically and quite arbitrarily in mid air) permit glimpses into another reality'.

Some of these witnesses claim that they could see through the portals to view an alien landscape and skies, as if they were looking into another reality similar to our own but separate from it. There is even a compelling video, which looks to be genuine, taken by Ryan Burns & Will Hoffman in 2013 which shows a large pulsating circular light, from which other smaller orbs of light appear around it each time it magnifies its pulsating action. It is difficult to see how far from the ground this light is, but it does look to be consistent with other reports made in the same area close to the Skinwalker Ranch.

The Giant Wolf & Black Dogs :

Possibly one of the most striking encounters with the unknown that happened at the Skinwalker Ranch was the appearance close to the Sherman family of a giant wolf-like creature which seemed to be intelligent. It was able to move close to people and almost mesmerized them with its large unworldly eyes, acting as if it was like a pet dog, showing no fear of humans by pacing confidently close to them. Yet, there was an air of uneasiness about the wolf (probably due unsurprisingly to its unearthly size which was out of proportion to other wolfs that the family had seen before in the area) and the Jekyll & Hyde attitude it displayed by being quiet and pet-like one minute and then trying to tear the head off a young calf in the coral, the next! Even when the 'animal' had been shot at point blank range a number of times with a gun that 'could bring down an elephant at 100 meters', and pieces of its stinking flesh (as if it was rotting yet alive) had been shot off the creature, it calmly moved away into the distance, as if moving from one world to another. No trace of the giant wolf was found and blood trails led to nowhere!

We do have comparisons of a giant wolf like creature close to the Settle portal area. In fact on School Lane, which runs down towards The Folly , at a 'dog-leg-bend' in the road, there is an account of a giant Black Dog with large glowing eyes. Black dogs often seem to haunt ancient lanes, track-ways, crossroads, old churchyards and prehistoric sites. Many of these places were associated with local superstitions and folklore. The haunts of the black dogs are also features said to denote Ley lines, it has been suggested that they represent some form of energy or natural phenomena moulded by the mind into an archetype of the black dog. These places were recognised by ancient man, and that is why black dogs (as some form of archetype) appear at places of ancient sanctity close to or at portals. There seems to be a case for these Black Dogs (which come under various names in Yorkshire as the Barguest, Black Shuck, Padfoot for example) as protectors of sites - which seems at odds with the creature-manifestation at the Skinwalker Ranch if indeed they are the same kind of entity? This certainly seemed to be the case at Ilkley Moor where a number of historical recordings of Black Dog appearances pertain, which indicate that where they position themselves (and where people unsuspectingly encounter them) around the edges of the moor on track-ways that lead to important ancient sites and stone circles, were exercised so as to either delay or put off completely anyone from travelling to those places at particular times. One such story involved a man called Philip Savile, who was nearing Ilkley on a dark and damp afternoon in the 1930's. Having joined the road which skirts the eastern edges of the moor, Savile came across a large black mastiff sitting in the middle of the road. Walking with hesitation towards the creature, snapping his fingers and trying to entice the dog to him, an odd thing took place. The dog just vanished into thin air. Savile was so terrified that he snatched his cap off his head and ran at full speed, never stopping until he got to Hawksworth village.

In the Skinwalker account we read about underground tunnels being connected with the giant wolf and other strange goings on in the area. This again, seems to be the predominant focus for Black dog legends from the North Yorkshire region too and there is good evidence to suggest that underground passageways seem intrinsically linked to portals. In these accounts, it seems that although terrifying, the phantom dogs stand guard over hidden knowledge or physical treasures until a time that the human investigator who shows he or she is deemed worthy of achieving and fully understanding the 'treasure' (as in the quest for the holy grail as an example), can by-pass the threats of the demon dog. A typical encounter of this type took place at Dob Park Lodge (originally called Dog Park), near to Otley in the Washburn Valley. The Lodge was shelled in the English Civil War by the soldiers of Oliver Cromwell and some old pewter plates had turned up in nearby fields during the turn of the last century. This led to locals thinking that there may be other treasures to be found in the ruins of the lodge and a walker one day stumbled across a secret doorway. He enters it and crawls down a long underground tunnel and eventually finds himself in a great hall under the ground. The hall is empty apart from three objects. A table upon which stands an empty golden cup, a golden sword hanging on the wall, and in one corner sits a great and terrifying spectre in the shape of a giant black dog. With its round saucer-like red eyes which revolved as if hypnotising the walker, the beast began to talk in broad Yorkshire dialect, offering him to take the cup or the sword? Being of greed, we are told, he tried to take the sword to cut off the Black dogs head and make off with the cup and all. With this, the dog brought a 'great terror' upon him, but his cries for help were to no avail. Dropping the sword, the traveller tried to make good his escape, but lost his way in a maze of tunnels. When he eventually found his way out from under the Lodge, the people he met could not understand a word he was saying, just a mass of gibberish as if he had gone mad in his ordeal and when he later searched for his family nobody recognised him as many years had passed by while he was under the ground!

Poltergeist Activity & Ghosts

Several members of the Sherman family experience poltergeist activity in their home - doors slam, objects disappear and are found later in another place, in or outside the house. Some incidents are just like bad tricks that a child would play. For instance, they find the salt and the pepper pot had vanished to turn up in another place. Another time, Gwen Sherman finds, back on the kitchen table, all the groceries she had carefully stacked in the cupboards and sometimes they hear voices laughing and mocking them in an unknown language.

Although what we term as poltergeist activity is mostly associated with mischievous human spirits as the cause, this kind of phenomenon has occurred at the Settle portal more than once to suggest a number of different kinds of entity or unseen energies may be at play here. Although human spirits have been recognised and recorded on tape and photographic film at the Horseshoe Trees vortex, we know that other kinds of entity which seem to be of the none-human kind, also generate poltergeist-like effects on the surrounding environment. One particular incident that happened in the summer months of 2014 concerned a video camcorder being turned on and off when I was recording a channelling session at the site. With nobody within two metres of the video camera, which was positioned on a stable tripod and pointing at Helen and I, the red light on it stopped working as soon as I began to receive information from my guide Sharlek. The camcorders light flickered on and off as if there was some kind of fault or maybe that someone was turning the device on and off record? We had been recording perfectly normally with it for up to 20 minutes before the channelling session started under the trees of the portal with no electrical faults at all and on inspecting the camcorder after the channelling, it began to work normally once again. More surprisingly and without any reason we could think of, the actual battery life of the camcorder had increased to full power, yet we had noticed previous to the session that it was half full of battery life!

This is not the first time this kind of thing has happened at that site. In 2013, three people watched as the flash on a digital camera went off on its own when nobody was anywhere near it and this was recorded as it happened on another video recording device.

Strange and inexplicable voices have been heard at the Settle portal site too. I was once investigating alone at the site in 2013 and out of nowhere, yet it seemed to be above me in the treetops maybe, I heard a familiar voice calling my name. It sounded like my own father Harry Mortimer, who died in the mid 1990s in Otley, some 35 miles from the portal. Other growling sounds like that of a large beast, maybe a bear, have been heard there too - but no bears have been inhabiting the area for hundreds of years, unless of course 'these bears' do not originate in this time or dimension.

Balls of Light & Strange Mists:

Soon after occupying the ranch in Utah, the Shermans start to see balls of light of various colours, moving around and over the cattle and their home. They frequently observe baseball-sized orbs, of bright blue colour, *"filled with swirling liquid, electrically charged"*, which dim the lights around when passing near the house.

The Balls of Lights (BOLs) phenomena are probably the most common type experienced by anyone at the Settle portal site. Mainly milky white or translucent in colour, the BOLs have been seen with the naked eye, photographed and caught moving on video film. They range is size from pinpricks of light (around the size of small flying insects) to soccer ball sized objects, the most common size being that of a tennis ball spherical object. Some of these BOLs are able to change shape, and although they mainly stay looking like a sphere, the edges of the object or light source is able to distort, sometimes larger at one edge, sometimes contracting, but never in a uniformed manner. It seems that the BOLs are alive in a way, able to pulsate in mid air as they move.

On infrequent occasions, the Blue BOLs have been observed at the Settle portal, mainly at night time or late evenings. I have sighted a turquoise-blue BOL in a tree at the nearby Giggleswick Chapel (in 2012) which remained absolutely still in the space between the branches and I was close enough to determine that this was not an object that had been suspended there by someone. This object was about the size of a water melon, seemed to be self-illuminating, which is evident on the photograph I managed to take of the object at the time.

Probably the best photographic case we have from the Settle portal area shows a massive BOL that seems to be shown descending in the early morning sky right onto the spot where the Horseshoe Trees vortex is positioned on the the slopes of Castleberg. This coincidence of where the object is observed and photographed taken from Giggleswick in possibly 2009 or 2010, is an amazing act of synchronisation due to the fact that the person responsible for taking the photograph (a local garage workman in Settle called Jim Stiles (pseudonym)) had no idea at all, where or what the Sun Dial Portal was, or if in fact, it had ever been re-discovered. Yet, here we see in his photograph an enormous illuminated round object with a smaller dark object inside its glow at the very site of the portal.

Other-worldy mists have often been associated with ghost stories and graveyards in fact and fiction, but there seems to be another kind of 'mist' appearing out of nowhere at portal sites and in most cases this is a white mist with tinges of electric blue, or as in the Settle portal case, a vivid sky blue mist of swirling energy. At Rendlesham Forest, which some believe to be a massive portal with several vortexes within it at strategic locations, Brenda Butler has taken dozens if not hundreds of photographs that show these unusual mists which form into recognisable shapes almost like a kind of ectoplasm; sometimes these shapes become any or all of the noted and recognised phenomena that has been witnessed in the forest over the years, greys, shadow people, monks, dragons, UFOs and even out of time (or in the wrong time) objects like Jeeps and mechanical devices!

The Window Portal :

An apparition of a sort of circular "window", floating in the sky was seen over the Skinwalker Ranch. These looked like strange orange structures that would appear in the western sky. All family members saw these structures dozens of times. They would appear in the sky and seemed to hover low over the cottonwood trees about a mile away. The family see this window always in around the same place, and on one occasion Terry Sherman claims that he can see inside the orange 'hole in the sky', where there is another sky for a land that was daylight while he observed it at night in this one.

This window phenomena is probably the most direct information we have that indicates the area around the ranch to be a gateway between worlds or dimensions. Without doubt the Shermans and later other investigators including those of NIDS made connections between the ongoing UFO sightings there and these strange orange openings in the sky. The portals were not only seen in the air however, there is at least one account where one of these that looks like a tunnel from which a strange dark lumbering entity emerges into our world, is observed close to the ground in the valley below.

Again, comparisons have been made at other portal sites. I do not think that soon after Helen and I made the re-discovery of the Settle portal site at the Horseshoe Trees in 2012, that we felt compelled to arrange a ring of rocks in a circle to outline where intuitively we felt the portal 'window' gateway to be located at that particular spot. In my minds eye, whenever we visit the site, I see more than is actually physically there. I see those same rocks joined together by an endless spiral of orange-red vibrant energy and this energy is alive. I see it at ground level and at the same time I see it above and below me, like a funnel (or tunnel) stretching out into the vastness of the beyond, but where it ends, I have no clue as of yet.

Those who have managed to observe these elusive portal doorways often describe them as looking like a round flat tablet or a disk on its side around 6 to 8 feet in diameter, reminding one of the kinds of portholes or the locking hatch of a submarine maybe. The archetype of something which divides this world from another one (or maybe several other ones) seems firmly entrenched within what we observe as a portal entrance and even popular movies like Stargate on some kind of subliminal level allow us to envisage portal entrances as round and circular.

The Freemasons connections :

When I read about the Freemasons connection with the Skinwalker Ranch in 'Hunt for the Skinwalker' in 2010, I was amazed that this connection had been discovered and included in their book by the authors Kelleher and Knapp. Right from the off, my own investigations into the Settle Sun Dial Portal led me to uncover a Masonic awareness of the sites of the local portal vortexes and what they were supposed to be used for, as has been explained earlier in this and my previous books. I found the Skinwalker episode so intriguing in light of my own discoveries, that it left me with a feeling that at some level, certain places like the Utah ranch must be important to these secret societies in one way or another. We have already seen that some of the Settle Freemasons at the Castleberg Lodge have an awareness of the Sun Dial portal and how it connects with the ancient mysteries of King Solomon and Jacobs Ladder, but what happened in 1886 in the Utah basin, really does begin to make one wonder how far their global interest in portals goes and for what reasons?

The story goes that after the battle of the Little Big Horn, in the August of that year, Major Frederick Benteen led the Ninth US Cavalry into north-eastern Utah with seventy five battle-tested cavalrymen. Every one of the seventy five troopers was black, the legendary Buffalo Soldiers, so-named after there dark skin and black curly hair. It was said that they took part in at least 177 armed engagements in the native Indian wars in the west and so, were honoured above many of their white counterparts. What is not widely known about the Buffalo Soldiers, is that most if not all of them, were 'full-fledged, ritual practising, secret-handshaking Freemasons. These soldiers became Freemasons due to a strange allegiance for a black slave named Prince Hall who emigrated from England to America and established African Lodge No.1 in Boston on July 3rd, 1776. Most tales concerning these elusive Freemasons tell of the frequent drinking forays into the countryside close to Fort Duchesne, alongside a place called Bottle Hollow today, after so many empty beer bottles were found it seemed an apt name. The ravine is now covered in water. No records of what the Buffalo Soldiers were really doing in this remote area have ever come to light, but Kelleher and Knapp mention something intriguing. At a geological feature known as Skinwalker Ridge, there can be found an unusual rock carving; an inscription located several feet below the top edge of the ridge 'as if someone had hung suspended from the top to carve it into the rock'. It is thought that the carving is at least a hundred years old, it is Masonic in nature and indicates that the Sherman Ranch was visited by the Buffalo Soldier Freemasons at that time with enough interest there to leave there symbolic mark at this prominent portal.

This brings to mind what I wrote about the Settle Freemasons interest in portals in my previous book and in it described a number of examples where Masonic insignia and symbols seem to litter the older buildings (mainly from the 1600-1800s period) close to the location of the Sun Dial Portal and betray the apparent interest of the Atholl Freemasons (a very ancient Scottish Rite, sourced as the Antients) at that time. One particular enigma is the Naked Man, now found on the front wall of the Naked Man Cafe in Settle; who seems to resemble a coloured or black skinned man wearing Masonic regalia. Then we have to consider, who was Prince Hall, the emanciated black man who travelled to the US to set up Lodges there? Is he one and the same as the image of the Freemason who's effigy is now hanging on the wall of the café in Settle, or does the image represent a secret allegiance to this person or someone like him? Further research is needed to establish any of these possible connections, but we have one more strange coincidence to consider.

Amongst the many photographs that I have managed to take at the Settle portal showing human and dimensional entities as they temporarily manifest into our reality, there was one which stood out for me because of what I saw appearing before my eyes, was quite unexpected. A large rounded face, large eyes and large white lips appeared, that was obviously of a much darker skin coloured man. I have always thought this to be the spirit of a coloured or black man of African origins up until the time in 2014 when I was informed by my guide that this was 'the Naked Man' -an inter-dimensional energy which had been observed by others through periods of time since the late 1600s in the area.

Ancient Sites, Rocks and Carvings :

Ancient Rock art, known as petroglyph's in the Utah basin region are something that connects both the Settle portal with that area and both have fine examples showing early man was not only fully aware of the mysteries of each seemingly separate environment, but may have been actively interacting with them. A new book in 2014, by NASA, "Archaeology, Anthropology, and Interstellar Communication", edited by Dr. Douglas Vakoch, the director of Interstellar Message Composition at the Search for Extraterrestrial Intelligence organisation, includes the suggestion how,

"different civilizations might create messages that could be transmitted across interstellar space, allowing communication between humans and extraterrestrials even without face-to-face contact. Only when people took seriously the possibility that chipped rocks might be prehistoric tools were they predisposed to look for them, and until then, this core piece of evidence for reconstructing extinct civilizations was simply overlooked by archaeologists doing fieldwork in Europe."

If we were to suppose that both the Skinwalker Ranch and Settle Sun Dial portals' were known to very ancient civilisations, which I proposed in my earlier books, then it would be probable to find similar rock carvings and stone circles made by them, at or close to each site. And we do.

Several important ancient archaeological sites in and around Utah, include Danger Cave; with evidence of human life dating back to 9000 B.C., False Kiva (Kivas are subterranean caverns or rooms which are found among ruins in the American south-west, indicating ritual or use by the ancient peoples of the region) known for its man-made stone circle of unknown origin and purpose, or Moon House with its ceremonial Kiva. In particular Horseshoe Canyon stands out, not just because its place-name is so similar to the one at the Settle portal vortex at the Horseshoe Trees, but due to what is found there. Horseshoe Canyon is located in a remote area west of the Green River. It is in the Great Gallery, a repository of petroglyph's that date back as far as 7000 B. C., and including more than 20 life-size panels of anthropomorphic figures, was left behind by a desert culture pre-dating both the Fremont and the Anazasi cultures. On one carved panel it shows seven upright figures, all shrouded in what look like robed garments with ties at the waist. They almost look to be floating in mid air. The Ancient Pueblo People of the region were known to believe in the existence of portals -places that were the point of origin of their people, and through which their ancestors passed to come to this world or dimension.

The stone circle at False Kiva, although of unknown origin, looks very familiar to Helen and myself. It is stated that although the site has been deemed to be probably connected with magical and ritual practice in ancient times, nobody knows exactly what its real purpose was. There are important points we need to look at here in connection with our comparative study of the Skinwalker Ranch and Settle portals and both involve the physical attributes of the stone circle and location of False Kiva in Utah.

Looking at the man-made stone circle at False Kiva, it can be clearly seen that it is a circle of around the same circumference and built up of singular boulders, as the circle Helen and I constructed to determine where the portal vortex was at the Horeshoe Trees at Castleberg in Settle. The False Kiva stone circle is not a typical one like we find the world over which, as we have seen, include upright often pointed standing stones. This 'stone circle' is almost modern in construction, like that of the dry stone walling found in Yorkshire in the UK. We are told that the ancient peoples who may have been responsible for building this circle of stones within the false Kiva believed that portals connected them with other dimensions and the land of the dead - exactly the same as we propose at the Settle portal.

Researchers at the Horseshoe Trees Vortex have remarked more than once that they get the impression there may be an underground cavern or artificial space at the site. Early attempts at Remote Viewing seem to suggest this too, with a large 'room made out of the rock' being detected. Could this be a similar kind of Kiva to those found in Utah? There is evidence to suggest that a Neolithic culture once inhabited the area and may have found the site sacred, placing a stone circle close to the vortex (the remains of which have been removed and only an outline in the ground of such exists today to the immediate south of the vortex) and we know that larger caves close by were once the homes of these settlers.

Conclusions:

Obviously we will never find every aspect of these far distant locations being reflected perfectly in all portal attributes or the mysteries that surround them, but there is enough evidence in a reported form to suggest that we can at least attempt to look for good comparisons, in order to better understand what might be happening at these portal sites (the world over) and why. Whatever the outcomes of any such study, it would be sensible to state that we can not always rely one hundred percent on the evidence being presented unless we know for certain that something happens in the way it is being reported. But, if we get enough comparable evidence, enough on site photographic images and video footage, enough witness statements, from more than one portal location at a time, then we will heading somewhere to a point where it becomes clearer that something truly unexplained is occurring at these certain locations.

In a way, this is just a condensed mini-study of just two portal areas, both ancient places with similar phenomenon and interactive events of a highly strange nature. There is much more we could add here to show further comparisons, like cattle mutilations, time anomalies, military interest in both sites, etc., but that would take up a whole book on its own. What needs to be done now, is for people like you, the readers of this book, to take this study further and look for that comparable data from your own portal area. Do this in an honest and truthful manner and I can guarantee that it won't be long before we all have answers to something that has eluded humanity for so long now.

CHAPTER SEVEN

Portal Science & Physics

In Physics, a wormhole is a shortcut or bridge through space-time that connects two points.

It has been said that any high school student of physics can tell you that our reality is an illusion. That illusion is perceived by the human mind as something we call physical matter, but in truth matter itself is not really what it seems to be for most of us. In fact it was Albert Einstein who said,

"Reality is merely an illusion, albeit a very persistent one".

All of that which we call matter is really confined energy. Modern science tells us that most of 'matter' is energy in one form or another, not absolutely 'confined' as it is allowed to change, but the point is valid. Tiny moving electrons and other energy particles (atoms) so small, they are invisible to the naked eye, form molecules of specific substances. Even though atoms and molecules form larger structures, these are mainly made up of spaces so vast that if we were to shrink to the size of an atom, the next one would look like a very distant star. It was thought until recently that because we are so much bigger than an atom, that billions of them in a cluster look like matter to us, but science tells us that this is not entirely true because we only see them as solid objects due to the angular resolution of the human eye. Electron microscopes can distinguish the individual atoms and their 'vastness' and so it's simply because of the density of light emitting /reflecting nuclei in the material we observe, that objects seem opaque to us. Of course we are formed out of those atoms too, and the perception of ourselves is that we are solid, living in a solid physical world. But that, at the level of quantum physics, is far from the truth. We all know that we cannot push our fingers through a brick wall, but we can push them through the smoke of a cigarette. This is because the molecules of atoms in the smoke are farther apart than those that make up a brick. This again is true to a certain extent, but science also understands that the reason we can't push our fingers through a brick wall is not just because the atoms are more dense, but because the bonds between the molecules in the brick wall are stronger than the force applied by the finger on the brick. For liquids and gases there are very limited attractive forces and so our hands can displace the molecules much more easily.

Mankind learned early in his evolution how to manipulate molecules and turn seemingly solid static objects into other forms by influencing them through chemical and physical processes. As if by magic, we can easily cut down a tree and change it into something else like a chair or paper. The physical form has changed but the molecules that once formed the wood into a tree, now take on the physical appearance of something very different. Yet, those same molecules remain as a part of the substance that forms the new object. In affect, we have learnt how to manipulate energy and in doing so, we have become in a way, shape-shifters of that energy, albeit in a simpler form. Again, modern science demonstrates how in this sense that we have learned to reconfigure material structures both microscopically and macroscopically.

If the energy patterns and states of the atoms making up the cells of your body were radically different from those found in the bed that you lay on at night, both consisting of millions of atoms, then it is quite possible that the two sets of atoms would intermix with each other and you would sink right through the bed to spend the night sleeping on the floor, or a worse scenario, you may even become a part of the bed! So the reason we don't fall through is down to the electrostatic repulsion between solid objects, on an atomic level the valence electrons from each material repel each other, creating a 'gap' between the two materials. This is the same principle that applies in the ability to pass your fingers through the smoke. It is all to do with particular states of individual atoms at any given time dependant upon the chemical make up of the object or person or thing. It makes sense to speculate that our sense of reality, which is itself made up of energies vibrating a certain frequencies, is a part of something else that is beyond our senses and capabilities to comprehend, but it could also be made up of energy vibrations at a different level or frequency to that which we do comprehend. For example, light has an associated electromagnetic oscillation frequency which is related to energy. These energies could coexist with us and even share the same space we occupy, without our ever becoming aware of them.

Latest findings in science has shown us that the light of higher or lower frequencies than we can measure at this time, definitely exists, but is currently immeasurable. These energy scales are the types of things being probed by ATLAS at CERN and at the levels of these higher energies you can get new exotic particles being formed that we could only theorize to exist before. It remains mind boggling that news to come out of CERN in the summer of 2014, whilst conducting the scientific hunt for the elusive 'god particle', is that one possible conclusion reached is that our own Universe should not exist today in any known form. In a new study, Robert Hogan, a doctoral candidate in physics at King's College in London and his colleague at King's College, fellow physicist Malcolm Fairbairn, tried to illustrate how cosmic inflation might work to create the universe after the Big Bang scenario. We learn that they used a model based around the properties of the Higgs-Boson particle, that is a manifestation of the Higgs energy field that pervades throughout the universe and which potentially explains how other particles gain mass, along with the measurement of the original gravitational waves from cosmic inflation. Amazingly to even themselves, the results were not quite what they were expecting. The newly formed universe and everything in it, should have been subjected to powerful shakes that would have destabilized the Higgs field, downgrading the energy levels until the it inevitably imploded and collapsed into none existence. Questioning if in fact the model is correct, then they were left baffled by what had happened to circumvent the inevitable collapse and allow the universe to remain.

"We are here talking about it," Hogan stated, "and that means we have to extend our theories to explain why this didn't happen. The generic expectation is that there must be some new physics that we haven't put in our theories yet, because we haven't been able to discover them," he added. Yet, here we are in 2014, not only existing in a world out of nowhere and one that the most current science states in all sense should not even exist and actual scientific method would have us believe that we exist within a world of illusion.

The Question of Portals as Dimensional Gateways:

Can we look to science to confirm whether or not extra-dimensional states exist, and if so, how would science explain the possibility of humans, E.T.'s, Inter-dimensional Beings & Elementals travelling through them or existing within them, or maybe being created by them? To try answer the first question, science would look to the principles of modern physics to determine this with two basic scientific laws:

a. Quantum Physics which studies the smallest objects in nature such as atoms, protons, neutrons etc., b. General Relativity studies the planets, galaxies and the Universe in general and c. These two areas' can overlap in studies which scientists then call "quantum gravity.

Before we can start to imagine if portals operate in a way that allows matter at best and conscious thought at least to travel through them, we need to understand what our reality is and how it might differ from other kinds of reality found in higher and lower dimensions. So, what is 'reality' and how can we measure it?

Professor Akram Khan of the Brunel University, London quantifies our current understanding of reality as 'the state of things as they actually exist rather than as they appear or might be imagined'. Yet, even he in his wisdom feels that this common sense approach may be somewhat flawed and concedes that 'it is our imagining that marks us out as being human'. All that this tells us is that reality is a problematic idea. Stephen Hawkins tells us that a well constructed reality creates a reality of it's own and this is the dilemma of how we perceive reality with the known senses. The dimensional parameters of three of distance and one of time in which we all live our lives, has only allowed us to realise in a cognitive way, responses to natures expression in a particular band of reality. We tend to

167

measure this in two ways, the reality that we can see and the reality that arises through consciousness. Fundamental to multi-dimensionalism within quantum physics is string theory. The string theory is likened to the theory of everything in the universe and it is based upon the concept that all objects in our universe are composed of vibrating 'strings' and 'membranes' (orbranes) of energy. Scientists call it 'super symmetry' also known as superstring theory, or M-theory. This theory can be correct if reality has 10, 11, or as many as 26 dimensions. Many physicists believe multi-dimensional space is extremely likely and most scientists agree that several extra dimensions to the universe must exist. It certainly seems to be this way if we are to include gravity into a Theory of Everything, but none the less, it has been theorised also that these extra dimensions will be very compact.

Student of theoretical physics at Manchester University Colin Smith (pseudonym) states, 'Be careful about extra-dimensional states. There are the obvious 3 spatial and 1 temporal dimensions that we know and love, but I do agree that there's nothing stopping the existence of higher dimensions that we do not perceive. Maybe time doesn't flow in those or flows too fast for us to realise. We can easily imagine a 2D world, unaware of our 3D one (like a piece of paper).'
He goes on, ' for science to explain the possibility of humans, E.T.'s, Inter-dimensional Beings & Elementals travelling through them or existing within these dimensions, or maybe being created by them, and assuming there are 3 space and 1 time dimensions, my idea of something that you describe as a 'portal' would be a wormhole. A wormhole can exist in 3D space, it only means that the space is curved in such a way that a tunnel is created between two, originally distant, points. Einstein's field equations imply that space-time is curved near massive objects (black holes) and in fact NASA are now prototyping a ship that uses this physics to travel faster than light (it basically creates a bubble around itself that distorts space-time such that light in the bubble behaves normally but the space itself moves faster than light speed.

The Question of Electromagnetic Effects at Portals:

The investigation of haunted places and portals would not be complete today without the measuring of electromagnetic effects and changes within the environments Electro Magnetic Field (E.M.F). There is a long history of paranormal events happening alongside natural and unknown changes to the electromagnetic fields of these places. This is one particular area of investigation where we are able to measure in a scientific way what might be taking place when these strange experiences happen.

An electromagnetic field is one that contains both magnetic and electrical properties that surrounds objects with an electrical charge. Electromagnetic fields are AC fields that are most often produced artificially by electrical power currents such as those found in our homes. In some instances, they may also be produced naturally by geophysical sources, such electricity produced through seismic pressure on conductive rock along fault zones as noted by Dr Michael Persinger in his Earth Lights theory (1985,), and very low frequency atmospherics, which are electromagnetic pulses produced from electrical discharges after a lightning strike for example. The E.M.F. is also naturally occurring as the movement of electrons within the Earth creates a field that surrounds the planet. This is why a compass works as it does. An E.M.F. can also be a man-made phenomenon, as every electrical device we have created emits some level of an electromagnetic field. This field is created when energy runs through a circuit and electrons pass through a conductor. In context to paranormal investigations, we begin by usually obtaining a baseline reading of the background electromagnetic field. When high readings are detected and a source is identified, we then look for alternative reasons for this. First, and most importantly, we look to dispel those answers with rational reasoning and only then attempt to gather evidence to suggest whether a location is haunted or has paranormal activity occurring there.

At the Settle Portal we have found the presence of residual energies from either a spirit or entity presence at the site, can cause a change from the baseline E.M.F. readings. For example, if an E.M.F. device detects a spike in the electromagnetic field at the same time that paranormal activity is noted, and we were able to record an unseen voice or photograph something at that moment for example, we would have a much better case for something highly unusual happening. It is difficult to debunk three pieces of corresponding data. Having said that, we should always be aware that coming into contact with unusually higher levels of E.M.F.s at such places (and there may be a case for these fields being altered to a degree by the phenomena at such sites) may have implications on the health of human beings. Some concern has been raised over the effects that electromagnetic field exposure may have on brain functioning and resulting mental health and at least some experimental studies have seemingly demonstrated an effect. For example, two studies have observed possible changes in brain wave activity on an electroencephalogram (E.E.G) following a brief (up to 2 seconds) exposure to E.M.F.s as strong as 780 milli-Gauss and higher and these are often similar to the levels we may find at haunt areas and portals. Indeed, I have personally found that whilst conducting mind channelling sessions at the Settle portal, there seems to be some kind of electrical interference going on which can not only effect my own ability to tune into spirit and ET entities, but has a subtle effect on some of the electrical equipment that we were using to record at the time. Also, it has been noted on a number of occasions by Helen and myself (plus others) that visits to the portal can lead to headaches of the migraine-like type at the worst, or maybe a sense of utter euphoria at best, both sensations coming 'as if out of nowhere' which might be related to the effects of E.M.s at the site.

The Question of Time Distortions & Time Travel :

"Physicists have always scoffed at the idea of time travel, considering it to be the realm of cranks, mystics, and charlatans, and with good reason. However, rather remarkable advances in quantum gravity are reviving the theory." - Dr Michio Kaku

I like Dr Kaku. He is someone who dares to explore where other scientists fear to tread (well almost), but I fear his statement above, in which he portrays all mystics in the same lot as charlatans and cranks may be shown in time to be without good reason. His own admittance that 'remarkable advances' in his own field of scientific theory, not only match what the mystics have always been saying, but it seems he is prepared to take on board the fact that 'their' claims have been revived by science today. To be fair to Dr Kaku, it is true that the question of the possibility of Time Travel is riddled with problems and paradoxes from the current scientific viewpoint. 'For example, there is the paradox of the man with no parents, i.e. what happens when you go back in time and kill your parents before you are born? Question: if your parents died before you were born, then how could you have been born to kill them in the first place?'

Even today, we tend to see and experience Time as a linear phenomenon and we are happy to measure what we think time is, using clocks and computers for example. It is due to the simple fact that we do things (and seemingly we observe things in the universe doing the same) in sequence, having a memory of what has just happened before and more distantly back in time in our human minds. But even with this there is a problem. The concept of the mind measuring time through remembering what has gone before (in the recent or distant past) is different for everyone, although we can agree by using time-measuring devices like clocks, or maybe looking and observing the passage of the Sun and Moon, that something has changed and seems to be moving forwards. It is our own individual concept of what time really is that becomes the problem. Imagine that you are living on a remote island and you have no means of telling the time in a man-made mechanical way. Yes, you could learn to use the passage of stars or planets to keep a record of time-related events, but how accurate would this be? Some would say, it could be very accurate. Say you measured time in this way for 10 years, alone on the island, and then along comes someone else with a calendar and wearing a working watch. Do you think that your recordings of the time passed by in those 10 years would be the same as your visitors? I doubt it very much. There would be discrepancies, even some large margins of error and even some coincidentally occurring similarities, but none of this would prove that you were both individually measuring the actual period of time in the same way. Yet, for both of you, using different means of measuring time, your own concepts would be as accurate as possible and the best version available to you at that particular time because you would not have been able to compare your version of time with the other persons!

But, what if time is an illusion? What if there is no forwards or backwards in time and this concept is something that we can only 'measure' within the mind in a way that is constricted by our own levels of human evolution? Isaac Newton believed that time was like an arrow; once fired, it soared in a straight, undeviating line, but this was postulated in the 1600's remember, some time ago. He and others since Newton for quite some time, have postulated that one second on the earth was one second on Mars for example. Clocks scattered throughout the universe beat at the same rate. Einstein gave us a much more radical picture. According to Einstein, time was more like a river, which meandered around stars and galaxies, speeding up and slowing down as it passed around massive bodies. One second on the earth was Not one second on Mars. This reasoning seems to demonstrate that time is something which we have yet to fully understand and due to that, there may be capabilities within the concept of time that we will one day be able to manipulate in order to 'work with time' and not against it as it runs past us through our fingers or the sands of an hour-glass.

Physicist, Colin Smith of Manchester University states, 'Wormholes and maybe Portals not only connect points in space, but also in time. Backward time travel would be definitely viable using this method.' However, due to the unstable nature of wormholes, using a method of travelling through one to reach another period in space and time is not, as we understand the science of wormholes now, very practical. For one, it would require an immense amount of energy, maybe the power of a star, to enable us to move through galaxies in this way. All is not lost though. Stephen Hawking once opposed the idea of time travel. He even claimed he had "empirical" evidence against it. If time travel existed, he said, then we would have been visited by tourists from the future. Since we see no tourists from the future, then it is likely that time travel is not possible. Because of the enormous amount of work done by theoretical physicists within the last 5 years or so, Hawking has since changed his mind, and now believes that time travel is possible and will be attained by mankind in the far off future if we survive that long. Black holes are very likely to be effective wormholes, warping space-time, but these could be nigh on impossible to harness, since time effectively stops at the centre of a black hole.

Portals and the nature of portal vortexes, suggest that there may be another way to travel through time and space. And that is by using them to travel sideways. In her book, 'Time Travel - Fact, Fiction & Possibility (Blandford 1994)', respected paranormal researcher Jenny Randles noticed something back then when she wrote the book, which has become more and more apparent in UFO and Portal experiences. She writes,

' There seems little doubt that some naturally occurring force that manifests as a glowing cloud (or mist) is appearing on a regular basis in the world around us. When someone gets too close the consequences may be amazing. They seem to include the possibility of a trip through space or time.'

As has already been noted in this book, we have encountered a strange blue mist or fog at the Horseshoe Trees at the Settle portal (and this has been captured on video film), plus there are many tales and legends supporting the idea that this strange cloud or mist indicates a process taking place which might be connected with the displacement of time at the immediate site of the event. I remember some years ago, possibly in the late 1980's, riding my motorcycle along the main road between Long Preston and Settle in North Yorkshire and suddenly after a bend in the road, going straight into an odd green coloured mist that lay just above the road surface. As I travelled about 10 yards into it (it became thick and dense, so I could not see anything around me other than a kind of green glow), I was forced to slow down. As I came to a stop, my motorcycle engine cut out and would not restart. Worried that some other vehicle might come into the mist and hit me in the middle of the road, I pushed the bike to the side where the mist looked to be a little clearer, enough for me to see a small cottage with a short pathway to the door. I began to take a look at the bike to see what was wrong with the engine, but it seems strange to me now, that I did not even question why the green mist was there at all or what it was? I could find nothing wrong that I could see, so tried to start the bike again. Nothing, not a splutter.

Having no tools with me to open the engine side panel to see if there was an electrical problem, I decided to ask at the cottage to borrow a screwdriver or see if I could get some help from a garage. I knocked on the door and it was opened by an old lady. She seemed very familiar to me, but I had never actually taken notice before of the cottage where she was living, so I put this down to her looking like someone I must have met in the past. Then things became very odd. I hadn't even asked her for the help, before she invited me inside, with a kind and pleasant smile. It was as if I went through the door into a small kitchen area with one chair and a small table. Without any words between us, she brought me a cup of tea, but I noticed that the cup was very old and very delicate. It looked Victorian. While I drank the tea, I felt that there was no hurry, as if I was in a waiting room while all of my problems were being sorted out. I felt calm, relaxed and in no hurry.

'You can get on your way now', said the old lady with white hair in a bun, ' thank you for visiting me again'. Even when she said 'again', although I knew that I had never been at that cottage or ever met this woman in my life before, it seemed normal for me to just say 'yes, thank you' and walk out of the door, back to my motorcycle propped up against a dry-stone wall next to the roadside. I got on the bike, kick started it and the machine instantly turned over the engine with no problems at all. I did not look back or into my wing mirrors as I set off down the road and there was no sign at all of the strange green mist. The road was as clear as it had been before I entered into that very unusual scenario and concentrating on the normal flow of traffic in both directions as I headed home, took my mind off what had just happened for a short while.

It would be less than a month later that I decided to journey back towards Settle to see if I could find the spot where this had all happened to me. To this day, I have never found that particular cottage or ever seen the green mist cover that road. It was as if the whole thing had never taken place at all, apart from one small thing. About six months later, I was servicing my motorcycle at home and could see something shiny under the seat. I unbolted and lifted the seat up to reveal a very old screwdriver, possibly some 50 years old which I had never seen before. The handle was faint and worn, but betrayed a layer of green paint that matched the same colour of the mist I had seen.

The question remains, had I travelled in time by entering that green mist and if so, does this prove that not only was I able to move through time, but the machine that I was riding at the time, was able to accompany me? What was taking place in the environment to create the green mist? Was it some kind of doorway into another state of being? I don't know, but there were factors that I now can see which might indicate that I had in fact time-travelled that day, or possibly some kind of intelligence was trying to give me the impression that I had received help from a different time maybe. It was as if two different locations within time and space had connected through a means not yet fully understood by us. We do now understand that this can happen on a very minute level of experience where the quantum entanglement of two particles are created which are 'linked in some sense'. Once an experiment is performed to record a property about one particle, the other 'knows' and adopts the opposite state. This is proved to happen over a very long distance and theory suggests that this distance is infinite.

The Question of the Light Spectrum & Colours at Portals:

Strange lights of various different colours have been sighted at the ancient site type portal areas since very early times in human history and may have been one kind of paranormal activity which assisted in the rise of religious concepts and wonderment concerning the position thinking Man took in his uncharted existence. Thousands of years of this recognition have shown us that unusual light forms, some in the skies, some in the waters and even some underground, are transient the world over. It is true to say that a majority of all reported UFO sightings are of light forms of one type or another and closer experiences with Unidentified Atmospheric Phenomena (U.A.Ps) through to illuminated balls of light and Orbs make up the remainder of these elusive phenomena. We know that humans only actually see a small proportion of the light spectrum that really exists as electromagnetic radiation and gives the ability of sight, some animals see other parts of it, and with the aid of technology, we are able to determine X-rays and Microwaves. There is another aspect of light which does not seem to sit well within the spectrum and that is something called Solid Light.

Solid Light tends to be found in the shape of a beam of light or a kind of rod of light, like we find that emerges from a torch maybe, but is different in that it can penetrate solid objects and come out of the other side. These lights are different to lasers in that they seem to be either intelligently controlled by an unseen source, or they hold some kind of intelligence within themselves to enable complicated manoeuvres. Witnesses have said that they have seen such beams of light bending around corners, coming straight out of the ground or coming down to the ground from UFOs like a ladder of light, which might make one think of Jacobs Ladder. Others have seen ET's waving wands & probes that seem to be made out of solid white light. As has been already mentioned several times, light forms of the Orbs type have been seen and documented numerous times at the Settle portal with one particular case in which a tennis ball sized round white light was seen to move into and pass through a person, emerging out of the other side of his body as the same shape and size. The sequence of this happening was photographed at the time, and even though this looked to be disturbing and an intrusion by something unknown, it left no ill effects after departing the person's back.

Light itself is produced in tiny packets called photons and these travel as particles and waves. This is known as wave-particle duality, a central concept of quantum mechanics. It was in fact back in the days of Isaac Newton (who may have been himself witness to the Settle Portal in Yorkshire) , & Christiaan Huygens that the idea was formed that Light was made up of particles and waves, but neither could agree with each others proposal. Today it seems something of a compromise has been reached in current scientific theory, holding that all particles also have a wave nature (and vice versa). A challenge to this scientific viewpoint (which is only one amongst a number of alternative propositions) is put forward by Steven Eric Kaufman and although mainstream physics would not entertain his theories due to the fact that they are what some would call of the fringe element, in connection with our portal research and observations concerning light forms at such sites, I personally find this compelling and thought-provoking. Kaufman proposes that wave-particle duality can be better understood through what he calls 'experiential creation'. In this model the phenomenon of wave-particle duality is accounted for by explaining it in terms of what he calls this Unified Reality Theory (U.R.T).

I would think that most current day scientists see the U.R.T as more of a philosophical argument than a wholly scientific approach, but their are some open-minded physicists out there who are beginning to become aware that the margins between the so-called solid foundations of scientific principles and those theories put forward like Kaufman's may be drawing ever closer. Kaufman states, *"reality is a state of existential self-relation. Consciousness and awareness is truly the source of physical reality, rather than a by-product, and physical reality is merely one facet of a universal consciousness".*

Kaufman's model of experiential creation explains the basis of all experiential duality including wave-particle duality by taking a holistic viewpoint using crossovers between science and spiritual & conscious awareness, (i.e., why all experiences, whether they be of the physical, conceptual, or emotional variety, always come in pairs of opposites, i.e., hot/cold, light/dark, good/bad, position/momentum, etc.) and it also reveals a fundamental limitation inherent in any observer's creation of experience that makes it impossible for a single observer to simultaneously create opposite or complementary experiences through relation to a single underlying actuality, owing to the impossibility of the observer's involvement in the mutually exclusive relations with that actuality necessary to create those opposite experiences. This experiential limitation is used to account for why the wave and particle experiences can never be created simultaneously and is also used to account for what science terms 'quantum uncertainty'. So by utilising the conceptual model of experiential creation, it does not take too much of the imagination to see that this is very similar if not the same as the ideas put forward by the ancient Taoists with Yin and Yang. If what we determine to be light is known to be made up from particles and waves -and there is no argument at any level that this is true - could it not be also true, as Kaufman states, that the concept of light by human conscious reasoning, allowing for what is already known about it, is what really creates and allows the wave-particle duality we perceive, when all reasons from a purely tested scientific standpoint, fails to answer this conundrum? If so, then it may be the case that not only do we actually create the light that we see, but all the Universe and everything else in it!

The Question of Sound & Vibration at Portals:

During the latter months of 2013 there were reports of very strange and unusual screeching sounds being heard all over the world. Nobody knew just where these sounds were coming from, but video evidence suggests that their source may have been high up in the sky. I have personally heard these sounds too above the Settle portal, they are likened to the grinding and scraping of metal on metal, as if some gigantic mechanical device is hidden in the clouds and operating there. The sounds last for sometimes only a few minutes and even up to over an hour or several hours. To date, no identifiable solution has been given to the cause of this phenomenon. There also strange low humming sounds heard near and at portal sites which can last for a few seconds to minutes and then stop with no apparent reason or source. These hums have been attributed in ancient times to emanating from within the Earth and maybe made by enormous mechanical machinery of an advanced civilisation from the inner-world. Apart from solitary reports (albeit the world over), there has never been any firm evidence to support these claims. However, a phenomenon known as the Taos Hum, which is a faint, low-frequency humming noise heard in and near the town of Taos, New Mexico, seems to be similar in nature to the inner-earth sounds. Even stranger, it is said that only about two percent of Taos residents - about 1,400 people - can hear the low hum - between 30 and 80 Hz on the frequency scale - has been described as sounding like a lorry engine idling in the distance or having a slow beat-note sound. Some people perceive it as being louder indoors than outdoors. Those people who find the hum annoying when it happens, have tried to block the sound out by placing ear-plugs in, but then find that the vibrations from it, are still registered by the senses. 'Investigations by scientists, including some from the prestigious Sandia National Laboratories, have failed to find a source or even a plausible explanation for the phenomenon. One theory is that the source is the U.S. Navy's ELF (extra-low frequency) communications system that is used to communicate with its submarine fleet. The Navy, of course, accepts no such responsibility.' And so, we are left with a mystery.

During the late 1980's I worked alongside Ufologist Greg Long comparing UFO reports, his from Washington State and mine from Yorkshire's Ilkley Moor, both regions having a comparable geological make-up and the predominant types of UFOs being Orange Balls of Lights (OBOLS). We have seen that this type of seemingly intelligently controlled phenomenon was also witnessed several times at the Skinwalker Ranch. Interestingly, Greg found through his research that unusual and strange sounds accompanied these sightings, but their source seemed to be coming from under the ground. When comparing notes with Greg, I found that several UFO sightings from the Ilkley Moor region were accompanied by odd sounds, like the 'humming of bees' which David Barclay heard in the middle of winter on the moors prior to seeing a shape-shifting UFO, or the whirling sounds of what seem to be helicopter rotor blades at the time only a ball of light has been seen close to the ground.

Most serious scientific investigators of these odd sounds agree that the 'Hum' is a very real phenomena, even if they are not absolutely certain what its source may be. It is true to say that in a very few cases, the hum has been sourced to quite mundane explanations, for example in the United States, 'the Kokomo Hum was isolated in a 2003 study financed by the Indiana city's municipal government. The investigation revealed that two industrial sites — one a Daimler Chrysler plant — were producing noise at specific frequencies. Despite noise-abatement measures, some residents continue to complain of the Hum.' So, a further investigation was instigated and eventually it was determined that in one instance, acoustical consultant Geoff Leventhall was able to trace the noise to a neighbouring building's central heating unit. In other cases the hum has been linked to high-pressure gas lines, electrical power lines and wireless communication devices, but not definitely confirmed. Only in a few cases has the Hum been linked to a mechanical or electrical source, out of the many thousands of reports the world over.

Most scientists would agree that, ' Sound depends entirely on the medium which is being vibrated', as Colin Smith states, so whatever the source of these strange and unusual noises seemingly coming out of nowhere, clues to finding out just what creates them should be found within the recordings of such -many of which have been made. The ancients used a number of different techniques to make sound and understood how it could be produced to change the communicative frequencies of the ether. Although this became a lost science long ago, we can still learn about the frequencies at which these sounds operate, their tones, and whether they contain within them some kind of hidden message? My wife Helen, who uses instruments and her own voice to produce sound vibrations at the Settle portal explains,

"By using sound (drumming, chanting, etc.) I believe this changes the vibrational waves of energy in the portals, allowing me (Helen) to connect with other evels of similar sound vibrations that are created by entities unseen. I think it is a good way of communication because it uses a vibratory sensing as well as the audible sounds that we hear. For example some deaf people can still determine the volume levels & frequencies of sound although they do not do this in the same way that people with good hearing do by purely listening to those sounds. It is as if another range of sensation is brought into play and they can still communicate using sound but not in the way we are used to. Extending this recognition concerning sound vibrations, I believe that we are able to communicate with other world beings by projecting sounds of various frequency levels which align with the sensory capabilities of those beings themselves or the other dimensions they may exist in."

The Question of Human Psychology at Portals:

In the good old days of the 1980's , when I was regarded as more of a 'sensible' UFO reporter, rather than a UFO experiencer and channeller (as I am today), the connection between Ufology and Dimensional Portals had not been made in the mainstream study of the subject by many people at all. Even so, for those like myself who (maybe rather unthinkingly for my own good at that time?) dared to venture into the fringe territories of investigating actual contact with E.T.'s, rather than safely logging sightings of anomalous Ariel phenomenon, I was very soon pushed to the sidelines by those who saw themselves as amateur scientist-ufologists. Even back then, I could understand why they would do so, for apart from my own testimony to actual contact with my Celestial Guide and other UFO related experiences, I had very little to offer in way of comparable evidence to back up my claims. But that was something which I always felt needed changing, so I would look for similar evidence in other peoples reports, for I knew that I could not be the only one who had made this particular type of contact. In her book, 'Science and the UFOs' (with Peter Warrington -page 169), Jenny Randles wrote of me in those good old days,

'Active British ufologist Nigel Mortimer commented to us that when he began investigation after his close encounter in November 1980 he was at first constantly looking for parallels between what he had seen and any new sighting. At first he was unaware of it, but then he recognised that he was biasing the version of events that he presented in his case reports by focussing on certain elements he believed to be important. With effort, this "Mortimer Effect" can be minimized. But can it ever be removed?'

Doubtlessly, Jenny & Peter present the fact that after my UFO encounter with an OBOL in 1980 (in the same year as the Rendlesham Forest incident, the Alan Godfrey and Zigmund Jan Adamski encounters in Todmorden) I started looking for similar evidence in UFO reports, is a correct assumption. Well, it is correct to a certain degree. You see, they fail to mention that not all UFO experiences are the same, in fact the majority are very different in all aspects, so to simply state that I was looking for comparisons in a bias manner, is wrong and the many UFO reports that I sent into Jenny's Northern UFO News at that time, would suggest so. Many reports were of simple Balls of Light, of different colours, some made sounds, some did not, some were seen over water, some were not, some the witnesses believed they saw Beings with, some did not. How could I look for the certain aspects of my own experience in these cases, when in most cases they did contain them?

In order to rectify what Jenny & Peter call 'the Mortimer Effect' is quite simple. It can be easily determined and proven that there will always be similarities within UFO cases by the very nature that they bring up similar kinds of strangeness. But lets look at the actual and factual elements of my own Orange Ball of Light (OBOL) experience in November 1980. We can bullet point the main parts (for a fuller account see my book 'The Circle and The Sword' or Jenny Randles' 'The Pennine UFO Mystery'(Granada 1983):

- Initial sightings of a small ball of light in the night sky
- Find myself getting up out of bed and viewing this BOL change into an OBOL.
- Object changed again into a blue-grey coloured saucer like shape in the OBOL.
- As I watched I had the sensation that this was a 'living' thing.
- I felt a sense of communication with the object.
- Went to sleep, went to work next day, no recollection of what had taken place.
- Synchronisation - told about the object being seen by another person. I took no notice of this as I did not think it was anything to do with me (no memory of this).
- Synchronisation - After work saw newspaper headlines 'UFO chased by police'. Still no memory of my own sighting.
- Revelation - Went into bedroom, saw that I had moved ornament from windowsill (so I could get a better look out at UFO) and then my own experience and sighting came flooding back to my recollection.

As you will see there are a number of points here which on there own could be, or may not be found in other UFO encounters. I am sure you will find many comparisons. There were two particular aspects that I certainly remained aware of that might appear in other people's cases and they were the fact that I felt the object I witnessed seemed to be a living 'thing' -not just a constructed object in the sky, and that there seemed to have been something happening during the experience, where my recent memory of it had been temporarily erased until a trigger point (seeing the moved ornament in my case) brought the incident back to my conscious recall.

To state that I was biasing my reporting in order to back up my own experience is looking at this the wrong way round. I was looking at the aspects of my own experience and then, if the individual case report merited it (i.e., if similar or the same aspects arose in the witness report by there own inclusion of the facts that happened), then these would be mentioned and yes, I would state that this was similar to what had happened to me.

Facts are facts. The *'Mortimer Effect'* as far as I myself, have always been aware (and I have never changed my own opinion or attitudes on this) is one in which evidence is gathered and always presented in an unbiased, fair and honest way and should we find 'coincidences or similarities' within any reports, then I say good, because by not leaving out any vital piece within the jigsaw, we can only gain a much better understanding of what is actually going on.

The above quote came from a book concerning Science and UFOs and written by people respected in the field, but was this really an example of the scientific approach to the subject, or just an attempt to move 'sensible and scientific' thought away from what was fast becoming a subject in which many many people the world over (during the 1990s) had begun to express their own ET contact views within their own UFO experiences. No longer were the UFO case reports at distance and open to a wide range of speculation the majority. The crazy contact cases were too frequently putting a daring foot into the realms of scientific debate, dividing ufology like a sword though butter. I have never seen it as pure coincidence that Jenny Randles who wrote about my UFO experience in her earlier books several times in the days before my claimed contacts, has never since included or questioned me on this aspect of what I regard is my own UFO journey; one which is as valid if not more-so, than what initially happened to me in 1980. The real '*Mortimer Effect*' is one I hope others will understand. It is the effect and consequences of telling the truth if we are to ever reach a point of honest scientific debate.

The Unknown presents itself to us in ways that effect our appreciative senses, often challenge our conditioned expectations and sometimes, depending on who you are, feeds our inquisitiveness and yearning for answers. Some people prefer to go nowhere near the unexplained and see it as something 'evil' or 'occult', while others love nothing more than the thrill of discovering 'what might be', no matter how strange it is. Of course this is the two ends of the spectrum and there are those people who will fall into a number of slots in-between. Could you spend a whole night in the middle of Rendlesham Forest on your own for example? Some could do so, easily and then we find that some people who in the light of day claim that they would have no problems, find out that certain places like the deep woodlands of Rendlesham can start to play all sorts of tricks on you. There are have been hardened soldiers used to combat in the Middle East who have fled the forest, giving reasons that they saw something from another world there and nothing has ever terrified them so much before in their lives! Then there are those who week after week visit the Forest with a sense of concern and respect for strange places; investigators like Brenda Butler and Derek Savory for example, who almost religiously spend weekend after weekend investigating the many different types of phenomena they have witnessed and photographed at Rendlesham Forest. So what makes some people 'braver' than others -if in fact that is what they are?

Psychologists tell us that people fear the unknown because of one main factor - 'the unknown'. Not knowing or having a lack of understanding about something triggers within our psyche a lack of control and a feeling of insecurity. People who are prone to investigate the paranormal tend to look for answers and in doing so, they start to develop more knowledge about that which they seek. Even if very little is known about a particular aspect of the Unknown, just by the action of 'looking into' whatever it is, enables one to keep a certain level of control. I can fully understand this. There have been many times that I have visited the Settle Portal, sometimes in the day, sometimes during the dead of night. Of course it is in the night time that the portal seems more alien to us and we take more notice of those small sounds or maybe twigs breaking. This is simply because the dark or lack of light which would enable us to see any possible dangers in the woods, presents us with a lack of understanding and control over our immediate environment. With that, a level of fear begins to set in. We all have different levels at which we are able to deal with fear. I might be able to sit alone all night at the portal in the darkness and I might be able to sit in wonderment as the apparition of the Blue Lady floats silently through the trees, but you ask me to put my hand into a barrel of snakes (which might be a completely safe thing to do if the snakes are all none poisonous and don't bite) and I'm afraid you will see me run a mile! Show me enough knowledge and evidence that the snakes are fine, something not to be afraid of and I'd happily leave my hand in the barrel all day.

That is one level of fear, but science shows us that there is another level of unconscious fear. In other words you might be afraid of the unknown just because there is something that you are afraid of but not fully aware of it. People who worry often might fear the unknown. While they might be thinking that they are afraid of something that doesn't exist, the truth is that their unconscious mind is just reflecting their worries. In this way, we actually build up the none-existent fear, as if we expect something to happen when there is nothing there to happen. These feelings can become a kind of phobia if not recognised for what they are.

People sometimes say to me, 'you claim to have had so many different paranormal experiences. I don't believe you, as you would be scared to death by some of them.' Today, I still have no answer why I have had many unexplained things happen to me, why I am able to channel my Celestial guide Sharlek, why I seem to be led to places like the Settle portal, or why I have seen ghosts, UFOs, Beings, etc., over many years. I am what is generally known as a 'repeater'. I prefer to be called an 'experiencer'. The question as to why I do not seem to get affected by the fear of the unknown or situations in which this fear can manifest is a fair and valid one. I know for a fact, I am no braver than anyone else. Certain things can still spook me, like if something is dropped onto the floor at the side of me and makes a loud bang, that will make me jump, if I don't know what caused it. But, it is just something that I have always been aware of all my life, since a young boy, I suppose. That at some level, I understand without being taught this, that there is nothing to fear and that fear comes from within us all. Things appear in the dark of the woods, sometimes paranormal things, sometimes not, and they just happen. I know that some people would fear this situation, but I am a firm believer that there are far worst things in the world known to us that are caused by the actions of human beings, out of which fear grows at the expense of a true sense of the lack of understanding we sometimes have for each other.

The Question of Physics and Metaphysics at Portals

Concerning the locality of the portals (and indeed other places where paranormal experiences take place) we have seen that there seems to be an awareness that something happens to effect in a measurable way the electro-magnetic fields there. At the Settle portal I discovered in 2012 that there was sufficient evidence in the way of ancient sites, wells and formations within the local landscape for a Ley line of energy crossing the north-south of the portal vortex at Castleberg (in the woods) and another line of energy (also known as 'ethereal energy') running approximately east-west through the vortex, including Giggleswick Chapel as a balancing marker for this energy. It seems that 'the first people' (who I talk about in my previous books) not only had a working knowledge of portals, but also understood that to keep these in 'working condition' and active, the natural Earth energies found within the locality and which ran in straight lines between one energy node to another, needed to be kept in balance. Through ritual, song and dance, they were able to project these subtle energies from and towards the portals at will.

Certain aspects of Portal Investigations, including the Ley line energies that seem to be associated in a direct manner with them, have to be looked at in a scientific way alongside the spiritual awareness that becomes obvious at these sites too. To ignore one for the other, will do very little to help us gain any semblance of a full understanding. The cross-over between the scientific and intuitive approach really has no boundaries other than those which have imposed by two different schools of thought. In fact, today most open-minded scientists would argue that quantum physics is not only showing us that these two seemingly opposing avenues of investigation are getting much closer , they do at times overlap. It seems that it is only the investigative language spoken and somewhat differing methodology that is viewed as being at odds for some, not the actual reality of the results. The secret of Ley lines and Earth Energies may be found soon in the study of electromagnetism and at the same time we may learn more from studying the etheric fields that are recognised by dowsers and psychics. Without a shadow of doubt magical beliefs will find their way into the mix at some point, but will no doubt be explained away in purely scientific understanding in an age where we are ready to understand this notion.

One particular area which has already been subject to direct scientific and military scrutiny is that of Remote Viewing. Investigator and friend Tony Topping has seen the importance in the ability to use the psychic ability (a sensing) to remote view places, people and almost anything else, through this method. His research has revealed that although Remote Viewing (RV) was known to the earliest of ancient races, it is still practised in such places as Indian, Peru and the southern America's. It is also in these countries that the subject of UFOs and the possibility of E.T. and Inter-dimensional life-forms visiting this planet, are openly discussed by their representative governments. The importance of RV was held by the British secret services even in the days if Queen Elizabeth I as something that could be used to spy on other countries activities during war time. The secret government group called 'The Entity' with the aid of the 'master psychic spy' Dr John Dee (who enigmatically was suspected as being the original character in real life for James Bond, due to his code name being 007), used trance states and alchemy to induce revelations from the ether, time travelling to places beyond the here and now, in order to gain insights into information that would give his Queen the upper hand in world affairs. Remote Viewing was the equivalent of the modern day NSA spying activities, but using psychics and seers in place of hi-tech mechanical computers.

It seems the USA continued the use of RV throughout the 1950's under MKOFTEN; the CIA conducting experiments on people (sometimes there own military and unsuspecting civilians) in order to find out just how far they could go with psychic research, exploring through drugs and sleep deprivation techniques, the world of the inner mind. 'Travelling' too far into the dream realms without the necessary understanding of what they were really dealing with, they discovered that there were places accessible by the human mind, which were out of this space and time and inhabited by demons. They called these demons 'None Human Entities' (NHE).

I myself, along with others like Tony believe that RV is one way that we can take portal investigations further and probably gain results that would otherwise remain hidden from humanity. In a sense, it may turn out to be the case that dowsers have actually been remote viewing under a different guise as the techniques look to be quite similar -in particular CRV or Coordinate Remote Viewing, which the military have used to look at and sense with the subconscious mind real events on the battlefield. Many years of map dowsing, using a pendulum to focus my mind to information gained from divining over a map of a particular area (which can bring forth places, dates, ages, in fact anything at all that is associated or connected with the location on the map) has shown me that not only is this phenomenon a real ability, but does indeed allow us to find out about people, places and things, the normal five senses are unable to alone. In the summer of 2013, my wife Helen had a vivid dream in which she 'saw' the location of the Horseshoe Trees at the Settle Portal. Her mind allowed her to access the normal environment, the rock strewn ground, the trees of the woodland, the narrow pathways that dissect the site that she was already familiar with. But, it also allowed her mind on this subconscious level to understand something else there which she had never seen before. Helen states,

"I had a dream which felt very real as if I was there. I found myself alone inside the hill at the portal which looked like a cave with a pool of water that had an enormous orange stone in it. I touched the stone, and I instantly felt as if I was being moved at an immense speed to the top of the cave and onto the massive rock that is at the summit of Castleberg. Then what looked like many threads or lines of energy shot out of the rock and connected across the valley at other ancient places, looking like a grid or a spiders web. Then, I was back down in the underground cave again and in the pool with other people I recognised who were also in the water. Then, I woke up."

What is interesting, Helen told one of these friends after her dream about the experience in the cavern. She told Helen that she too had had a very similar dream, but did not recall all details as if it was more vague to her, but she did agree upon the location and that this left her with the impression that something at the portal could be found under the ground at that site.

Another portal investigator from the US, Aaron Turner had drawn a picture several years ago and had stated that it represented a hillside somewhere unknown to him, that had portal vortex's on it. When he saw photographs of the hillside at Castleberg (the site of the Settle portal) he informed me that he had 'seen' the place years before and regarded it as a portal. Looking at his drawing, it is clear to see that this is very similar to the same hillside we know at Settle, but what marks it out as being amazing is the fact that he has drawn a circular shape exactly where the Horseshoe Portal vortex is positioned on the densely wooded hillside and mentions that another hill higher up the landscape, is associated with a 'sugar loaf' shape. Aaron is absolutely correct again. To the east of the portal between Settle and Malham (on higher ground) can be found 'Sugar Loaf Hill'.

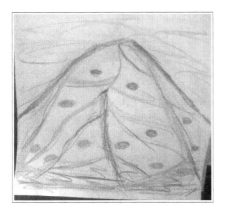 

Above: By remote viewing the Settle Sun Dial Portal Aaron Turner was able to determine that the second circle, second column from right of his drawing was exactly where Helen and the author had discovered the vortex on his sketch. This would correspond to the third stone down as seen on this old engraving (right).

CHAPTER EIGHT

The Secret History of Portals

During an extensive investigation and research program covering thirty years, I visited a number of places in the UK which, although I did not know it at the time, I now regard as being activated portals. One of these places was Rosslyn Chapel in Scotland, made famous in the blockbuster film, *'The Da Vinci Code.'* Much has been written about this enigmatic chapel with its Masonic and Templar influences found encoded within its walls, but far less has been written about the actual location where it still stands today. Like many other portal areas that I have described in this book, Rosslyn Chapel stands out as something which seems to hold the 'key' to the true mysteries of the portal that can be found in the vicinity of the 'place of worship' and it is not always the case that the chapel building is the portal, rather that it is positioned in the landscape in such a way, purposely built, so as to act as a kind of energy balancer for the portal vortex's nearby.

During the night of September 17th, 2004, I had a dream, one in which I had been transported to the borders of the Scottish lowlands. I was on a mission, finding myself standing atop a hillside which ran down through grassy slopes to a tree covered vale below. As I looked down the hill, I became aware of a torrent of water running alongside the line of trees to my east , a flowing stream of sparkling blue.

Earlier that week, my friend Sophie (pseudonym) also had her own dream. By strange coincidence she recognised herself at the site of Rosslyn Chapel situated between Peebles and Edinburgh. In the dream, she was standing in a small darkened room surrounded on four sides by cold stone walls. A kind of box shaped cell. The room was insignificant, but as she looked around an image appeared with a sound which she found difficult to comprehend, for it seemed to be a voice calling her name with the richness of musical orchestration. The image formed into the shape of a person surrounded by beautiful light, appearing to walk forwards from out of the wall in front of her.

During the course of the week, my friend and I discussed our separate dreams wondering at their meaning and significance, if any at all?

Our visit to Rosslyn Chapel had been planned several months after those dreams and we both felt it important we made the trip north from our home town at that time of Keighley in Yorkshire. It almost became like a calling for us and the dreams we had remembered, although odd in their content, seemed to be part of this inner 'calling'. I felt assured in myself that we would find something there, yet I did not know what that would be. It was important, yet remained hidden. A secret and whatever its purpose, it lay in the depths of the chapel's distant past.

On Saturday 19th September, we arrived at Rosslyn about midday. The weather had been changeable all of that week but blue skies began to break through the darkened rain-clouds as we entered the chapels' north door. Along with about forty other visitors, we headed straight towards the eastern end of the 12th Century building, finding the busy commercialisation of the chapel not what we had imagined at all. It seemed that on that day of all days, the world and all of its sons had descended on Rosslyn in search of their own holy grail.

After looking around the chapel and taking a couple of photos of one another standing aside the Apprentice Pillar, we came to a set of stairs which had been roped off at the south-eastern end of the building. One or two people were by-passing the roped off area and descending the steps to a lower region comprising of two small rooms . I urged Sophie to follow me down these steps and into the first of the rooms that looked empty apart from a large wooden chest-like unit which had been carved with an amazing assortment of heraldic and religious symbols.

There was nothing too unusual about that room, so we decided to head back out. Upon crossing the threshold of the door I looked down and was amazed to see a symbol which had been carved into the stone slab adjacent to it. The reason why I became so excited was because I knew this design. It was exactly the same as the marking that had appeared mysteriously on top of my left foot in 1999.

In 1999, I was living in the Wharfedale village of Menston, not far from Ilkley Moor. During the course of the night I had dreamt that I was being taken to a quarry at the back of my home by Grey E.T.'s in the typical UFO abduction scenario. In reality this quarry did not exist and I wasn't aware of there ever being one there in the past at a place which was then occupied by streets and housing. I did not see who it was that led me to the quarry, a tall entity that I sensed and she was female covered in a blue light. She moved me to the quarry surrounded by her ET helpers. That is all I consciously remember and I don't know what happened when I got there or indeed, how I got back again. The next morning I woke to find spots of blood on my pillow and it was later that next morning when washing, that I realised this had bled from my nose during the course of the night. I began to wonder about the dream and looking down at my foot I saw a strange marking just under the surface of the skin. I checked to see if I had scratched myself but this was not an injury. Looking more like a tattoo, but underneath the top layers of skin the shape, about an inch long, looked like a birds foot made up out of four straight lines. Amazingly, after I had shown this marking to my sister Sharon, the marking simply vanished during the hours of the following day, with no trace of it at all the next morning. Years later, I discovered that the origins of the symbol were Runic and this simple yet enigmatic design was recognised as an amulet for psychic protection. Who or what had caused it to appear on my foot remains a mystery.

Off to the left side of this room at Rosslyn, known as the Lady Chapel, there existed a doorway arch with no door. I led Sophie into this small opening, a room no more than 6ft long and 4ft wide, big windows to let in light, it remained a hollow, serving no recognisable purpose? As we entered the room, the whole chapel became quietened. It was as if everyone who had been moving around it had been transported away and we had been left alone in this cell cold and damp, with the hint of ages past still lingering in the stale and undisturbed air. I was a bit disappointed at first, but then began to recognise this as the darkened room in my dream. I felt like we had to be there and wait for something to happen.

We stood in the centre of this small empty space, face to face, and I began to feel the warmth of energies unseen that seeped through my feet from beneath the cold stone floor. At a steady ebbing flow, it raised up through the length of my whole body, increasing in its warmth and intensity to the point where I could hold back my emotions no more and tears of elation welled up in my eyes. This 'effect' was felt by Sophie too.

Just what that feeling was remains a mystery, but seemed to give off a sensation which seemed spiritual, indeed it had that effect upon the both of us. There was the distinct impression that the source of this energy lay somewhere beneath the floor of the chapel, maybe in the lower vaults said to be present as a crypt underneath the building. As soon as the experience passed, after say two to three minutes, people began to walk passed the room. As before, voices of tourists echoed around the walls of the chapel.

We both felt somewhat light-headed so decided to rest a while by the Apprentice Pillar, then followed others towards the western end of the chapel. Along the way, I paused to look at one of the carvings that decorate much of the interior walls. There is a strange mix of pagan, eastern and Druidic symbolism here, which along with Masonic and Templar insignia, completely overshadow any reference to this being a place of Christian worship. At first glance one carving looked to depict some kind of horned god, but a closer inspection revealed this to be the biblical figure of Moses, yet the horns and circular crown above his head suggested an Egyptian pagan influence behind the story. Could it be that the creator of this bust was stating a direct connection between Moses and his possible Egyptian origin of birth which some scholars place close to the reign of the heretic Pharaoh Akhenaton - who was first to introduce a monotheistic religion in the biblical eastern lands.

Interestingly, it seems that others who have visited Rosslyn Chapel have experienced and recognised this feeling of light and elation, along with other unusual feelings. Some people have had strange experiences in the same dark atmospheric crypt of the chapel we had entered. One person I spoke to felt a mysterious wind come from nowhere while alone in the crypt. The chapel undoubtedly has a strong atmosphere, but it could be said that some of the strangest occurrences have very little, if any, scientific evidence to back them up. Two weeks before the visit, I told Sophie that I had heard a 'voice' which informed me that she would have an experience at the chapel that would herald the finding of something important there. I was informed through channelling, almost like a prophecy, that she would hear the sound of a trumpet, and upon this would see the apparition of a woman dressed in white who would point out the location of a hidden 'something' within that mysterious building. And guess what. Nothing of the like occurred when we visited the actual chapel at Rosslyn. Yet, several days after the visit to Scotland, whilst traversing the electronic highway of the internet, I came across this astounding piece of information,

'There is a story that if you stand on a certain step within Rosslyn Castle and blow a trumpet, treasure will be found'. A similar story has been told about blowing a horn within the chapel to reveal the secrets of Rosslyn. The ghost of a white lady is also said to frequent the area. "(Rosslyn Chapel, History, Haunting's and Mystical Connections - Rosslyn Chapel Website 2004).

With everything that happened on that day at Rosslyn, it came as no big surprise to find ourselves peering at a painting in the northern upper gallery of the chapel almost waiting for something else paranormal to happen. The scene in the framed picture described the view of the chapel from the south east painted in oils. There could be observed a sloping landscape running up from a heavily wooded area. At once, I knew this scene. It was the one I had dreamt and told Sophie about prior to the visit. Before I could mention this, both of us caught two distinct flashes of blue electric light, in narrow lines running across the painting, appearing like the contours of a stream or small river. We looked at one another, confirmed that this had been no trick of the light from within the darkened chapel and *even* agreed that we had both 'received' the impression that this sign had been given to the both of us at the same time.

'We both suddenly realised together that there was water, a beautiful blue, crossing the landscape below the chapel and it looked almost magical.'

As we had no prior knowledge of the Rosslyn *(Roslin)* region before the visit, it would have been impossible for either of us to have known whether or not an actual stream or small river really did exist at the spot shown in the painting. We later learnt that this area of stretching woodland is called Roslin Glen, and there certainly is a small river which runs through it called the North Esk.

Roslin Chapel sits high on an outcrop above a deep rocky river gorge called Roslin Glen, some say a powerful telluric line called the Rose line, an electrical geological fluctuation which confers power on the ground beneath the chapel originates in the Glen. The region which lies to the west of the chapel is known as Hawthornden, comprising of sheer rocky cliffs over ninety foot high that plummet down on both sides of the River Esk. Along the eastern edge of these red sandstone cliffs we find evidence of Neolithic carvings over 8000 years old, most of which mimic those found in Ireland at Newgrange.

The gorge *(the Glen)* is heavily wooded and the overall layout of the immediate landscape is reminiscent of the Settle Sun Dial location at Castleberg and adjacent Giggleswick Chapel. I do not think the positioning of Rosslyn Chapel (like the one at Giggleswick) is positioned to the west of this ancient and sacred gorge by chance. High up on the eastern side opposite the chapel and below Hawthornden Castle, can be found Wallaces Cave, supposedly the hiding place of the Scottish hero William Wallace.

I am convinced that this area is of importance to archaeology with many spiral carvings, concentric cup and ring motifs and more recent copies carved into the rocks of the Glen, than science has given the area credit for. It is mainly down to the endeavours of armature archaeologists in recent years that the site has become recognised as a major Neolithic place of worship. A two page report by Childe & Talyor published by The Society of Antiquities of Scotland in 1936 describe a cursory investigation, which reveals some of the details of the etchings. The authors describe triangles, an S motif, a shield and other geometric marks, and suggest that these carvings are earlier than other known "cup and ring " markings from the Iron age within Scotland. They bear closer stylistic affinities to earlier Irish and Bronze Age art, dating to 3000BC, and may be from the Palaeolithic era. From what these carving reveal, it seems that the worship that took place there thousands of years ago, was of a kind that embraced both the natural elements and the supernatural as if it was one. That sense of the unknown within the dark recesses of the Glen has not changed in all of that time and reigns heavily within the atmosphere there.

The glen running approximately north-south past the chapel on the higher ground is filled with legend and haunted with ghosts and apparitions. Like the portal at Ilkley Moor in Yorkshire, we find similar aspects like phantoms that guard certain locations, balls of lights that have been seen manoeuvring above the treetops, and strange mists that appear out of nowhere. Like the Settle portal woodland of Castleberg, the glen is home to apparitions of monk-like figures and there have even been sightings of 'the blue lady' as she floats in and out of the maze of trees and boulders. Something, like we find at the other portal sites, is allowing similar phenomenon to take place within the ancient woodlands of Roslin Glen. A clue to what this might be can be found in an enigmatic rock carving located close to 'Lovers Leap'.

Left: 'Easily seen from the path is a striking carving of a face, thought to be that of a fish or a monkey, the origin remains unclear. It could be a carving of a "Green man" - a Druid or Celtic deity who represents the male aspect of the forest and fecundity, it also strongly resembles Sumerian and Babylonian artefacts. Or could it be reptilian in nature, and could have an unearthly history and be descended from alien creatures?' (Silver Fish).

Certainly, the carved face could look like many things depending on the context it is taken in and these have been touted as 'a lizard, a snake, a time traveller, a ninja turtle, and even an owl'! One thing that it absolutely shows is that Man was present in the glen thousands of years back and was so impressed by it, that he felt that he should leave a depiction of something there. Maybe something that although aware of, he found difficult to express in any other way? The Green Man carvings (which are found in Rosslyn & Giggleswick Chapels) may be pointing towards this earlier attempt of a similar carving and that the Roslin Glen 'fish' carving is something like an 'original' attempt to place humanity firmly within the energies of nature and the landscape. If that is the case, we still have a problem. Why don't we find such carvings all over the place, certain places, usually scared and ancient places, have them, while others do not. This is a puzzle, but it seems more than coincidence that the Green Man keeps cropping up at places of worship and at close by ancient portal sites.

Another legend from Roslin that fits in well with other portal sites like the one I worked with Helen at in Settle, tells of the Black Dog or Spectral Hound that is said to guard a treasure at nearby Rosslyn Castle. The story with the longest history suggests a phantom hound who haunts the woods of the Esk around the castle on dark and stormy nights, heralded by its eerie baying. It is said that on,

'February the 24th 1302, the site was the scene of a major battle between Scots and English forces. One of the English knights was master of a large war hound, and when the Englishman was killed by a Scottish knight, the hound attacked him so viscously that Scotsman was forced to kill it. That very night as the Scots rested in the confines of Roslin Castle, the spirit of the hound appeared in the guardroom causing panic amongst the troops. After this the dog appeared nightly, and the soldiers nicknamed it the 'Mauthe Doog'. Eventually the turn to guard came to the man who had slain the hound's master. Walking down the passage with the castle keys he let out a scream above the noise of a snarling hound, and fled back upstairs in blind panic, he never spoke another word and died three days later. The shape -shifting hound was said to have disappeared from the castle after this event, although the sound of baying can still be heard.'

'*(More Highland Folktales 1964 by R. Robertson MacDonald.)*

As we have seen at the Settle portal in Chapter 5, such ancient sites seem to be inexplicably linked with secret underground tunnels and the ancient woodlands of Roslin keep up this tradition with records of mysterious passageways running from both the chapel and castle. In the heights of the Hawthornden cliffs there are several caves and such tunnel systems which are said to date back to ancient times (at least the Bronze Age) which were said to have been used by Wallace's troops in the war against the English at the Battle of Roslin on 24th February 1303. One of these caves, 'Wallace's Cave' is found on the sheer edge of the western cliff below Gorton House. In the summer of 2004, I visited the cave and was surprised with exactly what I found there.

I was staying at Gorton House, which is now a guest house for sightseers and walkers and while I was there, I spoke to the owners about the history of the place. It turned out that a track from the gardens of the house led to the top of the inaccessible rock ledge from the bottom where the river was to where the cave was situated. Almost like an indicator that the cave is hidden there, a carved spiral of ancient age and others close by of more modern design, pointed the treacherous path towards Wallace's Cave. The sheer rock face looked like something from a long forgotten sacred Australian Aboriginal landscape, almost like a historic record in stone, spirals and concentric circles, depicting a lore and sense of the unknown only a few left can now comprehend the meaning of. This precipice, high above the River Esk is an extremely powerful, sacred and magical place and it has been said by other than me, that it 'crackles and buzzes' with energy.

Wallace's Cave is a cruciform grotto cut out of the bare rock of the cliff. Archaeological surveys & notes conducted in 1957 for OS Maps, state that it is an 'artificial cave (i.e. man made) capable of holding 60 to 70 men, is said to have been a hiding place of Sir William Wallace and others. Its entrance is situated on a ledge 20' high on the cliff face, about 60' from the level of the Esk. The cave extends some 38' into the cliff, with two recesses. Little can be suggested as to the period of occupation as no relics have been found.' In 1975, no further information is forthcoming about the cave or why it was associated with William Wallace. A clue might be found however, not in the actual cave, but in the grounds of nearby 17th Century Gorton House.

While I was staying there, I mentioned that Wallace was renowned to have carried with him a magnificent long sword into battle against the English. There remains some dispute as to exactly where this sword relic can be found today and indeed, if the sword that was said to belong to Wallace is the one situated in the Wallace Memorial in Stirling , genuine or not?

You may be wondering at this point what the Scottish hero William Wallace has to do with our investigations into portals. Well, a lot and it concerns the sword that he is said to have carried with him. There has been a story handed down through generations of the families at Gorton House concerning a lost golden sword. It was lost by a Knight in what are now the ornate gardens there and awaits to be re-discovered one day. I was amazed to hear this story so close to Roslin Glen and the chapel, as it reminded me of my own golden sword visions that took place in the late 1980's at the Ilkley Moor portal. Described in my book *The Circle & The Sword*' we find that certain historical heroes often carry with them ceremonial swords of great strength and power. One such on Ilkley Moor, was King Hakon The Good of Norway, the Viking foster-son of King Athelstan around 894 AD; who wielded a golden sword called *Quernbitter.* The sword was supposed to be so magnificent that it was able to slice through a quern stone (a type of milling stone) to the 'centre eye'.

Here at Gorton, I found myself looking at old maps of the gardens and grounds within only hundreds of yards from Wallace's Cave. There was something else that seemed significant and that concerned the layout of the gardens in Victorian times. Within the north-eastern extremes of those gardens made up of arbours and cultivated plant beds, there could be made out the remains of what looked like a circular embankment similar to what we find at Giggleswick Chapel in Yorkshire. Of course no ancient stones remained that I could find in the vicinity today, which might have pointed to this site being an ancient stone circle, but I did find it intriguing that the line of the embankment has been preserved by placing a circular hedgerow around it. This can be easily discerned from the sky and lines up west with Wallace's Cave.

So, to take all things into account we have the probability that at the geographical position of Gorton House we may find the remains of an ancient stone circle site which lines up with Rosslyn Chapel on the western high ground about a mile away. Between those two landmarks we find on the cliffs above the Esk ancient carved rocks and cavern systems. There are legends that suggest that all of these places are connected together with an underground maze of tunnels. You could almost be forgiven in thinking that I have just described the landscape of the Settle Sun Dial Portal in Yorkshire, so similar are the geographical, historical and supernatural aspects found in both.

Tales of underground tunnels are the stuff of folklore and legend, but may hold more truth than we realise. We have seen how the locals of Settle alleged such accounts linking the portal at Castleberg Woods with the chapel and other significant buildings in the area. This seems to be the case at Rosslyn too.

A local legend that has lasted many years is one which says that a hidden tunnel runs from the chapel down to Rosslyn Castle. A piper was said to have ventured into the tunnel and was never seen again. In an attempt to determine whether or not such a tunnel exists, ground-scans have been carried out, which have confirmed that a passageway leads away from the chapel beneath Gardeners Brae in the direction of the castle grounds above the woodlands of the Esk. Like the portal location at Settle, it has been suggested that these tunnels have been built imitating Solomon's Temple of Jerusalem as described in the lore of Freemasonry. Mark Oxbrow and Ian Robertson in their book 'Rosslyn and the Grail', state that,

'in one Masonic ritual, a 14th degree Mason identifies a passageway, deep underground, which leads from Solomon's Temple to his palace'.

Archaeological findings concerning the tunnel suggest that it may be the remains of a medieval drain, yet this has not been confirmed. Much symbolism is also associated with these caves and tunnel systems at Roslin Glen. Caves have long been thought to be the domains of the resting and the dead, of burial and rebirth. More importantly to our study of portals and where the dimensions meet, they are the meeting places for humans and the divine. In ancient mystery schools, caves and tunnels represented the miracle of resurrection and were used for initiation rituals. To the Celts, caves were the entrances to the magical Other-world.

While walking through the magical woodlands of Roslin Glen in 2004, I saw what I took then to be a ghost or spirit. Through the glade of trees close to the castle grounds, by a footbridge over the river, I saw what I can only describe as a floating apparition of a woman in a long flowing blue gown that was tied at the waste with a golden braid. Her hair was long and dark, flowing in the gentle breeze that day , in an almost slow motion. She looked ahead, looked once at my position some hundred meters away and then back ahead of her again with no change in her expression which was one of calm and almost automated. Floating another twenty feet or so, she simply vanished from sight into thin air, gradual as if walking through an unseen doorway. Throughout the whole experience, the 'blue lady' made no sound at all.

I actually saw this apparition of the blue lady again in the woods of Roslin while I was visiting the chapel as described. She moved and acted in exactly the same way each time, but was sighted in different parts of the glen. Even more amazingly, the blue lady has been sighted by others at the Settle Sun Dial Portal in the woods on the slopes of Castleberg. Her description is the same each time.

Checking the accounts of ghost stories from Roslin Glen, it appears that an apparition closely resembling the one I witnessed there has been seen more than once, but a major difference being that she wears an ethereal white colour gown instead of blue and such is known as the 'White Lady'. Legend tells us that the White Lady waits in the depths of the glen with the purpose to reveal a magnificent hidden treasure to the right person, knowing where it is located she has waited hundreds of years. She is said to be a maiden of the St Clair line who was bewitched by an evil spell and made to stand guard over the treasure. Upon a table in a secret chamber. lie a magical golden sword and golden hunting horn. She is guarded from leaving her prison by a dark demonic creature, which has to be overcome by some righteous Knight.

Hunting this treasure became popular in the 18th century when fortune hunters descended on Rosslyn from all across Scotland. Part of the legend says that only a blind man was able to attempt to seek out and find the actual treasure as the 'angel lady' who guarded it was of 'such a dazzling purity, that mortal eye could not look upon her and live'.

Two things come to mind here concerning this treasure and the 'angel lady'. Obviously we can see the mention of the golden sword associated with the lost sword of the glen thought to be in the vicinity by the modern day owners of Gorton House, in this legend. Also, there is a mention that the vision of the White Lady was such that it could bring about misfortune to life if she was gazed upon by physical eyes. When I read this, I jumped up in my chair! I was informed by Brenda Butler in 2013, that she had been using a camera technique at Rendlesham Forest (where a portal is said to exist) in which she takes photographs with the camera held over her shoulder and her back towards anything she might pick up in the viewfinder. She mentions that she channelled this instruction by E.T.'s that use the portals at Rendlesham, who said many of them do not appear to the naked eye, face on, because they give off a high level of energy which is like our radiation and this if looked upon for any length of time, can damage the pupils and can cause skin cancers. Taking this technique up myself, I found that I was able to gain frequent close up photographs of E.T.'s and other energy beings at the Settle horseshoe trees portal. Is this the reason why the White Lady of Roslin tends to keep her distance and mainly 'operates' within the confines of some subterranean hidden chamber?

Is the White Lady really an Angel, indeed, is she one and the same as the Blue Lady I saw floating through Roslin Glen and Castleberg woods? At both portal sites, although hundreds of miles apart and in two different countries, we do find some evidence to suggest this may be the case. We may even have to evaluate what an Angel is in this context ? Common to both places there are significant carvings of angels that seem to appear in odd situations outside of chapels and churches. In Rosslyn Chapel there are dozens of carved angels with books, angels with scrolls, angels praying and playing medieval instruments. At Giggleswick Chapel we find a solitary angel within a tunnel entrance, carved into a stone wall on the main road to Settle. But what is an Angel?

The word 'angel' is derived from the Greek word, 'aggelos', which translates as messenger in Hebrew from the word, 'mal'akh'. In the bible, angels are neither male nor female and are unable to reproduce. It is written that they angels are God's messengers on Earth. Angel forms have evolved over time within cultures and the female loving and nurturing angels we know of today was established by the Victorian era. She was dressed in pure white robes and bathed in divine light, a bright, magical shining being. The Rosslyn White Lady may have been such a beautiful apparition, maybe an angel, but the legend does not mention anything about her wearing any kind of halo or set of wings. She is often referred to in the treasure legend as the Enchanted or Sleeping Lady. We find reference to White Ladies in Faerie lore from all over Europe which might suggest that she is an energy being of light, elemental in nature, of which photographs exist from portals to suggest her kind haunt such places.

From the Castle of Spirits website, Anna Gamez, Everett of Washington, USA, gives a typical account of an encounter with the Blue Lady. She writes:

'This story takes place when I was about 10 years old. I lived with my Aunt and Uncle and my three cousins at the time of this experience, in which us girls still talk about to this day.

We lived in a quiet neighbourhood on the edge of Renton, WA, USA. In the middle of the circular arranged housing, there was the "woods". All of the kids would go into the woods to hang out, build forts and tree houses. It was our escape from the home life. Karen was one of my cousins and my best buddy. We were inseparable. Every day from school Karen would grab me and say "c'mon lets go to the woods". One day, we started walking down the trail going deeper into the woods, when Karen suddenly stopped and grabbed my arm. "Did you hear that?". " Hear what?" I said. "It sounded like a woman calling us". "Well maybe its your mom?". "No she's not even home yet and that didn't sound like her. "Your freaking me out Karen, stop it!". "I'm serious, you didn't hear that?". "No, Lets just forget about it ok!"

We continued down the trail. Karen still had a hold of my arm in a death grip. I knew in my mind that she was frightened by something, but what exactly? We approached our favourite tree in the woods. This was our special place, because whenever Karen and I needed to talk or just have our space, we would end up here at the old maple tree. Someone had built a rope swing there. So we started playing and swinging away. When it was Karen's turn, suddenly right in mid air, she screamed and let go of the rope. I came running over. "What's wrong?". " Look!" she points down to the bushes. My heart was pounding and I was suddenly weak in the knees. There was a woman standing in the distance with a long blue dress and her skin was glowing white. The woman pointed her finger at us. Both Karen and I grabbed each other in horror. We were so frightened that we couldn't move. The woman started to move towards us with her hand reaching out. Karen screamed and at that moment we both got our strength back and started to run like hell without looking back. For months afterwards Karen and I talked about the "Blue Lady" and we never went to the old tree to swing alone!'

There is here allegory to Christian characters within the descriptions of both the White and Blue Lady visions. We have seen that the white apparition has been described as an angel, a messenger from God, while the blue apparitions seem to suggest something else. We can turn to religion again, for an answer as to who this lady might be, or as is the case, we might find the true explanation somewhere else outside the limitations of the bible texts.

I must say, however, that on the last occasion that I witnessed the blue lady within the woods of Castleberg, I had very mixed feelings about just what I was experiencing and who I was observing. Of course all kinds of questions about who she was ran through my mind as I watched her float effortlessly approximately a foot above the ground, weaving in and out of trees to the immediate north of the portal vortex. Was she human? She looked human. Was she the virgin Mary? She looked like her from books I had read and films that I had seen. Was she an angel? Yes, she might have been, but again, what is an Angel?

There remains a sense of mystery about Scotland's Rosslyn Chapel. Just what lies at the heart of that mystery is yet to be discovered, but it would seem that an air of the supernatural penetrates the senses of those who are willing to participate in its activation. I would say that Rosslyn, for Sophie & I was a calling, an awakening towards something which cries out to be recognised, yet remains hidden from those who decide to take no heed.

For those who do decide to 'follow dreams', those revelations & hidden insights may come to light. The mystery which is at the heart of Rosslyn Chapel is one steeped in hundreds of years of myth, legend and pagan folklore; something which was at that locality thousands of years before any Templar decided to impart his own interpretation of that knowledge within its scared walls. Some say that Rosslyn holds the key to the final resting place of the Holy Grail, some the biblical Ark of the Covenant, and even for others, the crashed remains of a UFO! Whatever is to be found in the lower underground levels of the chapel vaults, it is certain to be a magical treasure of one kind or another, for that is what is being sought. Man has always had the knack of turning the ordinary into the extraordinary. Whenever he has chooses to seek out that which he is unable to explain, he reveals even deeper mysteries.

Alas, it may be a case of the dreamer dreaming on for a while yet, as up to present there have been no obvious plans to open up the vaults of Rosslyn Chapel for inspection. Any revelation contained therein, is to remain hidden for now we have been informed. I have a feeling though, that there are those who know what truly lies in the deepest corners of those darkened vaults and they wish to keep their secret a while longer. You get the sense that they choose to dangle the truth just under our noses, just enough as to keep us transfixed on something that may one day become accessible. For now, we remain ever wanting to push that little bit further towards seeking out what 'they' probably already know.

We have already examined the possibility that some portals may require an external device to activate them. This might be technology that has been made by humans in the distant long forgotten past or maybe in the recent past. There is even the possibility that a device like the Ark of the Covenant which we looked at in chapter one of this book, is a device that allows a portal to be formed and activated in another dimension by none-human beings. Another more down to earth scenario could be that the portal device is one which originates in the future and time travels back to moments we acknowledge as the past and the present. No matter what the truth of that matter is, if such a device did exist and was available to our reality (i.e. it was physical in nature at some point), then you can rest assured that there would be world powers wanting to show an interest in acquiring it for there own use and gain. According to researcher and UFO experiencer Mike Oram, this may have already happened. In his book *'Does It Rain In Other Dimensions'* Mike recalls how when he was with friends in the deserts close to the notoriously top secret Area 51 close to Groom Lake, Nevada, recently admitted by the US President Barack Obama to actually exist, he encountered E.T.s ; which appeared at the time that a Jeep carrying a portable 'portal generator device' was sighted just off the road ahead of him. Not only does Mike believe that the US armed forces he saw that day, possess a hidden technology that relates to inter-dimensional travel, but that he was also a traveller through this device!

"The truck held a long tubular device which seemed to have two wheels attached. At first I thought this was a cannon. This was not the case, because when I managed to see the other side of the machine there was no 'wheel' device there. I t was only on one side and seemed to consist of three raised sections that looked like a wheel."

Describing the device under deeper hypnosis, Mike states further, "there were three magnetic coils inside this wheel and that this device was known as a Magnetic Pulse Generator ......it could create a portal and that it was a Mobile Portal Creator."

Magnetic Pulse Generators have been mentioned before in connection with the famous Philadelphia Experiment concerning the disappearance and reappearance of the ship the U.S.S. Eldridge in June 1943. The experimental vessel was fitted with tons of electronic equipment including, it is said, 'two massive generators of 75 KVA each, four giant magnetic coils mounted on the deck, three RF transmitters of 2 MW CW each mounted on the deck, three thousand power amplifier tubes, special synchronizing and modulating circuits, and a host of other undefined apparatus. All of this equipment was employed to produce a massive electromagnetic field that would be able to bend light and radio waves around the ship, thus making it invisible. Apparently, at 09.00hrs on 22nd July 1943, these generators were put into action and the massive electromagnetic fields began to build up. A strange greenish fog was seen to slowly cover the ship, but then the fog itself began to disappear, taking the Eldridge and its crew with it. When the generators were turned off, the green mist appeared again and the ship with it. The crew were sick and disorientated, but as it had been deemed that the experiment had been a success, the generators were turned back on again. This time something terrible took place. As before the green mist enveloped the ship and made it vanish and reappear as before, but when the ship was boarded for inspection the crew were in a bad state. Some had gone mad, some were violently ill and some were fused to the metal structure of the ship and had become a part of it! So, what had begun as an experiment in electronic camouflage, ended up as an accidental teleportation of an entire ship and its crew. Since then, it has been rumoured that attempts have been made to teleport in hyperspace experiments back to the Eldridge in order to turn off the generators which are making the ship appear and disappear from locations miles apart from each other to this day. Are these generators causing a rift in time, manipulating matter and transporting this giant physical object through space and time? After noticing the portal device on the road to Area 51, Mike Oram claims that he and his partner Fran were forcibly taken into the portal created by the machine at gun point. The portal was created in front of their eyes, about 2.13 meters tall and about 5cms off the ground. so they were able to step into its thin oval shape of wavy lines of energy that rippled like water. As soon as they moved into the portal, pop, they were in another place underground in a base run by the military forces that sent them through it.

Mike Oram experienced this kind of oval portal close to his home, on a lonely lane near to Lake Windermere in the Lake District. He recounts how he felt an urge to go for a walk along this favourite country lane and sat down on a bench to meditate. While he was doing this, a man appeared with a dog on a long leash, who asked Mike if he could sit down next to him. They got talking about the area and the man said that he had lived there for 30 years, but Mike found this odd, as he had never seen him before. After telling Mike about a strange experience close to the lane in wintertime, when three mysterious young girls appeared out of nowhere to help the man push his car out of snow into a field and as quickly vanished into thin air, the man hurried away with his dog up and over a hill in the lane. Looking back, this odd character shouted back at Mike, "When I see the girls again, I'll tell them about you"!

Mike looked around puzzled at what had just happened and then noticed a figure standing next to him which he recognised as being his 'space brother'. This entity created an oval portal in the road, similar to that seen at Area 51, and asked Mike if he would like to journey through it. Mike declined on this occasion, as he felt that to do so, would mean he had agreed to move on from this world and he was not ready then, having more work to complete here.

Looking at video footage of the spot on the lane where Mikes experience took place, it is strikingly similar to the lane that runs from the Settle portal to Langcliffe in North Yorkshire. In 2012, UFO and other paranormal entities including a giant ghost owl were seen and photographed on this lane.

Secret Chapels, Masonic Halls, Underground tunnels and Ancient sacred sites. What could possibly be the connection between these places to portals? If we join the dots and dare to look a little deeper into the rabbit hole, we will see that these man-made and natural aspects, seemingly innocent in design, may hold the clue, the holy grail that is at the heart of portal research and investigation. In the concluding chapter, I will put forward my own theory as to why these elements keep cropping up time and time again and the very serious reasons why they are intrinsically woven into the very fabric of this ancient and modern mystery.

Helen & I could never have imagined the outcome of our visit to the Settle Castleberg lodge of Freemasons open night in 2012. When we first arrived there it was all the usual pleasantries, but then I got talking about my book about the Sun Dial Portal and the Masonic connection. I was shown that past masters of the lodge wore the hexagram which I have found all over the older buildings in Settle and in particular a mason showed me two paintings of Castleberg Rock that hung on the lodge entrance walls, but I thought little of it as the rock is a central landmark to Settle. These pictures showed just the rocky woodland landscape and nothing else. Next to each of these pictures I saw was other pictures of Solomon's Temple. Helen told the mason that her uncle had been a Freemason in another Yorkshire town and it turned out remarkably that he was well known to the lodge, another unexpected coincidence. This seemed to open the mason up in continued conversation and he asked me four times if I would like to join them. I refused, trying to be as polite as possible by explaining that I prefer to share openly any knowledge I may gain with others as equals to me as human beings and to join their secretive fellowship would mean me having to give this freedom up. No price, no hidden knowledge, is worth giving up our god-given right to freedom.

We wandered around the lodge looking at all the symbolism on the walls and carpets, and then out of the blue we were invited to go into a small back room which looked to be just full of stationary and books. The mason told Helen that we needed to look at another picture in this room. He pointed towards the open door, but we could not see any picture large or small on any wall as we entered it. Then, when we turned, puzzled, to come back out of that store room, there it was on the wall hidden behind the door and not in a place for everyone to see it at all. It was a large framed copy of the Buck and Feary engraving of the Sun Dial Portal; the governments misrepresentation of what was actually there on the Castleberg landscape in 1768. This was proof positive that the Settle Freemasons (at some level) know about the portal, I thought.

We even had time for a little frivolity in the lodge...there was an old organ in the corner of the ceremonial room upstairs and Helen was told that she could have a play on it, but normally women do not get the chance to enter that room, never mind play the organ. We just seemed to have been treated differently to other people who were wandering around the Lodge. How apt then, when she broke into 'Rock around the Clock' (sundial....clock...get it?) -which brought a wry, hidden smile to both our faces, but as Helen played on, I began to form thoughts in my mind as to the chances of finding the Sun Dial picture in this Masonic Lodge and why it was so important that we should be shown it at all?

Helen had finished playing the organ in the Castleberg Lodge, and I turned with some embarrassment towards the Freemason who was coming back up the stairs into the ceremonial hall. I had noticed earlier that this particular gentleman had been huddled in a corner of the room downstairs where others who had attended the open evening had congregated, and seemed to be watching us both. I found it a little disconcerting, that he would not take his gaze off me, even when I looked directly back at him and I found myself having to look away towards another part of the room. What did this mason want with us now?

"Come with me, I want to show you something else....". He offered to take Helen and I downstairs again and show us a small framed painting that was hanging on the wall near to the kitchen. At first I did not know it was a painting at all, until he pulled on a delicate golden coloured braided cord and two red silk curtains opened to reveal it. Instantly, I recognised the scene on what appeared to be a very old (possibly 1800's) picture.

"That's Jacobs Ladder", I exclaimed. It reminded me of something from my youth, for my grandmother Bray used to keep a small model of Jacobs Dream that was a 'ship in a bottle' ornament, itself so old that much of the wood making up the miniature ladder inside the green bottle, had rotted and began to float around in the darkened water in little pieces. But, there was something very different about this particular painting, something did not seem right.

Then it hit me as I looked at it again. Yes, there was Jacob with his head on the Bethel Stone, there was the troop of ascending and descending Angels and there was the ladder from his dream, but the scenery, it looked very familiar to me.

My jaw dropped and I looked at Helen. She thought I had seen a ghost! Jacobs Ladder had been painted onto the rise of the rocky hillside that is Castleberg, starting at the foot of the rocks between two pillars (the Sun and the Moon) and running up through the woodlands that were so well known to us both, right up to the last rung of the ladder stopping at a place we would estimate being exactly where the Sun Dial Portal vortex is today, at the site we call the 'Horseshoe Trees'. This could not be coincidence.....surely!

Was our Masonic 'friend' trying to tell us something here, confirming something that I had began to suspect and formulate theories about for the past two years in the Settle area? If what I was looking at was correct, then not only was the story of Jacob highly significant in allegory to the Freemasons, but maybe they had known all along that it was possible for some human individuals (like the biblical Jacob for example) were capable of extending the hidden knowledge of the ancients, in order to access through the mind and ritualistic ceremony the portal gateways within the natural landscape.

I convinced myself that this Freemason before me was testing me. He watched me look back at the revelation in the painting and waiting a moment for me to highlight what he already knew - that there was an actual physical site, positioned on the slopes of Castleberg , where what we might call Angelic Beings are able to move into and from this world and had been doing so for many thousands of years.

"You know too much already". A pause and then he repeated it again. Was he reading my mind? I had not spoken a word at this point concerning these amazing connections with my own research, but my thoughts raced as I felt an amazing sense of realisation that the quest for the Settle portal was something that was real and known to others. And it was important to those Freemasons too.

Conclusion: Reaching Out

In the introduction to UFOs, Portals and Gateways, I gave the standard dictionary meaning for a portal, ' *a doorway, entrance, or gate, especially one that is large and imposing, sometimes found in large buildings, at other times found between dimensions* '. As we have seen in the chapters of this book, a portal is much more than that which is found in the above statement.

Yes, it can be a door and an entrance, it is certainly a gateway, but I differ to accept that portals have to be large or imposing. In fact, the portals that I have ever encountered, in the sense of inter-dimensional portals, are usually experienced as being so sacredly fragile in their essence (or maybe that is how I actually perceive them) that they demand a level of awareness and respect in remembering that they are a part of the ether in our world and also made up from other energies that we have yet to fully understand in other worlds.
What I am trying to say is that I regard portals in a similar way that conservationists regard threatened species of animals.

Portals were obviously important to ancient man who understood far better than we can today about what these gateways are, and how they operated, having kept in memory the lore and instruction that would allow their predecessors, the first peoples, to travel at will between the unseen void. With the essence of measured time, the majority of mankind was forced to forget some aspects of their own world which once worked miracles upon them, the natural science of inter-dimensional awareness being one part of that. Only the few, the shamans of the worlds elite took it on themselves to secret and code the mysteries of the portals in those early times, but in doing so began themselves to lose the true purpose and sacred meaning of the ancient stone circle sites. As every human being, with only the ego to blame for their own self-indulgence in keeping the reality of the portals a secret amongst the brotherhood, lost touch with the 'instructions' laid down by their forefathers, portals became like a lost treasure, like an endangered species because mankind in the main continues to slumber instead of ponder on the very real meanings of the reality that he lives in.

The good news is that there seems to be an awakening in so many different ways around the globe today and the sudden realisation that travelling vast distances between different worlds does not necessarily mean we will have to wait until thousands of years have past, due to the lack of capable technology, to get to the nearest stars when we have been given an idea. An idea revealing itself at last from the depths of the long forgotten ancient past, that of inter-dimensional travel allowing mankind to reach out to his brothers and sisters, many of whom are doing the same in other places, other worlds, just the other side of those unseen doorways.

There are a few people who have expressed to me that it is wrong to open portals and they should be left well alone. I have even been threatened by some of those people as they see me as some kind of demon-possessed overlord intent on doing what I do (investigating the reality of portals and nothing else to cause anyone on this world or off it any harm) so that I can help to usher in some kind of evil invasion of the planet. This of course is ridiculous. I fully understand that there will be readers of this book who have never met me or Helen before, who will do a double take at some of the statements I have made in it and will cry out for good evidence from us or simply dismiss all and any of my claims about the portals. Using their own rights as a human being and the freewill to express such comments is something that I would never negate, but there is another problem that has been circling the cloudy skies of ufology like a prophet of doom for a number of years now, which does very little to help any of us to reach out, and try to understand better, what is truth concerning visitations of none human life-forms to this world and how that is possibly happening right now.

I have played the UFO investigators game for the past 30 years now and have been an active part of the UFO world of so-called and often self-acclaimed experts. Up until the early 1980's there were really two camps or two independent schools of thought about what acceptable investigation of case reports should take. One was the amateur-scientist approach taken by many of the well known and respected UFO groups and organisations (including their represented member experts) who saw most reports as something that they could look at much in the way a police investigation takes place and then log their results in self gratifying newsletters and UFO magazines, books, etc., and the other approach was much like the anti-political movements we have today, not only holding strong beliefs that they had made contact with other worldly beings, but that they were in constant communication with them. One party was mainstream, official and almost regimented in its membership and the other consisted of those who preferred the freedoms of living on the fringes of Ufology, even if this often meant that they would become the butt of underhand jokes, even from those in the more 'respectful' schools of thought.

In the last 10 years or so, that landscape has changed. Those who were once seen as living on the lunatic fringes of the UFO subject because maybe they claimed to be able to channel beings from unseen worlds make up the majority of people researching and investigating. Many of the 'old school' UFO groups have fallen by the wayside, not because they actually did anything wrong apart from some cases of what we now know were unfounded attitudes of social snobbery, but because they were not prepared to move with the times. When they saw this change happening, it was often remarked that Ufology was dead. That was once all their case reports had been filed away, over and over again, the results of which they had already gained over three decades since the 1970's, but like a breed of scientist-repeaters, they failed to take a grasp of the implications from their own data. Ufology was not dead, it was very much alive, living on through the continuous efforts of those fringe believers, brave people all over the world, who told the very real truth about their experiences with the unknown -not for self gratification, but for something which overshadows any of that. For the truth. For they were the UFO experiencers and they are the ones who take Ufology (and within that portals investigations) forward in a way that the 'old school' never could, or should we rightly say, never would.

Of course, I believe that all of this was supposed to happen. I was myself actually of the old school Ufology in the early 1980s (a director in BUFORA) , but then was disregarded by them because I told the truth about my own contacts with E.T.'s and channelling. Thankfully, there were a few wonderful people back then who understood because they had been Contactees too, amazing people like Diane Tessman who channelled a guide similar to my own called Tibus, and Laura & Mike Sayers, who were investigating portals and making contact with Celestial Beings in Lancashire even before I had any notion of this hidden world. These people will be shown to be the subjects' heroes in time, pioneers who took a firm grasp of the reigns of truth, and with the honour they deserve, ordered science may someday soon come to realise that wisdom comes to all of us at many different levels.

The investigations at portals continue. Most of us do not know how they work, we do not know why they are here on this planet, but we do know that odd and unusual things happen at sites we believe to be portals. The one thing I am certain about, is that portals pose no danger to any of us. They are as natural as the trees that grow in the forest. They are just like many other things we do not fully understand and may be a cause for fear and lack of control in us. It is a fact that humans are happier when they are in control of situations and tend to fear less that which they fully understand. It would be foolhardy to state that there is nothing to fear at all concerning portals. Of course there is something and that something is us! Will we eventually gain full knowledge about portals, will we be able to travel in mind and body to other worlds using portals, and will we act in a civilised way once we do so? They are the burning questions with regards to portals for me. What kinds of people wish to gain control of the portals, those with good and respectful intentions or those with bad?

There are beautiful intelligent life-forms all over this solar system, all over the Universe, and even in places we have yet to comprehend. You will never see them with current technology and modern day science will never find them, well not in the foreseeable future in any case. But, they are there. Waiting. On their side of the door they hold the golden key to the wisdom of the gates. It has been put into the lock and opens the door every now and again for them to take a peek through the portals into our world. They take on board the sadness of human life lost in war and misery, having left behind in their own distant past, the childish antics of hate, greed and power.

They wait. They hope. And they watch . . . .

References

Chapter One:
Mortimer, Nigel, Isaac Newton & The Secret Sundial, Ancient Mail Verlag 2012
Prince, Clive & Picknett, Lynn, The Stargate Conspiracy, Warner Books 1999
Knight, Christopher & Lomas, Robert, Uriel's Machine, Arrow Books 2000
Hancock, Graham, The Sign and the Seal, QPD 1992
Osman, Ahmed, Moses and Akhenaten, Bear & Company; 2 Reissue edition 2002

http://travelvista.net/hidden-dimensions-ancient-civilizations
http://www.thelivingmoon.com/
http://www.esolibris.com/articles/alternative_history/stargate_alien_gods.php
http://www.bibliotecapleyades.net/merovingians/blueapples/
http://www.biblicalarchaeology.org/daily/biblical-sites-places/temple-at-jerusalem.html
http://www.allaboutarchaeology.org/ark-of-the-covenant.html
http://www.domainofman.com/ankhemmaat/moses.html
http://www.jewishencyclopedia.com/articles/6779-goliath

Chapter Two:
Mortimer, Nigel, Spheres Of Influence, Privately published booklet 1986.
Size, Nicholas, The Haunted Moor, Privately Published reference book 1934
Mortimer, Nigel Editor, The UFO Reporter, Edition No.4, 1994
Mortimer, Nigel, The Circle & The Sword, Ancient Mail Verlag, 2012 (E-book edition)
Mortimer, Nigel, UFO Mysteries of Ilkley Moor (Unpublished MS) 2005
Whetnall, Paul & Randles, Jenny, Alien Contact (Window on Another World), Coronet 1983
Owens, Andy, Yorkshire Stories of the Supernatural, Countryside Books 1999
Randles, Jenny, UFOs and How To See Them, Caxton Editions 1997

Chapter Three:
Randles, Jenny, The Pennine UFO Mystery, Granada, 1983
Bord, Janet & Colin, Mysterious Britain, Paladin 1974 (reprinted 1977)
Curran, Bob, Werewolves: A Field Guide to Shapeshifters..... New Page Books 2009
Hyatt, Victoria & Charles, Joseph W., The Book of Demons, Lorrimer 1974
Parker, Michael St. John & Jamieson, Andrew, Beasts of Myth and Mystery, Wessex Books 2007

http://hauntedohiobooks.com/news/tokens-of-death-owls-cats-and-phantom-funerals/
http://hiddenexperience.blogspot.co.uk/2012/11/judy-carroll-gray-aliens-and-owls.html
http://hiddenexperience.blogspot.co.uk/

Chapter Four:
Buttlar Von, Johannes, The UFO Phenomenon, Sidgwick & Jackson 1979
Gordon, Stuart, The Paranormal, Headline (BCA) 1992
Hawkins, Gerald S., Beyond Stone Henge, Arrow 1977

UFOs, Portals & Gateways

Hynek, J. Allen, The UFO Experience, Corgi 1974
Keel, John A., UFOs - Operation Trojan Horse, Abacus 1973

http://mysteriousuniverse.org/
http://www.roswellrods.com/
http://pleiadians.net/
http://www.abduct.com/contact
http://www.bibliotecapleyades.net/vida_alien/alien_watchers05.htm-the Blue people
http://www.fatima.org/

Chapter Five:

Hudson, Rita & Phil, Giggleswick (Take a closer look at), Hudson History 2004
Shevill, Ian, A Brief History and Description of Giggleswick School Chapel, June 1996
Malhamdale - A New Guide for Visitors, Dalesman Publishing 1970
Langcliffe Millennium Group, Langcliffe -Glimpses of a Dales Village, Hudson History 2000
Maclellan, Alec , The Lost World of Agharti, Souvenir Press, New Edition (New) 1996
Horne, Alexander, King Solomon's Temple in the Masonic Tradition, Aquarian Press 1972
Hancock, Graham, The Sign and the Seal, QPD 1992
Grierson, Roderick & Munro-Hay, Stuart, The Ark of the Covenant, Weidenfeld & Nicholson 1999
http://www.redorbit.com/news/science/1112684881/jarusalem-figurines
http://www.environmentalgraffiti.com/offbeat-news/mystery-deliberate-burial-ancient-megalithic-stone-circles
http://www.uhcg.org/Jacob-pillar/
http://www.yaim.org/web/literature/eldertraina/342-thestoneofscone.html
http://www.themodernantiquarian.com

Chapter Six:

Kelleher, Ph.D Colm A. & Knapp George, Hunt For The Skinwalker, Paraview Pocket Books 2005
Mortimer Nigel, The Circle & The Sword (First unpublished copy -handwritten) -April 1991
Speakman, Colin, Legends of the Yorkshire Dales, Smith-Settle 1990
Skinner, Ryan, Skinwalker Ranch : Path of the Skinwalker, Ryan T Skinner 2014
Skinner, Ryan & Wallace, D.L., , Skinwalker Ranch: No Trespassing, Voodoo Creations 2014
http://skinwalkerranch.org/blog/
http://www.skinwalkerranch.org/

Chapter Seven:

Morehouse, David, Psychic Warrior, Michael Joseph 1996
Warrington, Peter & Randles, Jenny, Science And The UFOs, Blackwell 1985
Screeton, Paul, Quicksilver Heritage, Abacus 1977
Randles, Jenny, Time Travel, Blandford 1994
Taylor, John, Science and the Supernatural, Temple Smith 1980
Van Dusen, Wison, The Presence of Other Worlds, Wildwood House 1974
Vall'ee, Jacques, The Invisible College, Dutton 1975

http://www.nasa.gov/mission_pages/sunearth/news/mag-portals.html
http://www.smithsonianmag.com/science-nature/Opening-Strange-Portals-in-Physics.html
http://www.paranormalpeopleonline.com/the-nazi-bell-wunderwaffe-or-time-portal/
http://news.nationalgeographic.co.uk/news/2005/09/0916_050916_timetravel.html
http://www.natureworldnews.com/articles/5181/20131204/wormholes-and-quantum-entanglement-one-and-the-same.html

Chapter Eight:

Oxbrow Mark, & Robertson Ian, Rosslyn and the Grail, Mainstream Publishing 2005
Wallace-Murphy, Tim & Hopkins Marilyn, Rosslyn, Element 1999
Butler, Alan , Rosslyn Chapel Decoded, Watkins Publishing 2013
Sinclair, Andrew, Rosslyn, Birlinn 2012
Allan, Brian J. , Rosslyn -Between Two Worlds, 11th Dimension Publishing 2010
Oram, Mike, Does It Rain In Other Dimensions?, 6th Books 2007
http://silver-fish.hubpages.com/hub/Roslin-Glen-Ancient-Rock-Carvings
http://www.mysteriousbritain.co.uk/scotland/mid-lothian/featured-sites/rosslyn-chapel-roslin-castle.html
http://mysearchformagic.com/tag/roslin-castle/
http://canmore.rcahms.gov.uk/en/site/51808/details/gorton+house+wallace+s+cave/
http://www.castleofspirits.com/bluelady.html

Photographic Section:

1. Page 6: The Portal vortex at the Settle Sun Dial site, Horseshoe Trees, 2013. Nigel Mortimer.
2. Page 110: Illustration showing the different types of phenomena encountered at portals. Design by Nigel Mortimer, 2014.
3. Page 111 - 116: Plates 1 to 11. Settle Portal Archive. Nigel & Helen Mortimer 2013.
4. Page 117: Plate 12. Settle Portal Archive. Nigel & Helen Mortimer 2013. Rendlesham Ghost   Owl image courtesy of Derek Savory 2014.
5. Page 118 – 120: Plates 13 to 18. Settle Portal Archive. Nigel & Helen Mortimer 2013-14.
6. Page 130: B/W version Photograph of Helen inside the Freemasons Lodge, Settle. Nigel Mortimer 2013.
7. Page 179: B/W version Photograph of Helen at the Horseshoe Trees, Settle. Nigel Mortimer 2013.
8. Page 188: Photograph of Illustration by kind permission of Aaron Turner 2013.
9. Page 195: Photograph of 'Fish Face', Roslin Glen. Settle Portal Archive. Nigel Mortimer 2010.

Illustrations:

1. Page 26: Ark of the Covenant B/W inset - Settle Portal Archive 2014.
2. Page 34: Akhenaten B/W inset. -source http://www.brotherxii.com/egypt.html
3. Page 49: Swastika Stone B/W inset – Nigel Mortimer 2004.
4. Page 76: Black Dog B/W inset - http://paranormalstudygroup.wikispaces.com/Black+Shuck
5. Page 122: Giggleswick Chapel B/W inset – Nigel Mortimer 2013.
6. Page 131: Plan of Giggleswick Chapel - Settle Portal Archives 2013.
7. Page 159: False Kiva Sepia inset – Settle Portal Archives 2013.
8. Page 71: http://christianimagesource.com/jacobs_ladder_g119-jacob_s_ladder__image_5_p485.html

Further Information

"Together, We Are Opening Portals"

Portals:

Opening Portals - www.openingportals.moonfruit.com
www.facebook.com/groups/openingportals

UFO Groups:

Diane Tessman- website: www.earthchangepredictions.com
Diane's book: www.amazon.com/The-UFO-Agenda-ebook
Warminster UFO Skywatcher, Facebook Page.
The Truth is Out There - www.facebook.com/groups/s.p.a.c.e.1500

Paranormal Groups:

B.E.A.M.S – www.beamsinvestigations.org
Megalithomania – www.megalithomaina.co.uk
Ghosts and the Paranormal - www.facebook.com/groups/ghostsparanormal

Organisations:

New Horizons, Preston, Lancs.
New Horizons, Lytham St Annes, Blackpool, Lancs.
Truthjuice – various around the UK
PROBE UK, Lyham St. Annes, Blackpool, Lancs.

Publications & Internet Resources:

Phenomena Magazine – www.phenomenamagazine.co.uk
Planet X radio show - www.planetxlive.co.uk
Opening Portals Show – www.openingportals.moonfruit .com

INDEX

Made in the USA
San Bernardino, CA
21 February 2017